Advance Praise for

THE LONELY HUNTER

"An insightful and thorough investigation into one woman's loneliness and the systemic ways we're all becoming less connected . . . It might seem like a depressing topic, but I laughed so hard and learned so much."

—BLYTHE ROBERSON, author of
How to Date Men When You Hate Men

"I'm not sure how one could read *The Lonely Hunter* and NOT fall in love with Aimée Lutkin! Her memoir is at once a tender, vivacious consideration of modern romance and an incisive cultural study of American loneliness—a great and heartwarming achievement."

—RACHEL VORONA COTE, author of
Too Much

"At once heartbreaking and deeply funny, Lutkin's *The Lonely Hunter* captures the essence of seemingly endless singlehood in a world built for couples. As vulnerable as she is illuminative, Lutkin achieves what so many of us singles are looking for—she makes us feel less alone."

—REBECCA FISHBEIN, author of
Good Things Happen to People You Hate

"Wry, smart, full of bittersweet detail and vivid scenes, *The Lonely Hunter* is engaging without giving in to easy answers and is willing to ask the big questions—what makes a good life, and what do we want from each other?"

—ROSALIE KNECHT, author of the *Vera Kelly* novels

"In unflinching, honest prose that deftly weaves sociological and cultural analysis with her personal journey, *The Lonely Hunter* challenged everything I assumed about the nature of loneliness and what it means to lead an authentic life. . . . A deeply relatable story that will resonate with readers, lonely or not."

—DOREE SHAFRIR, author of *Thanks for Waiting* and *Startup*

THE
LONELY HUNTER

THE
LONELY HUNTER

HOW OUR SEARCH FOR LOVE IS BROKEN
....

Aimée Lutkin

THE DIAL PRESS

NEW YORK

A Dial Press Trade Paperback Original

Published in the United States by The Dial Press,
an imprint of Random House, a division of
Penguin Random House LLC, New York.

THE DIAL PRESS is a registered trademark and the colophon
is a trademark of Penguin Random House LLC.

LIBRARY OF CONGRESS CATALOGING-IN-PUBLICATION DATA
Names: Lutkin, Aimée, author.
Title: The lonely hunter: how our search
for love is broken / Aimée Lutkin.
Description: New York: The Dial Press, [2022] |
Includes bibliographical references.
Identifiers: LCCN 2021025546 (print) | LCCN 2021025547 (ebook) |
ISBN 9781984855886 (pbk.; alk. paper) | ISBN 9781984855893 (ebook)
Subjects: LCSH: Single people. | Love. | Loneliness. |
Interpersonal relations. | Man-woman relationships. | Couples.
Classification: LCC HQ800 .L88 2022 (print) | LCC HQ800 (ebook) |
DDC 306.81/5—dc23
LC record available at https://lccn.loc.gov/2021025546
LC ebook record available at https://lccn.loc.gov/2021025547

Printed in the United States of America on acid-free paper

randomhousebooks.com

1st Printing

Book design by Dana Leigh Blanchette

DEDICATED TO THE MEMORY OF MY GRANDMOTHER,
CARMEN AQUILONE, AND THE PRESENCE OF
MY MOTHER, PAMELA ENZ

CONTENTS

....

PART TWO

PART THREE

When Can I Say
I'll Be Alone Forever?

It was late in fall, long past the invigorating joys of vivid foliage. The clocks had been set back, and naked branches raked gray skies. There was still a long tunnel of darkness ahead before the twinkling lights of the holidays would emerge and illuminate a more cheerful atmosphere. These transitions were as familiar to me as the Brooklyn street I was walking down, carrying a bottle of wine in a black-and-silver striped bag, also familiar. The sensation of counting the days until the next thing and then the next thing was how I paced my life, with no expectations of more than what I already knew.

I knew the texture of the sidewalk, now with brown leaves ground into its porous cracks, the places where it bucked over tree roots. It led me to the door of a brownstone protected by a heavy, practically medieval gate hung with an actual bell that I'd rung many times. I rang it again. The brownstone housed a cooperative of six or seven people, depending on who was in town. I'd been invited to a dinner party and I'd arrived a few minutes before the hour it was supposed to start.

When I walked into the kitchen, nothing had begun to happen that would result in a meal, so I kicked off my shoes and sat at the dining room table, opening the ten-dollar bottle of wine and chatting with my friend Xavier, who'd opened the door. He'd come down from the upstairs living room a little flustered and sweaty, saying he'd been dancing by himself to shake off a bad mood.

The rhythms of this interaction were pleasant. It was another night in my uneventful life, a night that I imagined would be swept away along with so many others. Some members of the cooperative and other, less foolishly punctual guests slowly assembled in the kitchen, opening and closing cabinets, moving a stack of plates from a shelf to a table, volunteering for a deli beer run, until finally a feast was prepared. It was a nice dinner, and by the end, sated and a little buzzed, we turned the conversation to love.

One of my fellow diners asked me, "So what's going on in your life? With romance?"

This is not an unusual question, and it wouldn't have been particularly memorable either, except that I was feeling unguarded and open after consuming so much home-cooked food. And booze. So I answered honestly and said, "I don't really know if I'm going to date anyone ever again."

The friend who had asked, Rachel, was recently engaged. Her fiancé, Jon, was sitting at the table, too. I'd been friends with Jon long before I'd met Rachel, but she'd made an impression. They'd dated when they were much younger and had broken up. About eight months before this dinner party, Jon had emailed her out of the blue to say she'd appeared to him in a dream.

Usually, if someone tells you they just had a dream about

you, it's a euphemism for wanting to have sex. With Jon I really believed it. He had an otherworldly aura, an angelic calmness that soothed everyone around him. He was the sort of person you could imagine moseying through the landscape of dreams, checking in on old lovers to see if the fruit of a relationship had finally ripened.

They went on the second first date of their two relationships, and this time love stuck. They would be married in a few months, in the same house we were all having dinner in with the permission of their many roommates. Almost before I had finished my sentence, Rachel was rolling her eyes, responding with the dismissiveness of someone who had recently been plucked from singleness by a dream walker.

"Of course you will," she said, shaking her head.

My throat constricted, a kind of tightening that happens when I'm compelled to say something that will make me feel more upset than relieved.

"I think there's this idea that everyone finds someone eventually," I managed. "And I just think, realistically, there's no reason that would be true. Some people are just alone forever."

A ripple of reaction went around the table. In turn, everyone denied that I was facing the rest of my life alone: Xavier, who was currently dating a woman in an open marriage, two friends of Rachel's (completely unrelated women who looked like they came from the same wholesome, outdoorsy family), and a new redheaded roommate named Scott, whom I'd met mere moments before. He had taken a seat at the table during dessert to go through the household mail and weigh in on my love life.

"Have you heard of Tinder? Or OKCupid?" Scott demanded, clenching the pile of bills.

He was recently affianced, too, and clearly secure in his belief that everyone gets there eventually.

"Yeah, I've tried both, but I didn't meet anyone," I said, sounding pathetic even to myself.

He threw up his hands in an exasperated gesture, as though this were a longstanding argument between us and he was sure I was just obstinately opposed to dating. Scott turned back to the mail, done with my unrepentant stubbornness.

Xavier was a little quieter. I guessed that being in a relationship with someone who was already married had made him more aware of the challenges facing modern daters. His girlfriend didn't keep him a secret, but her husband wasn't thrilled with the arrangement. They still sometimes hung out as a group, going to summer events at the Prospect Park Bandshell and having dinners. I'd bumped into them in line for a screening of *The Triplets of Belleville,* a threesome navigating polyamory with the awkwardness of a coffee date.

The overall theme of the responses at the table that night was clichéd reassurance: there's a lid for every pot. Everyone who thinks they're never going to meet someone meets someone right then. It's when you're least expecting it, boom, love happens. If only that were true. How many varying states of expectation I'd lived in: sure, unsure, pretending to be unsure, hopeful, determined, entitled, defeated. No attitude had worked, law-of-attraction-style, to bring love my way. My current state was "acceptance," a word associated with grief. It can also mean that you're dealing with reality as best you can.

I was thirty-two years old. In the last six years, I'd had sex once—somewhere around year three. A quick fling in the midst of all that abstinence hadn't been the end of a drought; it was more like a mirage in the desert, briefly convincing me I was about to be saved from the unrelenting tread across burning, sexless sand. In a way, my singlehood was just as baffling to me as it was to everyone else at the dinner table. I wasn't going to be cast as the lead on a sexy CW show anytime soon, but I wasn't unattractive; I wasn't shy; I wasn't unpleasant (whatever you may think after reading this); I had many friends and deep connections. There seemed to be plenty of other single people who could say the same, but somehow, none of them were the right fit. One year single had turned into another, then another. Time had flown by, summer to fall to winter, with no spring romances. Without planning it, I'd become a spinster.

Unlike my friends, I'd had some time to acclimate to the current state of no affairs. I'd learned to shop in small quantities, to eat at restaurants alone, to arrive at special events without a plus-one. It was fine! It was absolutely fine, until I had to explain what was going on with my love life to a bunch of people who actually had love lives.

Each person in the room had lived through a moment when they thought they'd never meet anyone. They'd been proven wrong. They were certain, looking at me, that I was just them in the past, in that moment before. Soon, sooner than I could imagine, I'd be in the after. I just had to wait and be patient, because my special someone was coming as fast as they could. The conversation at the dinner table circled. They were progressive folks, nonjudgmental, kind, open-minded, but what I was saying about my life made them too unsettled to really listen. Or maybe no one wanted to agree with "Yeah, you're right, no one will ever love you." When Rachel repeated, "No one ends up alone *forever*," I finally shrugged and said, "Yeah, I know," so we could talk about anything else.

The group started clearing the table and doing dishes, moving on to other subjects. I felt exposed and out of place, like I was sitting at the table topless and everyone was pretending not to notice. Tears welled and I swallowed them. Gamely, I asked if anyone wanted tea and got up to fill the kettle. The sense of enjoying another typical, forgettable night had been disrupted, and I suspected even then I would remember this conversation for a long time.

Being alone wasn't so difficult to contend with. Yes, sometimes it was hard. Sometimes I wished I had someone to bring to holiday gatherings, to split the rent, to spoon me on the couch on a rainy day. But more often, being single wasn't the defining characteristic of my existence, which contained all sorts of delightful things: friendships, hobbies, parties, lazy weekend mornings, two long-haired cats, and the ability to make my own schedule without checking anyone else's. The hardest part of being single wasn't the quality of my life, it was really this lack of language to articulate the meaning of my own solitude as I saw it long-term.

What is so scary about someone saying that they might spend their life alone? Especially for people in relationships?

Love and relationships are often a marker of time. "Forever" is a concept we associate with love, though love was theoretically as tenuous as my single state. Like being single, being a couple can end any second, but we definitely don't look to the end of a relationship the same way people hope for the end of singleness. Instead, the calendar of human events is built around partnership: the ceremonious connection of families, anniversaries, children. The cost of housing or healthcare or the inevitability of taxes. A promise of care in old age, or of bringing a guest to other people's weddings, or even receiving an invitation to events and vacations upstate populated only by your coupled friends. The patches of ground where our bones will lie are often bought in pairs. Nearly everything prioritizes two over one. Some of these things are admittedly petty, but others are a matter of survival.

When I said, "I think I might be alone forever," people in relationships could be hearing something much more threatening, something about how insubstantial these support structures really are. I was suggesting that we don't find love as part of cosmic destiny or because we deserve it. If you're in love, if you feel loved, you're mostly just very lucky. It's your ticket into a "normal" life as society understands human cycles. Few want to think about what they would do if their luck ran out.

By the time the kitchen was clean and the counters wiped down, our camaraderie was restored, if not my peace. I hugged Rachel, Jon, Xavier, and even Scott goodbye and walked back through the creaking gate into the small courtyard. The air was damp and smelled like someone had lit a fireplace. I yanked my hat down over my ears and walked to the train, mulling over all the things I wished I'd said, trying to construct the perfect explanation for how it feels to be alone year after year and never to have that acknowledged as a valid experience, only as an intermediate period it's better not to discuss. My breath steamed out in front of me, blowing back into my eyelashes in an angry mist.

Getting dumped was a good example of the difference between my "condition" and what coupled people go through, I thought. In my years of semivoluntary celibacy, I'd had several friends who'd been in multiple relationships, some of them quite passionate and committed, with barely a pause in between each one. The immediate sense of loss after a relationship is painful, but at least there's a label for it: heartbreak. I had no way to describe the slow, dull ache of separation from physical and emotional intimacy after years without it. What I felt had no simple words.

Ruminating on the evening, I realized why I was so agitated: the underlying message of those platitudes about pots and lids was that I needed to just keep on wishing and hoping and waiting and eventually I'd get to join in. Just wait, and wait, because something better than the life you have now is guaranteed. Love is guaranteed, if you just believe in it.

I wanted to cry at that dinner table, not because I was alone or even sometimes very lonely. I wanted to cry because I was exhausted from keeping up the farce that I was still waiting for someone to come find me. Waiting meant staying still. It meant diminishing the life I did lead, suggesting it would never, ever be enough as long as I was still on my own. I would never be free to say, "I think I'll be alone forever," only that I was in a holding pattern until real life began.

And when I thought of how I'd been letting the seasons change around me, letting one day bleed into the next without stirring into action and demanding something different, I did wonder if it was true. Was I waiting or was I living? Were the barriers to connection something internal or built into everything around me?

Like that, the path diverged and I looked in a different direction.

. . .

That evening started a ripple effect in my life, one that would tow me along on its undercurrents all the way back to dating, even back to falling in love; as a result of that dinner, I began to steer the next year of my life out of where it had run aground on the shoals. And when I reached the open waters, it became evident that my situation was indicative of something much more expansive.

One single woman at a dinner party full of couples might feel like a misfit, but if we pull back further, the balance between my circumstance and those of my relationship-blessed friends shifted. Earlier that same year, Rebecca Traister published her opus on the rise of single women and their influence on humankind, *All the Single Ladies*. One of the key points of the book is that in 2009, for perhaps the first time ever in the history of the United States there were more unmarried women than married, as much as it might have felt otherwise to me. There was nothing so unusual about my being single at all.

Singleness, as any peppy self-help book will tell you, does not equate to loneliness. Yet they're words often used synonymously. In an editorial for *The Washington Post*, author Bella DePaulo, who has written a number of books on the bias against single people, pointed out that this conflation promotes this bias, painting singles as isolated and even self-centered. If you think of "single" as synonymous with "lonely," it assigns negativity to a single person, or a negative value to being single. But it's unlikely every single person thinks of themselves as lonely, or that loneliness doesn't find its way into relationships.

Another reason people conflate the two terms may be because finding a partner is still considered the antidote to not only singleness but loneliness. We're considered somehow incomplete, missing that special something, the final piece to fulfillment as long as we're outside of a relationship. How could loneliness plague someone who is satisfied by romantic love?

But loneliness, feeling the ache of solitude instead of its pleasures, is a biological response, like thirst. There was a time in human evolution when refusing to participate in society was as perilous as refusing to drink when you're thirsty, and this innate psychological alarm bell pushed us back into the crowd. That's important: loneliness pushes us back to other people, not to a monogamous romantic relationship. That development came much, much later, under the pressures of social forces, rather than chemical ones.

In recent years, it seems that chronic loneliness is beginning to be understood better as something outside of dating or marriage, in part because so many more people are openly admitting that they're suffering from it. In 2017, a report from the Jo Cox Commission on Loneliness said over nine million people in the UK often or always felt lonely. Loneliness was declared an "epidemic" and by 2018, the country appointed its very first minister of loneliness. By 2020, the UK had gone through three of these ministers, each ordering new studies that tried to gather more information on how many people were lonely and to then implement programs to alleviate some of that loneliness. They introduced projects like paying younger people to work with older people on digital technology, and public health campaigns to reduce stigma around the issue.

In a *New York Times* opinion piece, *Going Solo* author Eric Klinenberg responded to the UK's rush to declare loneliness a catching disease, warning that it was actually the poor, the disenfranchised, the elderly, people without access to medical or in-home care, who would be those most likely forgotten in the ministry's approach to "solving" loneliness. Klinenberg argued that it's a positive thing that loneliness is getting the attention it's currently receiving—it is a huge issue connected to a variety of social ills. He then pointed out that the "epidemic" label is based on faulty, overly general data. "When Britain announced its new ministry, officials insisted that everyone, young or old, was at risk of loneliness," he writes. "Yet the research tells us something more specific. In places like the United States and Britain, it's the poor, unemployed, displaced and migrant populations that stand to suffer most from loneliness and isolation. Their lives are unstable, and so are their relationships. When they get lonely, they are the least able to get adequate social or medical support."

What Klinenberg is saying is that loneliness can't just be treated as an individual failing. It has to be seen in the context of society, as a result of decisions being actively made. Being alone is a state that is pushed on some people far more than others.

When Brigham Young University psychologist Julianne Holt-Lunstad, a leading researcher on loneliness, addressed the 125th annual convention of the American Psychological Association in 2017, she presented evidence that social isolation and loneliness significantly increase risk for premature mortality. "The magnitude of the risk exceeds that of many leading health indicators," she said. "With an increasing aging population, the effect on public health is only anticipated to increase. Indeed, many nations now suggest we are facing a 'loneliness epidemic.' The challenge we face now is what can be done about it."

The research paper Holt-Lunstad was presenting to the APA is regularly cited in aggregated articles on loneliness, which often boil it down to a report on potential health effects; one of the paper's most repeated talking points is that loneliness can have a greater negative effect on your health than obesity. Actually, Holt-Lunstad and her colleagues emphasize the same thing Klinenberg did, which is that people most at risk are the elderly and socially isolated, who may already be suffering from various mental and physical ailments that can't always be meaningfully distinguished from health problems caused by loneliness itself. The phrase "loneliness epidemic" caught on anyway.

Making societal loneliness into an illness is dangerous in that it obfuscates larger problems, even if chronic loneliness can be considered a mental health issue, even if being alone correlates to or causes physical illness. It's almost too convenient. Most illness is treated as a personal problem rather than a systemic one, despite the massive influence that everything from geographic location to access to food and basic medical care can have on health. Describing lonely people as being "sick" in some way means pushing *lifestyle changes* instead of alleviating larger economic and social problems. It also puts it into people's heads that loneliness is catching, which can only compound the problem for those experiencing it.

Being single was definitely my personal problem as far as my friends were concerned. Many of the single ladies shifting the U.S. census numbers that Rebecca Traister analyzed would likely marry eventually, holding to the expectation that they do something about being alone. So might I, because life is long and full of surprises. But if not, where would I turn as I aged and statistically became more exposed to the social isolation Holt-Lunstad warned about?

Many people depend on children to function as a safety net in their old age, but the number of babies is declining, too. In 2017, federal data from the CDC showed that the U.S. fertility rate was at its lowest point ever. For every thousand women between the ages of fifteen and forty-four, there were only 59.8 babies. For comparison, the 1950s baby boom had a birth rate that was twice as high. When people do start families these days, they're also considerably older. Forty years ago, the average age for a woman to give birth was twenty-one. In 2000, it was around twenty-four. In 2017, it was about twenty-six, edging toward twenty-seven.

Canadian journalist John Ibbitson and political scientist Darrell Bricker wrote in their 2019 book, *Empty Planet,* that the lowering birth rate is actually a planet-wide phenomenon, which they largely attribute to the increased access to knowledge via smart phones. An increase in education will often lead to a decrease in family size.

That might be interpreted as a reflection of women pursuing careers instead of raising kids; however, it seems to me that anyone with an awareness of their own economic precarity would be hesitant to have children. In the United States, the expense of having a child in a hospital could ruin a family before it's even begun. Affordable childcare is practically non-existent, which often draws women out of the workforce as the simplest solution. Public services like education (public school being the closest thing to universal childcare in the United States), are being defunded in nearly every state, and to extend this list of potential expenses as far as college, the cost of a degree for the next generation is staggering. And if you are particularly grim about what's ahead (clearly, I was on that autumn night of the dinner party), the looming disaster of climate destruction must make potential parents think about what they're promising a child born right now.

With fewer children being born, there's a huge care gap ahead that may quickly mount to a crisis as seniors find themselves without supporting family. It's currently estimated by the Institute for Public Policy Research that by 2030, the number of elderly adults in the UK who need care will have doubled since 2012. That's two million people without adult children to care for them, and potentially with no backup plan. That's also a shortage of young people in the workforce who might be available to care for elderly communities as a career.

In *Going Solo*, Klinenberg doesn't advocate for people to pursue coupledom and make a baby to avoid the isolation of age. That's because he found in his research that most people do die alone, even people who get married or have kids. Many elderly people live completely alone because they can't afford some form of assisted living. Furthermore, in the United States, nursing homes can be not only prohibitively expensive but poorly run and dangerous for occupants. Klinenberg suggests that the solution for an aging and increasingly lonely population could be found in state-sponsored assisted living facilities that bring safety and dignity to aging. But this is a suggestion, not an existing option. Aging without family care is a form of loneliness anyone can face, whatever choices they've made, but the myth persists that coupledom and children will save you from social isolation. Once again, a major gap in public services becomes an individual's problem.

There are so many ways in which people's choices are policed, and it's so we can point to where they went wrong rather than where they were failed. The stereotype of the career woman who refuses to settle down and then regrets waiting too long haunts popular culture. This characterization implies that there is a choice in the matter, as though the breadwinner model of household division is a manageable option for most people. Delaying settling down is more often a survival tactic than an attempt to buck traditional values. For millennials like myself, graduating into the crash of 2009, a full-time job with healthcare, benefits, and stability felt as out of reach as winning the lottery—or meeting someone willing to support me as I cared for our home. Even if I was never financially in a place to support myself and a child, the stigma of "waiting too long" would follow me.

When I first started thinking about these issues in 2016, I had no idea what was coming only four years later. It is still too early to tell how COVID-19, prolonged quarantines, and the restructuring of social behavior around "social distancing" will affect family structures in the long term, but the data is not looking good.

By the spring of 2021, many studies reported a significant drop in the already falling birth rate. The BBC reported that the United States was experiencing its greatest slump in birth rates in almost a century, and it was even worse in Europe. Some people admitted in a survey that they had chosen to delay having a child in 2020, but in Italy, one of the hardest hit places early in the pandemic, 37 percent of people said coronavirus had changed their plans to have a baby altogether. This doesn't even account for the people who may have been hoping to meet someone to start a family with before quarantine rules were put into effect, limiting socializing—and certainly making it nearly inconceivable to try to meet new people—for nearly a year. Many single folks ended up completely isolated, separated not only from human interaction but from the dream of meeting someone new.

The pandemic put into stark relief so many of the issues affecting the lives of single people, the isolated, and the lonely. Among younger people, loneliness skyrocketed. In November of 2020, Viviana Horigian from the University of Miami in Coral Gables told Medical News Today that in a survey of 1,008 people between the ages of eighteen and thirty-five, 80 percent reported significant depressive symptoms. These are people in an age range that is supposed to be the prime of their social lives. Many of the older ones might have been living alone or with a few roommates, but most college-aged people ended up returning to their parent's homes to go to

Zoom University. Others lost their jobs and returned to live with their families out of necessity, compounding economic setbacks with social ones.

Psychologist Richard Weissbourd told the *Harvard Gazette* that this disruption could have long-reaching consequences for people at an age of transition from their "inherited families to their chosen families," which are supposed to become "critical guardrails against loneliness." There is now a whole generation with a gap in their experience of bonding with others as growing adults.

These shifts are a continuation of trends in loneliness created by economic insecurity. Even before the COVID-19 pandemic, the gradual disruption in full-time employment options on a massive scale has been changing general socialization for years. Financial instability and the gig economy might be ruinous for your bank account, but what's more rarely discussed is how they annihilate the social advantages that come with having a steady job. We get to know the people we work with. Co-workers can come with all sorts of personality issues, sure, but they also fulfill the very important function of widening the circle of people we exchange daily greetings with. When people are constantly circulating from one gig to the next, those social circles are upended again and again. After a while, you might stop trying to create those workplace relationships.

With many forms of gig employment—and again, after many companies pivoted to full-time remote work at the onset of the COVID-19 pandemic—working outside of a traditional office setting has become the norm. As someone who has worked from home for years, I can attest to what a significant shift this is in the daily pattern of life. There are no shared lunches, chats in the break room, after-work drinks, or basic familiarity outside of the text and thumbnails on your screen.

There has been some acknowledgment of this disconnect in the design of offices—for instance, those in the infamous WeWork co-working spaces. WeWork was heralded as the perfect solution for small businesses that sought an open environment with the potential for networking. It offered a kind of cheap simulacrum of a Silicon Valley start-up, with millennial-targeted wallpaper prints, pop music playing in the toilets, a beanbag room, shiny snack displays, and beer on tap. In 2017, *Forbes* reported that the company was valued at $20 billion. In May of 2019, *Vox* said it was valued at $47 billion. By late 2019, WeWork was collapsing due to mismanagement and a whole host of accusations against its CEO, Adam Neumann. Before its collapse, though, many social scientists applauded the company for its attempts to encourage people to socialize, and Neumann's CEO mantras like "Make a life and not just a living."

But the rooms of WeWork's spaces were cleaned and restocked by a workforce who frequently striked and protested against working conditions under the WeWork banner. Union-busting and underpaying staff are antilife, because what actually makes a life is the ability to cultivate one when you're not at work and earning a living wage when you are.

The plush lifestyle of white-collar workers is often facilitated by unprotected minimum-wage employees, but the balance of work and home life has been gradually degraded in every department. Snacks and other perks might make office life feel friendlier, but they're usually just ploys to keep people at work longer, shorten their lunch breaks, and make them more willing to take jobs that pay less on a permalancing basis. WeWork might be one of the most spectacular rises and falls in the exploitative co-working membership game, but plenty of other companies consider community design flow before they consider employee welfare. A company that wants you to have a lounge but no healthcare is not a company that supports a thriving community.

And WeWork was probably one of the more generous of the "sharing" economy models when compared to gig monoliths like Uber, Lyft, and Airbnb, or delivery services like DoorDash, Instacart, or any of a number of apps designed to keep millions of workers on call with no guarantees. The sharing economy is more like a middle-management economy, inserting itself into every aspect of life and draining money off its workers and the consumers. Work is no longer a place to reliably build community outside of family, nor is it a place that supports healthy family life.

This shift in work culture and the relationships within it has largely been facilitated by technology, though that's not the first thing people usually think of when connecting the dots between loneliness and their phones. That would be the negative influence of social media on people's perception of themselves and others. Social media is not a replacement for love, family, or a fulfilling work life, but it is frequently asked to fill the gap in all those things for people who are feeling disconnected. While doing that, social media finds so many ways to drive wedges in real relationships via political disinformation campaigns, conspiracy group message boards, constant argumentative discourse, and simple FOMO.

This isn't at all to say digital culture is uniformly bad. The rush to blame smartphones and the Internet for loneliness has been as suspicious to me as the promise of a Happily Ever After. There are a million ways in which I could say access to the World Wide Web and social networking were a boon to communities everywhere, but in 2016, the pressure of the election made many of us more nakedly aware of the rancor present in humanity via Twitter and Facebook. There was this unrelenting imposition social media seemed to have on daily thoughts. Even if you wanted to look away, it felt dangerous to try, like you'd miss World War III being announced under Twitter's trending topics. The political divisiveness there led to an even greater sense of separateness, a rift that could not be healed.

The rise in media consumption and individualized choices in entertainment have long been blamed for the dissolution of other options for building community. In his book *Bowling Alone: The Collapse and Revival of American Community,* Robert Putnam connects the disbandment of civic groups that used to be so popular across the country to the proliferation of entertainment alternatives. Loneliness is on the rise because people don't invest in social clubs, instead going home after work to bask in the glow of TV and phone screens. But if we review all the factors above, who on earth has the time or money to commit to another activity outside the home?

And so the ingredients to a full, connected life—extended family, a stable living, ties to your neighbors and community—have been completely shredded by the dehumanizing demands of capitalism. There are people who manage to maintain all of these things anyway. It's not unworkable. In an increasingly stratified society, though, it's no wonder that a sense of loneliness and alienation has become a widespread malaise.

None of these issues were even really new; they were only being visited upon a wider range of the population every year.

For generations, people have been driven into isolation through structural inequality: the separation of the elderly to isolated communities; the exclusion of disabled people from accessible work and education; the racist prison-industrial complex that disenfranchises incarcerated people from basic human rights even upon their release, preventing them from voting in many cases, or making housing and employment almost unobtainable. If loneliness has begun to be noted as a widespread ill, it's because the inhumanity of the current social order is touching people who thought they'd avoid it their entire lives.

All the barriers to connection would make anyone question how we manage to connect at all. The fact is, we do. It could be that the biological response still drives us back to the herd more than we realize, even under appalling conditions for reuniting. With some understanding of the scope of that undertaking, the question for me isn't "How do people do it?" but "Why has this been made so hard?"

At the time of the dinner party, I was wondering why it was so hard for me, specifically. I was a white, cis, able-bodied woman living in a metropolitan city, miraculously earning about $65k a year, and it seemed that the lack of material challenges meant I should have figured it out already. After that small dinner-party confrontation, the aggravation I felt wasn't about injustice. I didn't even really understand how much loneliness is the inevitable outcome of the way people are forced to live. In my head, it was just my problem.

The morning *after* the dinner party, I was totally fine, already moving on to whatever new thing would annoy me that day. I worked as a blogger from home, which meant rolling out of bed to sit at my computer three feet away for eight hours straight. Most of my day was spent combing through the news, but occasionally I was given free range to pitch stories, ideas, feelings, photo essays. Not long after that fateful night, I was offered a chance to write an "end of the year" post.

That difficult conversation hadn't been something I'd actively given a lot of thought to. When I considered what I'd write to sum up another year, however, I found it had been percolating inside me and was finally ready to be poured out for a wider audience. It was the end of another year alone, and I thought that deserved to be acknowledged.

From a crasser standpoint, talking about loneliness and the unease between single people and their coupled friends would probably generate a lot of clicks. My job was to share information for the comments section to tear apart. Loneliness seemed like a conversation starter, based on my one evening of trying to talk about it. I wrote a very abridged version of the scene and my feelings about loneliness, and it was posted on Jezebel under the title, "When Can I Say I'll Be Alone Forever?"

I was in a cab headed to Midwood to see my grandparents for Christmas dinner when I realized my editor had decided to post my piece about loneliness during what can be one of the most emotionally trying times of the year for single people. My phone started to light up. When your work is lished online, you know it might be big when peopl tagging you on Twitter. They care enough about what you're saying to seek you out, share what you've written, and usually either thank you or curse you to the depths of hell. The notifications were a sign that Something Was Happening.

Emails started rolling in. I was being inundated by messages from strangers who also felt like they'd been alone forever and who saw no sign that a change was coming. Some said they were trying to date but couldn't seem to connect. Some were literally unable to meet anybody due to geographic location, or even unable to leave the house due to disability. Some had been in love, but the person they loved passed away. A few were cobbling together relationships that didn't quite meet their needs; they couldn't figure out how to find something better, or were scared to start looking all over again.

A man named Gary told me his dog had just died. "I too share the loneliness and I'm realizing that I just may be alone until I die. The Holidays are most difficult—it seems the whole world is coupled up. I don't embrace my solitude. I'm so, so tired of living alone. I'm sixty five. I just lost my dog of fifteen years this month," he wrote, absolutely gutting me.

And I wondered, "Is this me?" Clearly, the folks messaging me had seen something of themselves in my story, but I hadn't meant to seem abject. I liked my life, most of the time. I'd just wanted to express something about this one very particular way in which it was hard, and to say that it was made much harder because I wasn't allowed to talk about it without being force-fed silencing reassurances.

Apparently, I had revealed more than I'd intended. Perhaps the only real difference between me and the loneliest people filling my inbox was time. Then I noticed that though these people were lonely for a plethora of reasons, their focus always seemed to come back to love and sex and romantic relationships. It began to seem like everyone was certain that being chosen by somebody else was the only path to relief from that loneliness.

And again, I asked myself, "Is that really true?"

PART ONE

CHAPTER 1

Stasis

For many people, 2016 was one of the worst years that had happened in a while, or that's how it felt on Election Day. I was probably at the most financially successful point in my life, which was very messed up. I lived in a newly remodeled apartment with one other roommate who met her boyfriend about three months into our lease and then promptly disappeared. I would only know she'd come home for a change of underwear by the hint of stale smoke in the air.

Before that apartment, I'd lived in three different houses that could loosely be called cooperatives—lots of roommates invested in one another's lives, sharing food, throwing events, and pooling resources. By the time I'd downsized to cohabiting with one other person, I was completely sick of communal life. I wanted to put stuff down and later find it where I'd left it. I wanted things to be clean. I wanted space in the refrigerator. I wanted silence.

Scaling down the number of roommates had scaled down my life. There were many activities in my weekly calendar, but when I had lived with fourteen people, I rarely spent an evening or afternoon or morning alone. Weekends meant dance parties, trips to the beach, picnics in the backyard, house projects, and massive breakfasts cooked over hours together in the kitchen. The sustained energy required for that level of socialization had waned as I'd aged, but I hadn't contemplated how leaving a communal living situation would put a huge hole in my sense of *home*.

Now life at home was very quiet. My singular roommate and I barely ever sat in our cavernous living room. The hand-me-down couches, both upholstered in dingy, mismatched gray, emphasized the utilitarian plainness of the high-ceilinged white-box rooms. There was no carpet, nothing hanging on the walls, no standing lamps or friendly plants. We'd furnished it as though we planned to leave at any moment.

As a child, I'd been a pack rat, like my mother. The apartment I lived in until I was seven, a four-room railroad on East Twelfth Street in New York City, was overrun with our collections. Mostly, I remember my mother's papers, which littered every surface. She did her writing longhand on lined yellow pads, perched at her tall wooden desk that doubled as a dining room table. The apartment's massive claw-foot tub was set in the kitchen, so I would often float in cooling water and watch her scribble intently in the light that filtered through the courtyard window.

In those years, my mother was always busy and dynamic, managing my care with a distracted air. She wrote plays that were produced in black box theaters, sometimes featuring my father, who was an actor when he wasn't waiting tables in a fine dining restaurant near Union Square. Money was always an issue, one they seemed to regard as the price of making

their art. I was too young to know the difference, and if I noticed anything amiss in our little universe it was my dad's pro-
pensity for cleaning. How he loved to straighten up papers,
shuffling them into confusion, then throw my toys in a box out
of sight, and vacuum so we couldn't hear ourselves think.

Things changed abruptly when my parents divorced and I
began rotating from apartment to apartment annually. What
remained of my adolescence was consumed with years of custody arguments, phantom child support, and all the other
rigamarole that accompanies childhood trauma. By the time I
was a teen, the burden of emotional care had shifted to me, as
the financial stress took a toll on my mother's health. Diagnosed with multiple sclerosis as a very young woman, my
mother had persisted in walking and generally living a functional life, but as time went on, her need for pain medication
and her worsening symptoms consumed more and more of
her time and mental energy. This also made it more difficult
for her to maintain social connections. I remember her going
through an intense period of isolation when I was in high
school, withdrawing to the confines of her bedroom to watch
reruns of *The Price Is Right*.

"People are nicer to you when they think you're going to
get better or when they think you're going to die," she told me
once. "When you're always sick, they get bored."

Living on SSI, my mother could only legally make so much
money every year without risking her benefits being taken
away. She might have been happy to develop her writing career over a monthly government check, but that check was
also tied to her ability to access the Medicaid insurance she
needed. A person on disability SSI will have the income of

their spouse added to the assessment of how much they get, which meant that she was essentially outlawed from remarrying. "Marriage equality" in the United States only extends to able-bodied people, and that's just the start.

For another glaring example of the barriers erected around financial equality for disabled people, during the pandemic, activists pointed out how quickly accommodations were made so people could work from home when it hurt employers' bottom line. The Americans with Disabilities Act is supposed to guarantee a disabled person receives "reasonable accommodation," but that only applies to businesses with fifteen people or more, and bigger companies have all sorts of loopholes that alienate disabled employees so they get fired or quit. The pandemic, and so many companies' sudden pivot to remote work, made it nakedly obvious that accessibility could become a priority whenever businesses felt like it.

Growing up and witnessing my mother's economic uncertainty, to say I had low expectations of future financial success would understate the case. It didn't alarm me for most of my twenties, because leading a scrambling existence seemed perfectly ordinary. I got into a magnet high school for visual art, then was admitted to a small art college in the city where tuition was covered for everyone accepted. I took out student loans for living expenses that I would pay off over the next fourteen years, and I worked part-time in a bookstore. After college, I acquired one of those unaccountable résumés that adds up to nothing: theater admin, painting fashion showrooms, working in the kitchen of a vegan restaurant, photo assistant, catering events, waiting tables, fact-checking at a magazine, teaching at after-school programs in public schools, giving Photoshop lessons at a college, and one heinous day at a children's shoe store.

I got my first writing job just before I turned thirty-one. I had been working part-time at a reception desk, when a woman I knew who already had a lucrative career in advertising stopped for a chat and mentioned she'd been asked to apply to a much-lower-paying position at a blog site, but she wasn't psyched about the prospect. I begged her to send my wonky résumé to them with a word of recommendation, and she did. After a trial period, they hired me full-time.

That was the first and only staff writing job I had, with vacation, paid sick days, and even basic health insurance. For the first time in years and years, I went into an office every day, at a WeWork in the financial district. We sat in two tight rows in a single space, silently staring at our screens and communicating via Slack. If someone typed "LOL" you knew they really weren't.

As a person with an aptitude for many things and actual proficiency at very few, I took to blogging frighteningly well. If I had a talent in life, it was the ability to process written information and reshare it in the voice of a particular blog. A dubious skill, but it made me an excellent workhorse writer. When the company started having traffic competitions with gift certificate rewards, I won them month after month. When, after a year and a half, I didn't get the promotion I wanted, I headed off into the wilds of freelancing.

In retrospect, perhaps I should have held on to a full-time job, though that company would give up their WeWork office not long after I left, letting person after person go until they were a bare-bones operation. I was quickly hired by a series of

similar websites that paid about the same, but with no demands that I commute anywhere—and no benefits of any
kind. I could also do many jobs at once, writing for three or
four websites a day. By 2016, for the first time in my life, I was
making a reasonable amount of money to live off of in New
York City.

Starting at 7:30 every morning, I wrote. I frequently wrote
as many as ten posts a day of varying lengths; my output was
probably around four thousand words a shift, not counting the
time I spent learning the content-management system of each
company and inputting those words according to their style
guides. It certainly wasn't coal mining, and I worked from
home, but at the end of the day, I'd often feel numb from my
right eye down to my hand, a soreness in my lower back that
made it hard to sleep, and an acute mental exhaustion that
made me want to stare slack-jawed at the ceiling until bedtime.

I'd joke with friends that the Internet was polluted water
running into a sink, and I was the filter in the drain catching
all the chunky garbage. The garbage was then repackaged for
the masses with eye-catching headlines and clickbait photos.
Many of the sites I wrote for, even knockoff Buzzfeed-style
viral blogs, were focusing on Donald Trump, and that meant
constantly experiencing a stream of news that ranged from
bad to inhumane. It felt ridiculous to be so burnt out from
blogging, but I was literally plugged in to receive every news-
flash instantaneously for the majority of my waking hours and
then every response to it on Twitter and Facebook. The result
was a wild emotional state that had me vacillating between

sobbing and hysterical laughter many days in the privacy of my bedroom office.

Being at home alone during the day exacerbated that feeling. If I didn't go out in the evening, I could have gone days and days without speaking to anyone. The thing that kept me going out was comedy. In my early twenties, I'd resisted the pull of live theater for the most part, not wanting to inevitably slide down the same track my parents had traveled. Even in art school, I'd been much more attracted to photography and making experimental videos, telling stories instead of embodying headier intellectual practices. Blood will out, and I started to exhibit the genetic pattern of exposing myself on stage for politely supportive friends and family.

At first, it was awkward performance art. Then I took my first improv class in my late twenties, spending a tax refund check I should have used on groceries. Eventually, I started interning at the theater, then working in the tech booth so I could take classes for free and watch show after show from behind the switchboard. I'd never been in a sorority or social club, really; I imagine they have a lot in common with the comedy community. Any night of the week there were free shows or rehearsals or my own performances to attend. The year I wrote my essay about loneliness, I was often surrounded by people when I wasn't staring at a computer. I had a running sketch show I'd co-written with two other women that we also starred in and that, combined with improv, took up a lot of the time I might have filled with a lover. As everyone knew, I didn't have one.

Some of the people I met in that theater would be my

friends long-term. More than that, there were hordes of folks I'd known tangentially for years whom I could catch up with, wave to, gossip about, and feel loosely connected to. I think this feeling of being part of a constellation of connections is often what people are looking for in certain hobbies or pursuits or even church. We want to be recognized as a part of something by like-minded members of that same something.

Boy, was I tired. Even my extroverted ass was drained by the effort of maintaining all these relationships and trying to promote myself as someone who "did comedy" and wrote and acted and had four jobs and still wanted more than what they already had. Especially because it felt much of the time like I was stuck on a career plateau, despite all the frantic activity. And I was getting older every year, the way one does.

I met my friend Dylan in an improv class, and shortly after, he moved to Los Angeles. Periodically, he urged me to move there and see some new horizons. For Dylan, New York was just a stopping place; for me, it was home and family and my whole life. How do you know when it's time to say goodbye to those things so you can look for them somewhere else? It was feeling closer and closer to that time.

With all of this going on, I didn't think about dating very much at all. When I did, I recognized that my approach to romantic and sexual love had taken a swerve in my midtwenties and never straightened itself out.

Sometimes I wandered back through my history of love and dating, trying to figure out where I'd gone off track. The last time I'd felt truly treasured had ended when I was still in college. Owen and I had known each other since we were preteens, and he dated my best friend, Billie, during our sophomore year of high school. Our relationship began only after I got her blessing, the summer just before college started. Billie married her second boyfriend, whom she met in high school, and had already had one kid by the time I was dressing up as Brienne of Tarth for a *Games of Thrones* satire performed in front of a drunk audience in a basement comedy theater.

There was a safety in being Owen's girlfriend, and an innocence to our courtship. Reflecting on it in my thirties, I was touched by how unafraid Owen was of commitment. Even when we made each other wretched, he seemed willing and able to stick with it. He wasn't good at discussing his feelings, but he was good at tolerating my angsty ups and downs. When he suggestively joked that he was going to buy a wedding ring, I was both blushingly pleased and terrified. I was only twenty years old. The idea of being with only Owen for the rest of my life began to feel like living in a steadily shrinking enclosure.

Then, marriage seemed like the period at the end of a sentence. It indicated that some aspect of my life's journey had come to its conclusion. Even when Owen and I were in love, I believed there was something else still to come.

After almost three years together, Owen and I broke up. I went to Paris on exchange my senior year, like in a Molly Ringwald movie, and he immediately entered another long-term relationship. Each year, I waited for that feeling that I was mature, certain, *finished*, to pop up. When I was ready, it would happen. That's what marriage meant to me—it was a sign of maturity. But I never reached whatever that moment of being sure was.

After Owen, I dated a lot. Men, women, whomever I found

myself attracted to. Some of them I cared for, even loved, some of them I forgot after we parted ways. I had only one other official serious partner, just before my six-year period of near celibacy began. Morgan was sixteen years older than me. He was a highly functional alcoholic, except for when he couldn't function at all. Having to get him and his bike home every three months or so when he'd cyclically go overboard had been a drag, but I didn't really break up with him because of the drinking. It was because he wanted to move back to his hometown, Philadelphia, a city I felt zero connection to and, based on our visits there, where I would have ended up culti-vating a lifelong drug problem.

Or that's what I joked when people asked about our breakup. Actually, we could probably have gotten along fine, him drinking, me picking him up off the floor. He professed a passionate love for me—except there was something about it that seemed off. He wanted to settle down. This was a man who wanted to be In Love, to make a commitment. It was oddly impersonal. It felt like this determination took prece-dence over the actual object of his affection, like I was filling a slot. I later realized that Morgan and I were just never really in love. After we broke up, he started dating someone new al-most right away and married her within the year.

That doesn't mean I never fell deeply in love after Owen. Right before Morgan and I started dating, I'd been obsessed with one of my roommates at my fourteen-person commune, the kind of inevitable infatuation that pops up when that many young people live in such close proximity to one an-other. It ended in such a spectacularly appalling fashion that I still remember explaining to a friend that it felt like my "love receptors" had been damaged. Like, whatever the wiring was that allowed for that intensity of adoration had been fried to a crisp. The human mind isn't really a collection of wires, because it has the capacity to heal. In time, mine did, and I could even see that roommate and not really feel anything about him except a sentimental fondness for the exhilarating insanity of love.

I tried to date a little after Morgan. Then I tried less. Though I thought I'd recovered from my roommate fiasco, I began to wonder if something essential had changed. Perhaps it was the ability to suspend disbelief long enough to take a chance on someone. Everyone else was falling in and out of love all the time, but I didn't. As time went on, it seemed like love was a feeling of the past, never the future.

Without planning it, I stopped trying. I had begun to suspect that commitment in love was more a matter of timing than anything else, and mine was all off. What started as a slight step out of sync had grown exponentially until I was off the radar. When I wrote about "being alone forever," it was entirely possible that this would really be the case.

A few days after my essay was published, I was in bed with my cats, reading a book. The week between Christmas and New Year's was a foggy time. I had no personal chores, most of my friends had left town for the holidays, and my freelance work was sporadic. As I turned a page, my phone lit up with a text from a friend asking me how I was.

"I read your essay," she continued, and I expected a message of congratulations to follow. There had been a few on

Facebook and in texts, and it had been very nice to be recognized by people in my life. Sad to say for my ego, this friend wasn't pleased. She was worried.

"It's like you're valorizing depression," she texted.

She wasn't the only person who had been critical of my essay, of course. My writing is on the Internet; obviously I'm used to getting negative comments. But after I posted the essay, I received far more letters and messages from people who related to my situation. And I got a lot of notes about how I should just lose weight, or be less picky, or go to therapy, and the right person would come along when I was finally *fixed*. Even a love guru wrote to me, offering to help me find my perfect mate. There were people telling me that I sounded awful, negative, and like somebody no one would want to be with. And now my friend was telling me I was *depressed*.

It was intriguing that so many people believed that becoming self-actualized inevitably leads to a great relationship when so many relationships are made up of codependent, unhappy, and even (gasp) depressed people. To me, these sorts of ideas only expose the bias against single people more starkly—the assumption that something is wrong with us. No one loves a lonely person. Only people who are fulfilled and happy get to be loved.

Hearing something like this from a friend is different from hearing it from a stranger, so these texts genuinely upset me. I knew this friend had had depression herself. I knew that since college she'd had two long-term relationships without much of a break and was now with the man she was planning to marry. Either she was recognizing the signs of depression in me, or she had no idea what I was talking about, since she'd never really experienced perpetual romantic loneliness.

It could have been both. I had been depressed in the past and had taken antidepressant medication for about a year and half. However, that was following the sudden death of a close friend, a man named Raymond whom I'd met my first day of high school. I knew how I was feeling now was very different from the sadness of that awful period of bereavement, when it had seemed like the thinnest layer of ice lay between my feet and the black well of despair underneath.

Loneliness and depression are often paired together, the latter seen as an outcome of the former. The implication of this criticism irked me. There was, according to my friend, something wrong with me. A mental health condition, even. Which meant there was nothing wrong with the way things coalesced around couplehood.

Where was the line between personal responsibility for changing my solitary state and the external pressures that made being solitary untenable? If I was "sick," it was on me to get "better." If this is just a very unpleasant place for people existing outside of a heteronormative family structure, that's a different story. That might mean there's a lot that needs to change everywhere; that loneliness shouldn't be treated as an individual feeling or failing. It's an issue we all need to recognize, even when we're not experiencing it.

And to be honest, I wasn't even socially isolated! On a day-to-day basis, my life was filled with activities, friends, and family. I didn't face discrimination for my race or gender or sexual identity (everyone deduced I was straight, because long hair) and I was making enough money now to feel safer than ever before.

Yet through all my busyness there did run a thread of fear that, as time passed, many of those connections would fade. My older relatives would pass away. My friends would become more deeply immersed in their relationships and growing families. My physical health, which allowed me to easily navigate and engage, would deteriorate. Instead of the ebb and flow of human relationships, I sometimes saw only a steady decline ahead.

Was that depression, or a realistic assessment of what happens to single women burning through their thirties?

For the next few days, I was in a bit of a mope. I was irritated with myself for not believing what everyone was telling me: that love would come and I should be psyched about that, because love was the answer to loneliness. And I was irritated with everyone else for continually insisting I pretend to believe it despite my two thousand words on why that's obnoxious.

On New Year's Day, in bed again, I got a much better unexpected text from an old roommate named Lizzie. She reminded me of our tradition of going to Coney Island for the Polar Bear Swim. We hadn't really spoken since June, after moving into separate apartments. She knew it was last minute, but did I want to hop in her car and go?

Lizzie picked me up in her rusted old Volvo, nicknamed Dolores, and we giggled all the way to the beach. It was temperate out. The bright blue sky made the prospect of the dip much easier. As usual, parking was difficult, and we ended up having to walk several blocks before we reached the roaring crowd swarming the launch point. Many people wear bathing suits at the New Year's Day dip, but lots also dress up for the occasion—as mermaids, as monsters, as adult babies in diapers. I'd always liked to strike a balance between costume and practicality, so I wore a blue mechanic's jumpsuit and a pair of shoes I never wanted to walk in again.

The sheer exuberance of the surroundings was always enough to carry me into the ocean. Lizzie and I yelled "one-twothreeGO!" and then lost each other as we ran through the bathers and photographers. The most difficult part was going all the way under, putting my head beneath the water as my entire body screamed at me to stop and reconsider. On the other side of this torment was some sort of brain-chemical reward, the natural reaction to feeling close to death and being spared.

Lizzie and I met dripping and breathless on the shore again, then immediately decided to run back to the waves together. Afterward, the warmth of the day and the adrenaline allowed us to stand soaking wet for a minute and take in our surroundings. Teens screamed in shivering groups, costumed women wiped makeup from their eyes, dogs ran barking up and down the beach. The clouds thinned to let the sun touch upturned faces seeking heat.

I felt good, a thousand times better than I had in days. Despite the traditional midnight kiss, New Year's is a rare holiday that isn't focused on love, couples, or family. It is very much a holiday of self-reflection, self-commitment, and personal growth. It is likely the easiest holiday to celebrate as a single person. No matter how many lonely nights there were in the past, there is still a chance to wash it all off and start fresh in the morning.

Who knew what could happen? On the beach, surrounded by hordes of people greeting the new year, it seemed entirely possible that something special actually was on its way.

What was I hoping it would be?

All the conversations and comments and unwelcome texts in the wake of publishing my essay were stirring up something inside me. I wanted to be different. Maybe there *was* something wrong with me, and if I could just get over myself, I'd find the person who would clear away all my worries about the future. Maybe if I just tried to do all this stuff people were telling me to do, love really would come, and I'd never be lonely again. I'd finally be a real girl.

And what if it doesn't work, an inner voice hissed malevolently. *What if you change and nothing else does? That would really show them.*

With these two conflicting drives—to get better and to prove there was nothing wrong with me—I entered a new year the way many people do: intending to change my entire life.

CHAPTER 2

If You Don't Love Yourself . . .

"Lower," Daniel, my personal trainer, commanded, meaning I should squat deeper as I crab-walked back and forth along the wall. Being told to go lower made me want to stand up, so I did, briefly. Daniel waited patiently. We only had ten mins left together. It had been about a month since he'd been randomly assigned to work with me at the gym; Daniel understood there was a limit to what I would do. The limit was physical discomfort of any kind.

Like half the western hemisphere at the start of the new year, I signed up for a gym membership. This was the first time I'd made such a move in seven or eight years. Not sure of where else to begin in transforming my life (if such a thing was possible), I'd selected the place most haunted by resolutions: a gymnasium.

This would be my seventh year without a relationship. Saying so out loud to thousands and thousands of people felt very different from acknowledging it in private. Frankly, the feedback I'd been receiving was getting to me, though I would rather have eaten glass than admit that. I'd wanted to believe that I was immune to the cajoling, the opinions, suggestions, and solutions to loneliness. I wasn't. This year could not be like the ones that had preceded it—of that much I was sure.

Whoever said that true change starts within hasn't been subjected to comment after comment suggesting your looks are the only thing standing between you and romantic rejection. The solution to my whole problem, at least according to the standard anonymous Internet troll, was that I simply wasn't attractive enough to find love.

Like an idiot, one day I googled myself, and I saw my loneliness essay on Reddit. It had been posted on various subreddits, some of which were dedicated to psychology, some to dating, and some, for lack of a better description, to misogyny. Reading the comments is a stupid idea most of the time, but reading the comments on r/thelastpsychiatrist was a nightmare. From my essay on loneliness, I was diagnosed as a pathological narcissist and someone who was mentally and emotionally damaged from self-neglect. This may all have been true, but I'd have preferred to hear it from a paid professional.

Over the years, I've found that a common misconception about writers is that they share stories about their lives because they think they are good people; actually, I share stories about myself because I know that some people are bad in the same way I am, and talking about it can make us better. It's also the only way I've figured out how to earn money. Even believing in my own sincere intentions, the assessment from trolls disturbed me.

"Imagine if the genders were reversed."

"She seems very invested in her image as an unloved victim of circumstance. Ugh."

"If she were a man, she'd be an incel."

Though the criticisms sometimes hit the mark, I noticed they frequently implied that for people to have a reasonable expectation of love and care from others, they must have already reached some perfect form. It was an upsetting notion, because it wasn't just a fringe idea on a message board. "Working on yourself" is very mainstream.

Rarely do people work on themselves and not offer some proof of that work to others for validation. That's okay. Most humans want to feel seen for their effort. We don't live in a vacuum. If we did, no one would do crunches. It was just so common to hear "work on yourself, concentrate on yourself, love yourself" in response to complaints about singlehood that it had begun to seem like code for "no one will want you like that."

I resented it, this subtle suggestion that learning to love yourself really meant "make yourself lovable." The day I signed my gym contract, I felt torn between a wistful hope and a dreadful sense of capitulation.

My gym was one of those chain places that offered no classes and barely any accommodations, but they had weights, StairMasters, and ellipticals. That was plenty for Daniel to torment me with. I'd bought their personal training special: half-hour sessions twice a week if you committed to monthly enrollment. I justified the expenditure by comparing it to a gym membership at a place that offered towels. Signing up was a huge gamble, since the idea of exercising was petrifying. I'd tried and failed so many times to get myself to work out. The money was a bet that the shame I'd feel about wasting cash would propel me to appointments.

It worked. I showed up to meet Daniel, a nice man whose initial enthusiasm for our sessions quickly diminished. He led me from the StairMaster to the leg press to the mats, measuring the length of time on each by looking at the stopwatch on his phone. He was also looking at his Instagram feed, and I didn't blame him. It had to be dull to watch me struggle to do squats and lunges, and jump rope for no more than twenty seconds at a time. It was so discouraging. I wasn't just weak— I was clumsy as a baby and prone to tantrums.

After my crab walks, Daniel told me to lie down on the ground and do my crunches. It was early in the morning. We usually saw each other in the afternoons, and I was quickly discovering how a period of seven hours between waking up and doing jumping jacks was a necessary buffer.

"Elbows out," barked Daniel. "You can get higher than that!"

By the tenth crunch, I was pretty sure I couldn't. I was pretty sure that anyone asking me to get higher was an asshole, even if I was paying them to ask it. I sat all the way up, panting, "This is harder for me because I'm so much older than you!"

How tragic I was, old and worn out, falling apart at the seams. Too many crunches would send my stuffing flying everywhere; couldn't he see?

"I'm thirty," he said, with a contemptuous glance.

Oh my god, I thought. I was thirty-two, and I looked about 102 years older than this man. He had the buoyant energy of a teen running into the house after track-and-field practice and my joints ached from the pressures of simply being alive.

The moment was a turning point in my sense of personal vanity. That week, I started to finally go to the gym *in between* sessions with Daniel in the hopes of mortifying myself slightly less when I saw him. More importantly, I went to slow down my aging.

Vanity and my health (and delineating between the two) became my new obsessions.

I *tried* not to focus on an outcome of all this exercise, like potentially being hot. I tried to think of it as an experiment, like a scientist testing the hypothesis that "exercise feels good."

Interesting, I thought, watching myself do squats. *Very interesting.*

Week by week, my strength grew. The half hours I spent with Daniel were hard, but not crying hard. I started to see muscle in certain places. At first, this actually was a relatively private enterprise, the changes so subtle that only I could really tell—tracing the sore spots along my obliques, feeling the heat of a shower soothe the aches. I was afraid to advertise the effort I was putting into myself in case it turned out I couldn't actually change anything through that effort, so I didn't post gym selfies or buy cute spandex outfits, though Instagram's data mine somehow caught wind of my new hobby and started targeting me with ads for them.

Daniel usually directed me to focus on my lower body, saying that the larger muscles of the legs burn more calories. As my thighs and butt and nothing else began to gain definition, I thought about how personal trainers have a lot of say in the body shapes of their clients, especially new ones who don't necessarily have a grander end in mind besides "getting fit."

Fit for *what* was not explicitly stated; based on how big my quads gradually got over the next few months, I was training for a footrace against an emu.

Then, during a week when Daniel was on vacation, I scheduled with a substitute trainer named Mason, who had me work on my undeveloped shoulders. "Muscular shoulders look nice in a sundress," he said encouragingly, revealing his own biases. This was an annoying comment, but Mason could get away with it. Whatever his interest in sundresses, he was obviously deeply committed to helping people build muscle. He told me he'd only been a certified trainer for about eight months. Before that he'd worked as a line cook in a restaurant. He was fifty-six years old and he, too, looked way younger than me. His six-pack was so deep and cut, time would never erase it. Moreover, he had changed his entire life in his fifties. He was body goals and life goals.

"I wish I'd been your trainer from the beginning," he said, as I screamed doing bicep curls. "You would have been my masterpiece."

This was said without any detectable salaciousness. Mason really did view my body as something with potential, clay that could be formed into something worth triumphantly advertising. There was still no answer to the question of what such a transformation would be for or whom it was meant to please. *Me?* I wondered, flexing my arm and fingering the slight bulge beginning to grow.

Before the new year, as another resolution, I had been thinking of spending a month not eating dairy. In this susceptible state of mind, I wandered into a conversation in the greenroom of the comedy theater where my sketch show was set to go up. Everyone, including myself, was in costume. The show was set in the regency era. The other women in the room were in high-waisted cotton gowns printed with flowers and tied around the waist with bows. I was dressed in black, playing the maid, my hair tucked under a frilled cap. I'd written and cast the part myself, but when I would see everyone else in their graceful finery, I resented being the frump.

One of my castmates was reciting a list that didn't make much sense to me.

"No alcohol, no grains, certain oils, no soy, no dairy, no sugar of any kind," she said counting on her fingers. "Oh, and no legumes!" she added.

"What are you talking about?" I asked, intrigued.

"It's the Whole30," she said, explaining these were all things you couldn't eat on the thirty-day elimination diet. "And a bunch of us are doing it for January."

"I was gonna do no dairy. . . ."

"That's good, too!" she said enthusiastically. I looked in the long mirror in the corner, covered in scraped-off stickers and lipstick kisses. My eyes appeared sunken, my skin patchy, my neck bloated. It wasn't just the outfit. I turned back to her.

"Okay, I'll do it, too." Even though she hadn't asked, she fist pumped the air like she'd made a sale and promised to add me to the Facebook group of friends embarking on the Whole30 starting January 1.

The Whole30 is rebranded dieting. Established in 2009, the elimination diet plan is marketed as a way to get "in control" of your eating habits, by identifying what you consume that makes you feel *unwell* and then cutting through your food "addictions" to things like sugar and dairy. On their website, the Whole30 corporation paints a picture of freedom through restriction: "We cannot possibly put enough emphasis on this simple fact—the next 30 days will change your life. It will change the way you think about food, it will change your tastes, it will change your habits and your cravings. It could, quite possibly, change the emotional relationship you have with food, and with your body. It has the potential to change the way you eat for the rest of your life."

What a promise.

Those grand ideals, or the support of my friends in our online forum, or just a determination to change something, pushed me, and for the first time in a long time I stuck with a diet. I roasted vegetables and bought a crockpot and meal prepped. I read the posts and comments of my friends on our Facebook page, and we texted one another and joked about the Whole30's guarantee of "tiger blood" euphoria around day fifteen of our one-month commitment. I felt included and supported, even though I suspected we might be supporting one another in a kind of mania when someone posted about rejecting a slice of cake on their birthday.

It was hard. It was not as hard as I thought it would be. Every time I wanted to eat cheese, I told myself, It's just thirty days. You can do things differently for just thirty days. Having a time limit on changing my daily behaviors made those changes more manageable. If they didn't take, if nothing happened, I could just go back to the way things were and forget I even tried. That was soothing.

Toward the end of that month on the Whole30, I was in the greenroom, once again in costume, when another castmate remarked on my appearance.

"I don't know what you're doing, but you look amazing," she said, waving her hand in front of my face like she was wiping a windshield. The answer was mostly that I had lost ten pounds, but I said, "Thank you so much!"

She nodded, adding, "There's just something radiating out of you."

The praise warmed me, even as I recognized that a physical change was being labeled as something coming from my very spirit. It does feel good to stick to a routine and get your blood flowing and eat lots of vegetables, but it doesn't transform your soul. Fundamentally, nothing much had changed, and yet people had begun to treat me differently. It was very seductive to imagine more was happening than muscle gain. It was also easy, because "wellness" trends have been conditioning all of us to attribute much deeper meaning to losing a few pounds.

The weight-loss industry has gone through some revisions in recent years, absorbing the language of the body positivity movement to make a confusing hybrid. Reading the Whole30's cultish propaganda and following their Instagram handle certainly made *me* confused. I wasn't allergic to legumes, my stomach processed dairy just fine, and eating a piece of fruit had never done anything harmful to me. Following all those restrictions did stop me from snacking. I ate less and I ate it less often. It was definitely a diet, just the first diet I'd ever done where I could claim it was about "changing my relationship to food" rather than helping with weight loss. I did lose weight. And all diets are about disordered eating habits, no matter how they're packaged.

In her 2017 essay on the transformation of corporations

like Weight Watchers and Lean Cuisine for *The New York Times Magazine,* Taffy Brodesser-Akner expounds on how people's general perception of weight loss has changed so dramatically that traditional weight-loss companies don't even want to be associated with their own purpose. Instead, they use the language of body positivity and the new emphasis on the less easily defined umbrella of "wellness" to sell the same products: "Women's magazines started shifting the verbal displays on their covers, from the aggressive hard-body stance of old to one with gentler language, acknowledging that perhaps a women's magazine doesn't know for sure what size your body should be, or what size it can be: *Get fit! Be your healthiest! GET STRONG!* replaced diet language like *Get lean! Control your eating! Lose 10 pounds this month!* In late 2015, Women's Health, a holdout, announced in its own pages that it was doing away with the cover phrases 'drop two sizes' and 'bikini body.' The word 'wellness' came to prominence. People were now fasting and eating clean and cleansing and making lifestyle changes, which, by all available evidence, is exactly like dieting."

This change had certainly made pursuing weight loss more palatable to me. When I was a teenager, it was still both appropriate and expected that any girl would want to be thin, then thinner, then so emaciated she practically faded away. My mother would sometimes force me to run laps up and down our very crowded street in exchange for an allowance. She frequently berated me for overeating. She told me I'd lose weight in my stomach if I stopped eating bread and corn and rice; if I stopped eating anything, essentially, since I had the unrefined palate of a carb-loving kid.

Over time, my mother's perspective changed. She became

less inclined to criticize my behavior or looks as they related to weight, though she still hates it when I cut my hair short. Perhaps she recognized the way beauty standards had shifted, or perhaps she learned to shut her mouth to save our relationship. She made a living in her twenties as a model and grew up in a household where her mother guarded her daughters' figures like they were security deposits. I could forgive my mom for her former critical habits. The cycle of self-loathing over having a gut was harder to break. Thinking of working out or changing my diet as a form of self-love rather than of self-abnegation opened a small, new neural window that allowed for a different reaction. The hours at the gym, the fiercely monitored meals were all possible if I considered them a gesture of love and care toward myself. Even if that messaging was still corporate diet-culture bullshit.

As Brodesser-Akner observed, capitalism has an uncanny ability to soak up meaningful cultural trends and turn them into marketing ploys. In early 2017, "self-care," wellness's distant cousin, exploded into the mainstream as a response to political upheaval. Everyone was urged to develop daily habits of caring for themselves to escape their awareness of the direction the globe was heading. The way self-care was being used in the media then felt like a replica to me of the "work on yourself" mantra so frequently pushed upon lonely people. It was a hyperindividualistic solution to a major structural problem (i.e., having a fascist for a president).

In a 2007 article on fitness and feminism, author Carol-Ann Farkas quotes the work of Shari Dworkin and Michael A. Messner, after explaining that fitness magazines tend to work as a salve on individualistic concerns: "The kinds of individ-

ual empowerment that can be purchased through consumer-
ism seriously reduce women's abilities even to identify their
collective interests, [leading to] a radical turning inward of
agency toward the goal of transformation of one's own body,
in contrast to a turning outward to mobilize for collective action."

There were many collective actions to participate in at that
time, and I did, but I was in no way impervious to that individualistic salve. For me, the self-care trend post–Trump's
election gradually translated into more exercising and more
focus on food, because losing weight was the first thing I'd
done in a long time that felt transformative. These habits were
also being marketed to me as something healing, something
that would give me back control, something that would help
center and strengthen me. But "self-care" developed from the
idea that entire communities were not receiving the *external*
care they deserved.

In a piece for *Slate* in April of 2017, writer Aisha Harris
noted the rising popularity of the term, mentioning that in the
week after November 8, 2016, Americans googled the phrase
"self-care" at twice the usual rate. Harris traced the original
concept to doctors of the sixties and seventies who primarily
"prescribed" self-care to the elderly or people who required
long-term medical attention that kept them home- or bed-
bound. It then found its way into academic circles as a theo-
retical tool to combat stress in difficult jobs, like social work.
Self-care meant acknowledging that one had to slow down
and be sure to take enjoyment in life, because without health
within oneself, how could you promote health in others?

Self-care became an important tenet of activist groups

during the civil rights movement, eventually becoming a part of the Black Panther Party's work to bring health programs into their communities. As Harris writes, the programs instituted by the Black Panthers were about much more than taking a break and being kind to yourself:

"These nationwide clinics recruited nurses, doctors, and students to test for illness and disease rampant within the Black community (including lead poisoning and sickle-cell anemia), as well as to provide basic preventive care. For Black people and especially Black women, this kind of self-care was brought to fill a desperate need. The 'survival programs' of the Panthers were about just that: survival."

The politically meaningful use of "self-care" coincided with a rise of "wellness" culture in the seventies. There is a long history of wellness ideologies that can be traced back to European "cure towns," as writer Sarah Treleaven explained in a piece for *Elemental* in 2019. There, people would drink mineral waters said to have healing properties and engage in rest and relaxation practices that often involved an ascetic diet. These destinations evolved into the sorts of spas someone might now attend as a luxury, like Canyon Ranch. The term "wellness" was actually coined in the fifties by Dr. Halbert L. Dunn, and it became a mainstream phenomenon over the next few decades.

In the late seventies, as writer Daniela Blei recounts in a piece for JSTOR, Dan Rather interviewed Dr. John W. Travis, founder of the Wellness Resource Center in Marin County, on *60 Minutes*, releasing the concept on a much wider audience. He introduced the segment by saying, "Wellness. There's a word you don't hear every day. It means exactly what you might think it means: the opposite of illness. . . . It's a move-ment that is catching on all over the country."

"Just because you aren't sick," Travis explained in the in-terview, "[and] you don't have any symptoms, and you could go get a checkup and get a clean bill of health, that doesn't mean that you're well."

That sounds like a threat to me. It's even reminiscent of the idea in the Whole30 that there is some secret flaw in you that can be rooted out through a specific diet. Wellness has an ele-ment of vagueness that allows for it to absorb whatever it wants as part of its program. In the seventies, white hippies were appropriating Eastern medicinal practices like acu-puncture and yoga as a part of wellness, and trying all the non-FDA-approved treatments available—everything from cra-niosacral therapy to sound baths to crystal healing—basically, all the alternative therapies that are often mocked as Goop nonsense, even though they are based in ancient spiritualities.

On a more positive note, wellness promised a different form of medicine that connected the spiritual to the physical; it was a more holistic approach to health that contrasted with the alienating aspects of Western medicine and offered people a sense of control over their own bodies and health.

Regrettably, as it's become more mainstream, wellness seems to have absorbed the deeper meaning of self-care into itself, diluting the radical, community-driven aspects by over-use of the term and its application. I first understood the idea from the book *A Burst of Light* by poet, novelist, and civil rights activist Audre Lorde, who wrote that "Caring for myself is not self-indulgence, it is self-preservation, and that is an act of po-litical warfare." Lorde wrote those essays as she battled liver cancer; the gravity of her condition combined with the esteem in which I held her work made self-care seem like a rather serious undertaking meant for people on the front lines of saving the world. But three decades after *A Burst of Light* was published, after Donald Trump's election, it seemed like everyone who did a mud mask was posting a selfie on Instagram tagged with #selfcare, and they were only half joking.

It struck me as ludicrous and self-indulgent. It also looked really nice. I am human, and I was worn out. I needed care of some kind, and turning inward seemed safer than anything that was happening on the outside. Wouldn't being a better person be good for everyone? Wouldn't I be a better person if I felt better? Wouldn't I feel better if I looked better? It seemed not only possible but life-affirming and responsible to continue to focus on my packaging and to call it necessary for my health. My skepticism about the entire undertaking had been eroded until I barely remembered my hesitation about "working on myself" as a philosophy.

After a few months of meeting with Daniel, he started to pay more attention to what I was doing when we were together. One afternoon, he caught me looking at myself in the mirror as I pulled on the rowing machine.

"I see you checking yourself out there," he joked.

"I wanted to see my form," I insisted, reddening.

"No, you're looking good. Keep going, you're doing good work on yourself."

Daniel's praise pushed me even further away from my reservations about "working on myself" as a solution to being alone or an alternative to making the planet a better place. Close to my birthday, I was lying in bed watching *Arrow*. Katie

Cassidy plays Black Canary on the CW version of the DC Universe story. I found her absolutely entrancing. I might have just had a crush, but it had been a long time since I'd felt much interest in embodying femininity as it's presented on basic cable. My curiosity about her felt meaningful. I wanted to know what lipstick she wore, her conditioner, how her eye shadow changed so seamlessly from day to night. I wanted to walk in her skin—and not because she was a superhero. She looked so relaxed about being beautiful.

That weekend, I went into a Sephora and wandered the aisles, looking for that lipstick; something that would look like my natural lips, except better. By the time I left, clutching a Smashbox makeup set, four different eyeliners, and two lipsticks that would prove to fall short of my expectations, my face was smeared with glitter and streaky mascara, BB Cream congealing in the lines around my eyes. Hours had passed. When I got home, the purchasing fever continued. I bought a pair of high-heeled Cole Haan boots, plus some jeans in my new smaller size. I ordered a Drunk Elephant face serum that costs eighty dollars an ounce after reading in the "Beauty" Slack room at one of my jobs that it was the best one. I had never heard of vitamin C serum, but having the best one was now important. I decided it was all a birthday present to myself.

None of these "acts of self-care" would have been available to me without the sudden influx of money that came with all my freelancing. I was earning more than I ever had. If my financial history were a heart rate, it would have looked like a flatline hit with a defibrillator that year. Never before had I had so much disposable income, and I spent it as freely as anyone who is making bank for the first time—pretty stupidly, and without regard to the inevitable blow of self-employment taxes.

Money made it possible to buy high-quality food in large quantities, to pay a personal trainer for their oversight at the gym. Money made a big difference in the habits I could indulge in, the lifestyle I could enjoy, and the sorts of activities I categorized as self-care.

The workload was insane, but whatever unhappiness I felt about that could be soothed with purchases. These purchases were marketed to me via the same poisonous Internet info stream I worked for, either directly through ads, indirectly through the kinds of lifestyle articles that clog women's media, or through my own social media timelines; escaping the horrors of my Twitter feed to read a Reddit thread on different skin brightening techniques was a balm to my mind, as well as a way of finding something that could be bought for my face.

When you're poor, soothing yourself is limited to things that are free and things that are cheap. I hadn't been having sex, a delightful pastime that should be relatively inexpensive when practiced responsibly. The other, most accessible cheap thing after fornication was junk food. Stressed? I'd eat a bag of Goldfish crackers. Much more affordable than therapy. Bored and lonely? I borrowed a friend's Netflix password. Hurray! Six hours of my life passing in a binge-watch. There was also meditation, but that would have required listening to my internal thoughts. No thank you.

Suddenly, I could buy the sorts of distracting indulgences that came at a higher price. I hadn't paid anyone to color my hair in a long time, having been a hair model for aspiring aestheticians across Manhattan for years. There had been some disasters, but it mostly looked okay. Now I wanted it to look much better than okay. A friend recommended a hair stylist to me, and I was served a glass of prosecco in her chair. She looked critically at my reflection as I sipped.

"You see these bands?" the stylist said, poking my scalp with the end of her paintbrush. "You can see lots of people have done your color differently. We're gonna fix that." She took possessive ownership of my hair, adding balayage highlights to break up the discoloration, hacking away at the mass until I had a shaped shag instead of a dense curtain. I bought hair products that made it curly or flat as the mood struck me, and actually learned to use them.

"Your haircut is the haircut of someone who is starting something," an old teacher told me when she saw me at the theater. Everywhere I went, people commented on my appearance. "Your energy is really incredible right now," an acquaintance drawled when we ran into each other at a deli in Greenpoint.

Had I looked so bad before? I didn't know if I had or if I just now looked like someone who was desperately trying and needed a kind word of encouragement. Often, people discover the different ways that conventional beauty is rewarded by losing some marker of it, but I was going the other direction, becoming slowly addicted to the attention and self-assurance that came with conforming.

At the end of January, the Whole30 experiment finished and the Facebook group disbanded. From there, I tried a month of keto, and a month of the Slow Food diet, chasing the supportive structure that had carried me through the first month of the year. By the end of March, I had lost thirty pounds. I started eating more habitually, but the change had been made. Thrilled to admit my gym time had amounted to something measurable, I posted an updated pic of myself on Facebook, and an old hookup from years ago messaged me to ask if I'd like to meet up again. Though it would have ended my dry spell, I declined.

As hard as it was to lose weight or make the money to support my serum habit, letting go of the praise and support wasn't an option. It was easier to change my entire being than to reject the positive reinforcement I received for changing. I knew what people really meant when they said I seemed "happier," but my awareness didn't stop me from wanting or enjoying the benefits of their perception.

In her book *Bright-Sided*, Barbara Ehrenreich explores the history of positive thinking in America, showing how it segued from religion to business and eventually found a place in the medical industry. Ehrenreich writes that as she was battling cancer, she was battling on a second front against the insistence that she think positively as a way to fight her illness. The pressure to do so weighed on her like "a second disease," and any failure to fall in line opened her up to criticism from people who essentially implied that if she died from cancer, it was partly due to this refusal. Ehrenreich explains how one of the biggest flaws of positive psychology is that it is part of a general quest for happiness, that elusive feeling that we have come to think we should be experiencing constantly. She plainly states that most people who are happy, or generally satisfied with their lives, have pretty good reason to be. They're un-touched by many of the structural inequalities that make so many others justifiably miserable.

"Happiness, after all, is generally measured as reported sat-isfaction with one's life," she writes, "a state of mind perhaps more accessible to those who are affluent, who conform to social norms, who suppress judgment in the service of faith, and who are not overly bothered by societal injustice. . . . The real conservatism of positive psychology lies in its attachment to the status quo, with all its inequalities and abuses of power. Positive psychologists' tests of happiness and well-being, for example, rest heavily on measures of personal contentment with things as they are."

There is a lot of positive psychology folded into the confus-ing business of wellness and self-care, since being well must mean thinking positive things, right? You have to believe stuff like jade rollers and daily affirmations will change your life for them to work. If they don't, that means you don't believe it enough.

It's no coincidence that all the things I was doing that were supposed to be for self-care had the effect of making me more conventionally attractive, the same way getting "strong" and "healthy" has many of the same effects as weight-loss culture. That physical change influenced how people reacted to me. Being treated better inevitably makes you feel better, even when it's for the wrong reasons. People were treating me bet-ter because I looked better—at least, I looked like someone trying to fit a specific, limited standard of attractiveness. The good feelings that came from this treatment made the things I was doing seem like they were "working" on me internally, when it was actually a response to external support. Was that happiness? And would this type of happiness, the result of "working on myself," attract true love, as my Reddit accusers and Internet trolls believed?

It made me wonder if a relationship would function in a similar fashion, where I wouldn't so much be happy because I was in love as I would be relieved to be treated like someone in a relationship is treated. In a relationship, I'd suddenly be deemed valuable through the conformity of couplehood.

This habitual cynicism popping up was like hearing my thoughts from another era, and I dismissed it. I had the powerful sense that I had *done something* after many years of being stuck in place. That's why people on a fitness kick are so annoying—once they start seeing results, they feel like tiny gods with dominion over all they survey. Something that had seemed impossible actually wasn't impossible at all. What other impossible things could I do?

By the beginning of April, I knew what I was going to try. Much like when I started going to the gym, I didn't want to tell anyone at first. What if I failed? But what if I didn't? It was time to try to date again and see if that, too, might make me feel as good as everyone said it would.

CHAPTER 3

The One

The nail salon's bathroom was as small as a broom closet and frigid. Or at least I was shivering under a layer of thin black fabric that didn't quite have the opacity of acceptable outdoor clothing. I'd spontaneously ordered the dress I was wearing during my spending spree, and it had arrived quickly, slithering out of its plastic wrap into my hands. Sensuous to the touch, but too loose. My sense of my own dimensions was off.

The change in my body had resulted in more than a pressing need for a new wardrobe. Feelings that had long been dormant were coming to life, my physical thaw paralleling the warming city outside my window. I was three or four months into my self-improvement drill, hovering on the edge of making a dramatic decision.

Most dramatic decisions don't actually come all at once. They're created through a series of smaller decisions leading up to the final small decision, when you realize you can't turn back and jump away from the moment of truth in leaps and bounds. I'd been making small decisions for weeks, which had

brought me as far as that salon bathroom, and now I was trying to make another: Should I meet a man for sex?

I'd been hurtling toward this crossroads since early April,
when spring began to unfurl across the city. The first step
came from an observation I made in my bedroom one afternoon following a workout and a long hot shower, sitting in the
sweet-smelling breeze blowing through my window. The
apartment had been painted just before my roommate and I
moved in. The walls were a cool gray. As a younger person, I
used to throw up an accent wall or turn a whole room tur-
quoise. After too many moves, I'd resolved to let stand whatever color a place was when I arrived. It just wasn't worth
repainting when you moved out. As a result, life had become
muted, all my backgrounds in shades of taupe, eggshell, and
tasteful matte silvers. The neutrality was no longer suiting my
mood. I wanted to see neon flowers bloom across the wall, I
wanted rainbows to shoot from the floorboards. I wanted
twinkling fairy lights to drift down from the ceiling and to swirl
through my hair. I wanted to turn on the faucets and watch
liquid gold pour out until it spilled over the basin. In a word, I
was horny.

Why the suddenly oppressive walls of my bland bedroom
made me realize that is hard to say, but that night I redown-
loaded Tinder, committing to the tentative resolution I'd made
to try dating again. Over the years, I had uploaded and then
deleted quite a few dating apps, finding I was reluctant to meet
anyone in real life. It never felt right or exciting enough to follow through. I was busy with so many other things, like watching TV.

This changed with my recent explorations into Trying. Now I was trying to be different from the person who had given up on dating for so many years. The problem was that after that much time not connecting, I was as skittery as a virgin again. Action generally comes when want outweighs fear. The scales were tipping. It had become necessary to go further than I had in so long; it was time to put my mouth on someone else's mouth.

In the previous six years of mostly nothing, there'd been one thing: a single hookup with a guy I knew from my theater. He'd been the one to show me what Tinder was, and I'd downloaded it in the hope I'd see him there. I did, and we matched. That's what I'd thought the app was for—to check if people you already knew were into you. We used to ask our friends to do this work, but the robots had taken over. After he and I matched and spent the night together, I'd hoped we might have a bit more than that one night, but he wasn't interested. Perhaps if I'd kept swiping, that rejection wouldn't have sent me back into another three years of no sexual contact or dating. Instead, I'd quit the app.

Tinder had become far more popular in those three years. Apps were now central to people's dating life, no longer considered a fringe fad. Tinder launched in 2012, about two to three years after Grindr and Scruff became popular dating apps for gay men. Ashley Fetters reported for *The Atlantic* that once Tinder became available for Android, it was game over; by 2018 there were fifty-four million Tinder users worldwide.

Fetters interviewed a number of social scientists and couples' therapists, most of whom said the app hasn't been around long enough or studied rigorously enough to really give a clear

picture of how it's changing dating long term. Several inter-
viewees, however, noted that meeting your partner on dating
apps has become normalized. It was also mentioned that the
ways single people complain about dating have shifted. Folks
used to complain about not being able to find anyone single to
date. Now they have access to plenty of single people, so they
complain about not being able to find anyone they actually
like, probably because the sense of possibility that an app in-
spires is largely illusory. Those fifty-four million users are not
all located within a ten-mile radius of your house.

My profile hadn't been properly deleted, so when I opened
it again, I saw pictures of myself that were three years old. it
was like looking at a distant relative. My style, my body, my
hair had changed. It was harder to say how deep those changes
had gone. In those photos, I saw a person who was awfully
uncertain of their own appeal. I still felt that way, no matter
what size my pants were.

Since the Polar Bear swim, I'd made a lot of visible changes.
The success of those measures had encouraged some other
efforts that were less visible. Those efforts were very similar to
working out at the gym in that they were incremental and
mostly stuff other people had been telling me to try. I started
bullet journaling, which is like regular journaling with intensive structure and lots of aesthetic Instagram accounts to follow. In my journal, I planned out my days and broke up my
aspirations into manageable parts in a beautiful layout. Scrib-
bling down my targets for the year opened up my mind to
more possibilities: a one-woman show, a trip to see my friend
Dylan in Los Angeles, living alone. Fun things that didn't quite
seem possible, but that stimulated my mind to imagine.

And down below that list, I wrote: *dates???*

My logic in embracing new daily practices was that I might as well try everything and anything. The way I'd been living my life had driven me into this rut, so changing my daily grind would probably dig a much sexier new rut. And like going to the gym, these habits kinda worked. Journaling helped me track things like meditating, my mood, how many books I'd read. It was incredibly satisfying to check stuff off and make lists of items to collect my thoughts. Following bullet journal content on social media led me down more rabbit holes, and I ended up reading filmmaker Julia Cameron's 1991 self-help book *The Artist's Way,* which encouraged even more daily journaling. The book prompted me to buy plants, to say yes to a friend who was doing free Reiki sessions. Nothing was too woo-woo or silly to try, especially because once I started talking openly about doing those things I found so many other people who were on similar paths. It seemed like everyone was searching for something to make them feel better. For the moments when I was immersed in recording my own personality progress, I did.

So when I set up a new dating profile, I tried to make it look like the kind of person I wanted to be. A gym selfie, a picture of myself with my new highlights, one of me onstage. I tried to project confidence and optimism and sexiness, whether or not I was really feeling it, just like I was trying to imagine an out-of-reach future in my journals. I wasn't exactly sure who I wanted to respond to this self-advertisement. Learning to picture better things hadn't extended as far as imagining love, so there was no type of person in mind. Mostly, I wanted to see if I could break through my trepidation and into someone's arms.

After swiping for a few weeks, I matched with a man who was willing to do a colossal amount of work, at least via Tinder messaging, to soothe all my anxieties about meeting in person. He was handsome, had abs, and was new to the city. He lived alone in an expensive neighborhood, and he invited me to meet him near his apartment. I responded noncommittally. I didn't unmatch. A week later, he tried again. Nothing he said was creepy, but his intentions were clear. He wanted to put his mouth on my mouth.

In all the talk about being alone forever, I had, of course, meant that I might not ever have sex again either. Now I thought, *What if I could just flip the switch and be a sexual person again? That would be . . . something.* It still felt highly unlikely, based on my past six years. Yet, here was someone willing to meet up who appeared attractive to me. I wanted to try to see this opportunity through. Finally, I agreed to meet him.

Then I canceled, losing my nerve at the last minute. Then, a few days later, he asked again.

That was how I ended up in the nail salon that chilly night in late April. It was close to his home, and I went there on an evening he'd said he was free. That morning, I had told my Tinder beau that I would be in his neighborhood later. *Maybe we could meet up?* He agreed. As the day turned to night, I hadn't canceled. I was still *reallllly* stretching the definition of what could be called a "plan."

Once again, he demonstrated a remarkable tolerance toward my wishy-washy demands. *Let me know!* he messaged. Up until about a half hour before we met, I didn't let him know. I traveled to the salon, wearing my new dress and my new high-heeled Cole Haans. There was a birthday party for a friend just a short subway ride away, which gave me a reasonable excuse for being there, besides a date. I'd come to the East Village on a Friday night for a manicure on my way to a party, not to hook up with a random Internet man. Duh. Very stable behavior.

This subterfuge around my own feelings had brought me as far as huddling in the salon bathroom like a cornered ferret, my nails now a bright cotton-candy pink. I opened Tinder on my phone to make the next small decision, looking at his profile one more time. There he was, torso on display. My fingers were beautifully buffed icicles. They trembled as I typed.

Hey. I'm near your place. Would you like to meet for a glass of wine?

I told myself that if he hadn't messaged me back by the time I settled my bill, I'd head to the party. His response came almost immediately. Yes, he wanted to meet.

As I walked to a wine bar not far away in my fancy boots, my head felt like it was suspended five feet above my neck. The two blocks moved under my feet too fast, but it also felt like I was pushing through a viscous liquid. I wanted to go, I wanted to run away. The only reason I kept moving was because I couldn't imagine going through all those small steps to get to this first date a second time. If I turned back now, I'd have to start all over. This was it.

When I walked into the bar and saw my date, I understood I'd made a huge mistake with the heels. Starting in kindergarten, I'd always been head and shoulders above most boys.

Now, at my fully grown five feet, nine inches, I am frequently taller than many men, too. This guy wasn't just shorter than me; he looked like a perfectly proportional man who had been made at eight-tenths the size of the average model. His head barely rose above my shoulder, and I had to lean down to hug him hello.

It brought me back down to earth. It can't be easy being that petite and knowing every person you're meeting for the first time is discovering it, including the mammoth woman you're hoping to bone. Having spent most of my formative years being bigger than everybody, shorter men are often quite attractive. Once we were seated at the bar, it was barely noticeable. He was pretty and well mannered, and I relaxed with conversation. Talking to new people has never been hard for me, and I was soon able to forget the reason for us talking at all. Sort of.

My date had recently moved to New York to help establish the American branch of his company. His family was far away, and the time difference made it difficult to stay in contact. He was lonely. We talked about Tinder and traded online dating stories. I didn't have many. Because I was trying to hide that gap in my background, I kept deflecting the conversation from myself, obscuring identifying details. I still wanted an escape route, through anonymity.

How would a more personal conversation even go? *I haven't had sex in years, I felt like I was going to barf all day thinking about having sex with you, I'm worried I might not remember what to do so, maybe you should wear a helmet or something if we go through with this. I am definitely going through with this. It's time.*

We got a second glass of wine. I sat there, gradually unwinding in the candlelight. Once the decision had been made, I calmed down. Not because we were deeply connected, not because he was wickedly sexy. For a long time desire had slept, letting me live quietly in grays. Now I was awake, and I needed more. More life. More color. This awakened desire was voracious and could not go peacefully home to an empty bed.

As we saw the bottoms of our wine glasses again, the question was in the air. Would I take those final steps, back to his apartment?

"Yes," I said, obliterating the line I'd been redrawing for myself again and again all night. We walked shoulder to shoulder, me tottering high above him, around the corner, then up three flights of stairs. My feet screamed.

The interior of his apartment was spare, a walk-through looking out onto the busiest block of St. Mark's Place. The noise of folks out prematurely celebrating the fine weather pumped in, even through the closed windows. In one corner of the front room was a keyboard. He was a musician and an art collector. He showed me the limited-edition prints he had framed and not yet hung on the empty walls. He opened another bottle of red wine and poured me some in a jam jar and led us both to the couch. I took one sip before he started to kiss me. He pulled back.

"Do you mind," he whispered, "if I just go down on you?"

"Of course not," I sputtered. Having already made the drastic choice to pop the first-sex-of-my-thirties cherry, this was quite the upset for my expectations. I found I was much more relieved than disappointed. He pulled me up and led me to his bed in another bare white room at the back of his apartment, which smelled of some masculine cologne. This space shrunk sound as though the walls were padded, emphasizing the harsh edges of our breathing. The smell triggered echoes of the past, reminding me of how I used to be.

Once, I was someone who could meet a person on the dance floor and be making out with them before the song was over, I remembered. There was a time when I had the bravado to flirt with anyone, when I'd been sure the next person who would want to date me was right around the corner, because they usually were. I was someone whom a friend described as having an "awe-inspiring sexuality"—a remembrance that had become more ludicrous as the years went by. But I *was* once that person. A crisis in confidence, a disconnect from her body, some heartbreak, and the eroding effects of time had all conspired to subdue her; but she was asleep, not dead. That ravening past self took over.

Gamely, I let him disrobe me and toss the cheap black dress into a shadowy pile on the floor. He scrambled to get to my breasts. That, at least, had not changed since the last time someone took my clothes off. My breasts had always attracted fans. As he leaned over my naked body, the long silver chain and pendant that had been under his shirt fell down between us, getting in the way. He tore it off and threw it against the wall.

Whatever his reasons for wanting only to provide oral sex, this passionate gesture convinced me of his unbridled enthusiasm. He was good at it. Eventually, I asked if I could reciprocate. He murmured meekly, "Only if you want to."

I did want to, partly to be courteous and partly because, after all the buildup, it felt like I should have done more. He seemed amazed after he came.

"You're cool," he murmured in a stupefied way.

Afterward, we lay naked on top of his still neatly made bed. I don't know what I thought would happen next, but I was nonplussed when he pulled me close, sliding an arm under my head. Lying down, the difference in our sizes didn't matter at all.

The tremendous intimacy of being held again was almost unbearable. Immediately, I knew that this was the *more*, the thing that wasn't just sex. This was life pulsing against life, sated together and in harmony for a brief moment before reality encroached.

As I lay there, I imagined what it would be like to be held by this man regularly, to visit him on Saturday nights and wake up together on Sunday mornings. Would he bring me coffee in bed? Play a song for me on his keyboard as I read on the couch? I don't even read the Sunday *Times*, but in this fancy, I would, and we'd discuss the news over brunch.

And it would make such a good story. That I had waited so long, only to find My Person on my very first Tinder date in years, after making this huge fuss online about being alone forever. So funny! So ironic! Just when I least expected it!

Isn't that what people had been saying to me? Love comes when you least expect it. Love is a sly trickster, eavesdropping on your conversations to see if you've expressed just the right level of despair to leap from the bushes and yell, "SURPRISE, BITCH!" In a post-orgasm haze, I could see it there, poorly camouflaged and waiting for me.

I wasn't *completely* delusional. I realized it might take a minute before we had an actual relationship. I was happy to come over and enjoy oral sex until he realized I was an amazing catch.

There actually was that birthday party I'd been planning to go to, so I got up and found my clothes. Confident now, I kissed him lightly goodbye, assuming we'd see each other again, very soon. I took the train across the river to Union Pool, where my friends were standing around a firepit. I felt very clear-headed, like I'd just recovered from a sinus infection and could breathe again. His smell was on my neck, and the smell of the soap in his bathroom was on my hands. My large jacket felt like an embrace on my sensitized skin. I was alive! How peculiar that for so many years I hadn't been able to feel this way and now I could. The power!

I zipped from conversation to conversation like a child in the perilous hours after dessert and before bedtime, simultaneously replaying the details of my evening in my head and eyeing the crowd. Everyone looked so beautiful all of a sudden and I was greedy for more. I'd just been naked with one person. Why not another? I'd have to tell my guy that I wanted to date around for a bit before we settled into something exclusive, but he'd understand.

My friend Andrew was there. I cornered him and explained that I'd just had a hookup, eliding the oral-only details to make it bigger news. He knew, just like everyone knew, how long it had been for me.

"Oh my god," he murmured. "How do you feel?"

"Incredible," I said.

"Are you going to do it again?" he asked.

"I don't know," I said. "I hope so."

The hesitation made my vision of that future deflate a bit. Just the same, for the next few days, I rode the high of a successful encounter. Successful in the sense that it had happened, I'd enjoyed it, and it seemed like it could happen again. We had exchanged numbers. I waited until late the following week to text and ask if he'd like to meet again. He responded yes, how about that night? I wasn't free.

"How about next Tuesday?" I wrote.

No answer ever came. It took me longer than it should have to realize one never would. I did restrain myself from messaging him again. Despite having been out of the game for a spell, I knew unanswered texts aren't just forgotten. They're being ignored.

Ghosting someone is almost always unnecessary and almost always unkind, but there was no way for this guy to know how huge a letdown it was for me. He didn't know about my years of celibacy, the inch-by-inch journey I'd had to take to get to his bed. The workouts, the diets, the affirmations, the new wardrobe and hair and pages and pages of journaling. It was sort of like watching a rom-com montage where the heroine goes through a transformation, only to face-plant into an open sewer.

It was almost funny how personally I took it. Didn't he understand what I'd been *going through*? No, he had no idea. Nor did I know what he was going through, nor what happened to him after we met. Maybe he died. I didn't want that to be the case, but it would certainly have explained everything. . . .

In the weeks afterward, I wasn't sure how to proceed. I took to my bed, marathoning *Arrow* and eating macaroni. I tried to tell myself that no one knew about my little foray into dating; if anyone asked, I still lived on an island of singleness. No one had to know about my failed attempt to escape. Then I remembered blabbing about sucking a D at that birthday party and hit play on the next episode to avoid thinking about it.

Getting ghosted stung, leaving me lonelier than before I'd met that random man. It was scary. This person I'd known so briefly had managed to do all that to me. What if I wasn't able to try again, what if I collapsed under the disappointment? The fate of ending up alone felt more determined than ever.

I'd thought sex was all I wanted. In some ways, it had been satisfying to dip my toes back in the pond of physical connection. Then it had just stirred even deeper needs. I wanted more, but how would I get more without going through all of this again? How many times could I go through this?

A lot, I ultimately decided after a few weeks of journaling on the subject. I could go through it a lot. It had been unpleasant. I didn't want the same thing to happen again. On the other hand, I'd tried so hard to act differently in the last few months. I'd made steps that had seemed unachievable very recently. It was the perfect moment to question every seeming impossibility.

Finally, one afternoon, I got up, got dressed, and went outside to feel the sun on my face filtering through flowering trees. I even put on lipstick. The heart is a muscle, I mused, kicking a pebble down Eastern Parkway. For some people it's easy to build up the fortitude to find love or choose love or whatever verb fits for them. For me, it was a workout. I needed to build up the ability to connect with other people like I'd built up my ability to do a shoulder press, so that the next time it would be easier.

With that comparison in mind, I revised my dating resolution. I vowed to go on two dates a week, every week, no matter what. Whether I was tired, glum, gassy, scared, or fed up. Whether I met anyone I liked or not. Whether I had sex or not. Whether they called after or not. My reasoning was I'd get so used to the process that no rejection could ever touch my emotions again. My heart would develop a protective callus from regular handling.

CHAPTER 4

A Room of One's Own

"You look like Geena Davis," said the real estate agent. She was saying that because I was handing her an absolutely enormous sum of money. But it was okay; I enjoyed hearing I looked like Geena Davis.

"Oh, wow, thanks; she's a beautiful lady."

The agent turned to a man sitting on a chair far across the office, on his phone, waiting for his turn to give her an enormous amount of money.

"Doesn't she look like Geena Davis?" she called to him as I signed on all the dotted lines.

"Who?" he shouted back.

This was the first time I'd given an actual real estate agent any money, ever, having mostly moved from place to place by word of mouth and without a lease. Now I was moving into my very own apartment. My roommate was moving in with her boyfriend. For the first time in my life, I was living alone. It was a dream I'd never thought I'd achieve, and even with all the extra work I was doing I couldn't quite manage it; the next year of paying my rent felt like clinging to a ledge over a pit, though I did it with a smile on my face. Never having had much money, I had no idea how to manage it. It was a whopping financial mistake to pay so much rent, and I'd needed a real estate agent's help to make that mistake. At least the compliments were gratis.

"Goodbye, Geena!" she waved as I exited her office, leaving behind most of my savings and clutching a pair of keys.

My new apartment was on the top floor of a walk-up brownstone, four long flights that creaked and twisted so much that my friend Andrew yelled, "What is this, Hogwarts?" the first time he came over.

The ceiling sloped under the roof. The small space was divided in two by a sliding door thick enough to keep my cats, Bert and George, out at night when I slept. There were only two windows, both with deep-set ledges. The view was extraordinary, showing most of Downtown Brooklyn and the Manhattan skyline. A giant tree obscured that view somewhat, but the wind playing in the leaves was the lullaby that sent me to sleep each night.

The only problem with my new apartment was that it was too far from my gym. I had to bid a melancholy adieu to Daniel.

"Keep up the good work—you're getting good at this," he said, referring to my ability to jump rope for as long as forty seconds at a time without stopping. Leaving the gym for the last time, I said goodbye to it, too. It was a place that had begun to feel meaningful to me because I recognized so many people there, familiar faces who weren't quite friends.

There are a lot of people in our lives like that, people you might not even really notice are such an important part of your day to day until suddenly they're not. I had a transactional relationship with the men and women who worked at the desk, a light connection in which I was paying for a service. The people who lifted weights around me and nodded hello in the locker room, and even Daniel, had no idea who I was outside of that space. I still probably saw them more regularly than most of my actual friends.

These types of connections are called "consequential strangers," a term coined by authors Melinda Blau and Karen Fingerman, who published a book by that title in 2009. A consequential stranger is someone who can't be categorized as a friend or even necessarily a friendly acquaintance. They're just someone you're used to seeing in your life. Consequential strangers are co-workers, people at the dog park, the people who pass by your desk, who populate your yoga class every Wednesday, a neighbor you say hey to when you grab your paper in the morning, or somebody you see at your favorite coffee shop on their laptop in the afternoon. There are far more consequential strangers in your life than intimate relationships, and in some cases, you'll see the supposedly unimportant people more often than your best friend.

In an interview with *Time*, Blau explained the importance of people who aren't in your deepest circle. "We've been conditioned to think that our intimates are the most important people in our life. But both in our personal lives and in our business endeavors, the freshest information, the exposure to the most novel experiences, comes from people on the periphery. That's because our intimates think the way we think and they know what we know, whereas people who are what the sociologists call 'weak ties' don't. They're different from us, they link to other networks and different kinds of information, and therefore they are the place where we find opportunity."

The meaning of the word "opportunity" is nebulous. It sounds like Blau means more material opportunities, but connecting with people outside your echo chamber has lots of benefits that can't be translated into measurable results. In the neighborhood sense, knowing people around you makes your daily life safer and alleviates the sense of disconnection that is apparently plaguing most of the population. When the pandemic hit in 2020, much would be made of the loss of "weak ties," an updated term for a global disaster. For people who move a lot, the pattern of forming weak ties and then severing them is very familiar; in the first March of COVID-19, everyone got a crash course in how it feels to lose the small relationships they'd probably not thought much about before.

Blissfully unaware of this future in May of 2017, I joined a gym a few blocks away from my new apartment to re-create the method Daniel had taught me, adding my own embellishments. I was unconsciously trying to establish that same sense of community I'd had at my old gym. Then, about a week into my membership, one of those embellishments sent me falling to the floor clutching my leg in agony. I groaned like a harpooned walrus as the woman next to me calmly continued her barbell swings.

As best as I can describe the feeling, it was like a muscle in my thigh bent in rather than out, rebelling against God's design. Eventually, I got the barbell swinger to make eye contact with me and asked her to call the manager. She didn't seem too happy about it. He was not particularly impressed with my need for assistance either, so I dragged myself out onto the street, away from the cursed gym full of unknowns. They probably thought I was being an overdramatic dork, which is who I am only part of the time. They didn't know me, except as some lady whining about her boo-boo. I wasn't even the lady they saw every day who was now whining about her boo-boo.

My pain hadn't significantly improved by the time I made it to my building. A damaged thigh wasn't quite enough to make me completely unravel, though I did sit for a long moment at the bottom of that staircase, thinking about the hubris of renting a fifth-floor walk-up apartment. How confident I'd been in my energy, good health, and ability to hack it on my own. Exercising my body to the point of injury so brainlessly. Stupidly assuming anyone would be willing to help. I was so arrogant. If there hadn't been groceries awaiting me upstairs, I might have sobbed.

The pain of a pulled muscle took a week or so to fade. I was able to order takeout and buzz people in, though I usually crawled to meet them halfway down the Escher-painting stairwell out of guilt. My health wasn't something I took for granted, having grown up in a household with a parent whose health was always in jeopardy. Compared to my mom, I was a strapping milkmaid transported from the Swiss Alps. By the time I was eleven years old I'd shot up to be a foot taller than her, with width to match. When I was a teen, I remember people coming up to her and saying things like "she's bigger than momma" and "looks cornfed" and once, very memorably, "that's a bonnie lass you have!"—this from an enthusiastic elderly Irish man. He sounded like he wanted to saddle me.

It was good that I was strong. I always thought of my health in terms of my mom being sick, and my ability to help her. Whenever I was ill or hurt myself, I tended to slide into despair, believing it would go on and on and that there would be no one to help me.

It's deeply frightening to think about some calamity changing everything about how you work or socialize or even move from place to place without assistance. That's how a lot of folks are living right now, due to age or disability. Circumstances could change for literally any able-bodied person at any time, or time itself could be the cause. Managing to live a long life means almost inevitable shifts in mobility and accessibility. While alternating ice and heat, I let myself consider what it might be like if I never met anyone, never had kids, and grew to an old age. If that's what my mother had done, who would have taken care of her?

To keep these dark and arguably unreasonable thoughts of the future at bay, I focused on my self-proposed dating project. Laid up on the couch, I opened Tinder. Bumble. OKCupid. I started swiping on all of them, and soon there were a lot of matches to check. I messaged people. It seemed unlikely that anyone would go to as much trouble to eat me out as my last date had, which meant I had to be the aggressive one.

Who's next? I mused, looking through pictures, wondering if I'd see anyone I knew. Quickly, I learned that matching with someone was no guarantee there'd be a message response, a response didn't necessarily mean an engaging conversation, and conversation did not mean you'd ever go on a date. Apps had seemed like the most efficient way to meet new people, but after a few days I was questioning that presumption.

Why was it so hard? I had a very low bar for taking it from

the screen to the suggestion of a drink in real life: don't say anything hair-raising within the first five sentences, live nearby, and be willing to meet up within the next day or so. Not many parameters and they were astonishingly difficult to meet. In the past, when I'd hit a wall with connecting to people via app, I'd simply put my phone down. This was no longer something I was allowing myself, so I went harder, crafting enticing intro messages to every Tinder and Bumble match until my hand was cramping as much as my leg.

I finally got a man to agree to meet me for a glass of wine in Park Slope, around the time that I was recovered enough to hobble to the train station. With a thigh twinge, I wondered why I hadn't insisted he come closer to me. I'd told him I was slightly impaired, and he hadn't offered, so I'd been afraid to ask and lose my chance with him.

The day was warm and windy. The bar my date chose had a small fenced-off patio in front, facing the busy traffic of Fifth Avenue. It was lined with Astroturf. I bought a jar full of cheap wine and tried to get to know this unwitting human variable. I must admit that I no longer remember his name. It was something like Dan or Matt. One of the top-five guy names. He was of average height, wearing a plaid long-sleeved shirt over his faded T-shirt, hair slightly long, beard slightly grown in. Picture the most generic white man ever and you'll see him.

Once again, it was easier for me when I was face-to-face with my date, especially because I could sit down and rest my leg. After a gulp of overly fruity vino, I set about trying to get to know him. I failed abysmally. Every question I asked was met with a response of a single sentence. Any topic I introduced fizzled immediately. After that first drink, I knew approximately two things about my date. He'd recently been dumped, and he worked in music. I don't think he knew a single thing about me, because he seemed to have some sort of moral objection to asking questions.

Inexplicably, he still wanted to get a second round. I did, too. It was nice to be sitting outside with someone, and I wanted to try to give this a chance. It might be that you're supposed to be bored on dates, I thought, at least at first. This person wasn't special to me. We were there to see if we *could* be special to each other. Though I was already certain we never would be, just going through the motions felt kind of special in itself. It felt good, like stretching after a long car ride. That's all dating really was, it seemed in the moment—practicing treating people like they could be special to you someday.

However, by the end of my second jar, I didn't know Dan/Matt any better, so I said goodbye and limped back to the train. I'd done it, I'd gone on a date and it had been fine! I wasn't thrilled by the ordeal, but I felt proud of myself for seeing things through.

I was waiting on the platform when I got a surprising text from him.

So I guess we're not tearing each other's clothes off? he wrote.

I was baffled. I wondered, had he felt an attraction to me? He'd seemed just as disinterested as I'd felt. I responded diplomatically.

You seem cool, but it didn't feel like either of us felt any sexual chemistry.

Well, there was something holding me back, he replied.

What? I texted as my mind leapt to all sorts of possibilities: He'd been celibate for years, too. He turns into a werewolf after dark.

I noticed something on your lower lip. Is that ok? Wasn't sure what it was, he answered.

It's kind of amazing that someone you barely know can cut with a surgeon's precision into one of your deepest insecurities. What my hypochondriac suitor was referring to was a scar on my lower lip, the result of an accident from preadolescence.

It was one of those days in my childhood that holds so much shame, I can't think about it without becoming that kid again. I can see my dad angrily swinging his golf club, pissed off at me for how I'd handled driving the golf cart, though it had been at his suggestion. He had slapped me just before he took that swing, the only time I remember being hit in the face by one of my parents. His mother, my grandmother, pats my shoulder as I cry, my face is turned toward the green as she holds me. When my dad's golf ball ricochets off a tree, it hits me square in the mouth.

I can see him leaning over me with a bloodied T-shirt in the hospital parking lot, his face twisted by panic and remorse, looking at me and murmuring, "It's so bad, it's so bad."

I can see myself alone in the restroom shortly before submitting to fourteen stitches. I'm very young, six or seven, but I know, looking at the split in my lip going halfway down my tiny chin, that there will always be a scar. Now I'll never be perfect, I think. Over the years, I'll often think that when I paint over the scar putting on lipstick or bite down on it by accident inside my mouth. The scar diminished significantly over time; most people claim not to notice it. But occasionally, someone will ask what it is.

Receiving this message, I couldn't help but think for a moment that this flaw has been the thing keeping me from finding someone to kiss all this time. I'll never be perfect, and only perfect people are loved.

What I wrote was *It's a scar.*

So it's not contagious? he asked.

Have you ever known a scar to be contagious? I replied, loving that I was also being called a liar. *Don't stress, we are def never making out now. But good luck out there!*

I didn't really wish him luck. I wished him at the bottom of the sea.

My scar was something I mostly forgot about, having lived with it for decades; it was incredible that by allowing someone into my life for the time it takes to drink ten ounces of booze, I'd given them access to this dark recollection, along with the power to bring it to the forefront of my mind. Astounding that he would push harder, insinuating that I am not only contagious but deceitful and looking to deliberately spread my disease to innocent men, though I'd basically just told him I had no interest in ever pressing my deformed lips to his.

And I still had one more date to go that week.

By the time I got home, it was long past dark. I made my aching way up the stairs and unlocked my door. When I closed it behind me, I was incredibly grateful to be alone.

CHAPTER 5

Destiny

A few nights later, I met a woman at a different bar. I actually did find myself hoping I'd get to make out with her, assuming she wasn't grossed out by my mouth. My profile was visible to all genders. It had been even harder to get women to meet me off of dating apps than men, even on apps meant just for women. It made me think I was generally less attractive to the gals than the men, or that the potential for a one-night stand was less appealing to them. Women may more carefully guard their time. Trying to find two dates to go on every week had made my own perspective on dating pretty deranged. My time was free to give, as long as someone would take it, because I just wanted to get through this dating boot camp. I couldn't accurately compare myself to other women.

Anna was very tall and thin and more beautiful than me, and she seemed to think so, too. I'd ordered pizza as I'd waited for her, and she didn't appear to enjoy watching me eat it. She could not stand long against my persistent interest in her, however. She soon relaxed and began to tell me about her life. She was employed by a large tech company, though she declined to tell me which one. She did say her job entailed building models of human behavior. Because I am scientifically illiterate, I imagined her building an actual model out of paper and cardboard—little towns where tiny cutouts of people are pushed back and forth across a painted grid.

She cut through this whimsical notion by commenting, "Like, eventually an algorithm will decide who all of your friends are. So I try to model how that will work."

This is a completely obvious point to anyone who has ever thought about it before, but since I spent most of my time thinking about myself, I never had.

"What do you mean?" I asked, still grappling with the mental picture of it.

"Well, you know, Facebook is already working to determine who you meet and where, suggesting events where you're likely to meet a certain circle of people," she said. "Eventually, all of people's interactions will be monitored and directed by social media networks, so the person you end up with will be decided by technology."

This speculation, which wasn't very new, struck me with horror. I'd been conditioned by movies and TV to think of love as this semi-magical destiny trail, something that defies the odds. Love stories are so often focused on unlikely pairs, on people overcoming obstacles to be together, or the hand of fate intervening so that they can meet. Now it's the hand of Mark Zuckerberg, or whoever will be in charge of the next frontier of digital romance intervention.

Facebook Dating did launch in September of 2019, a bit late to the dating app game. It was built on a platform that already involved sexual networking in many ways. Who hasn't friended someone they met once at a party and hoped to meet again? Who hasn't sent a private message for a little late-night flirting? Facebook is the highly evolved descendent of Zuckerberg's original hot-or-not site FaceMash, a place to judge who is or is not attractive with a click. Access and avenues for flirtation are frequently what regular social media platforms are about, and Facebook Dating has many benefits. One is that you can easily filter out both friends and friends of friends and jump outside the folks you know or who know someone you know. The other benefit is building a "crush list" of people you *are* Facebook friends with. If you end up on their crush list, too, you get a little notification. Very nice.

It's also a pretty handy way to plug one more aspect of your life into Facebook, a company with a long history of invading users' privacy. At its launch, no plans were announced for how the dating app would make money, but as *Vox* reported, every user is giving even more personal information away, stuff that may be much more frequently updated and checked on than what you post for your aunts and uncles to see in your regular newsfeed. Facebook has a much deeper read on your private life than Tinder or Hinge, too. They can practically fact-check your dating profile to see if you really like traveling and long walks on the beach.

I'd certainly felt conflicted about opting in to the mass surveillance and data mining of social media. I'd still done it. Would the final invasion into my love life be so different? Would I even notice my behavior being directed and manipulated? It's not that unusual for people to spend time with other people who are already like them, already in the same socioeconomic circles, whom they meet through school or work or in their neighborhood. But the external influence of social media performing behavior modification on us all makes those circles even smaller and tighter, and they're making money off that insularity.

"Should we get another drink?" Anna asked, and I saw I'd drained mine without thinking about it. Anna and I were very different, too different to really be compatible, but we continued to enjoy our chat as I finished my slice.

As we started our third round, she showed me pictures of herself on her phone in latex fetish gear at a BDSM event. I could see why she didn't eat pizza—she'd have to buy a new weekend wardrobe. We mostly talked about dating and the constant deluge of people already in open relationships on Tinder and Bumble. She told me a story of willingly dating a woman with a partner, which kept her too busy to make time for their next meetup.

"I'm not going to wait a month just to have sex with you, you know?" she said. I didn't, but I nodded.

Suddenly she asked, "Do you usually do this? Ask people out so quickly?"

It was hard to say "Well, I'm doing this whole thing where I force myself to go on dates so maybe one day I can have a 'traditional' love life," or that she was one of the small handful of people I'd even gone out with in the last few years.

"You were communicative and responsive," I said instead. "Usually, if people are terrible, they reveal themselves quickly, unless they're deceitful. In which case, you won't know."

"Maybe I will try that on Tinder, too," she said. Then she leaned over to whisper a secret to me, saying, "I don't think this bar is very gay."

Anna was right. I had chosen the bar because it had said online that it was frequented by LGBTQ+ people. And because it sold pizza. Looking around, I saw that it wasn't very gay. I flushed when she pointed it out, feeling exposed as someone who didn't know what they were doing to such a degree that they hadn't even noticed their mistake.

"Well, we're both here," I whispered back. She smiled.

Anna told me more about the sex parties she'd been to. In theory, I was interested. In practice it sounded like going white-water rafting when you've only ever been on a paddle boat. Even though I was used to doing most new things alone, I didn't want to be awkward at a party where people were fornicating. I tried to explain that, and she assured me most parties are very intense about consent. I explained I was more worried about standing alone like a loser.

"That could happen," she replied. Soon after this discouraging answer, we parted ways. I wondered afterward if I should reach out. She'd seemed happy to spend the evening with me, but shouldn't there be some spark? Some certainty that this person would even say yes to a second date? I wasn't sure if a second date with the same person would count toward my two-dates-a-week objective. Going on lots of first dates isn't the same as trying to date the same person more than once. The latter was hard to conceive.

Dating apps are sometimes accused of giving the impression that there is always someone better, more attractive, more personable, and more fun one swipe away. Profiles tend to lead with the most flattering photos, making you suspect that the neighborhood is filled with lines of smoking singles. Actually, Tinder got into some hot water when people realized they were using the Elo score to pair potential mates. The Elo score system would rank people by attractiveness based on swipes, then show people of "high attractiveness" to one another and leave the rest of us uggos to chat each other up. They've updated their algorithm, though they're no longer terribly opaque about how the process of matching works now. There are probably users who were upset to think they weren't that attractive, based on the people they were being shown under the Elo system. I was more creeped out by what is essentially breeding people for looks.

Yes, technology was already controlling our sex lives in ways it shouldn't. My encounters, though, began to make me think that people weren't necessarily looking for someone better-looking or even "cooler" with every swipe. It was more like they thought the lines of people never ended. Dating has become a numbers game, and the number is infinity.

Except it isn't. Over time, I started to notice that I'd see many of the same people on all the apps. Sometimes I was shown the same person over and over, until I began to feel an affection for them. Here we both are, I'd think, trying our best to get out there, still with our profiles up.

I set a rule for meeting within a few days of matching partly because I had to hustle to meet my self-imposed two-dates-a-week quota, and partly because I noticed that if I left things too long without making a plan, one or both of us would fall off the conversation. It was like I could feel myself sliding down the queue. Even if there'd been some promise in our initial conversation, I couldn't compete with an abundance of new prospects burying me on their match list.

"Now or never," I'd tell myself, before asking some rando if they'd want to get a drink or coffee sometime.

After a month or so, I started telling people in my life what I was doing. I'd realized that part of the practice of two dates a week had to be admitting that I was trying, even if I was scared of being exposed as a loser if I never met anyone who wanted to be with me. Most people I told either were kind and receptive or ultimately didn't give a crap how I was wasting my Saturday nights. Some were doing the same Tinder dance. A few didn't really get dating apps, having met someone at work or through a friend of a friend. Coupled folks or luddites had hesitations about app dating, but they weren't worried about the potential for becoming romantic cattle, herded into the abattoir of algorithmic connection. They were literally afraid that people on apps were bigger jerks than the usual jerks one meets in real life.

Was using the algorithm of apps inherently worse or narrower in scope than meeting people in real life? Would I be treated better by someone who was accountable to people who knew us both? At one point, I matched with a former roommate and shyly asked if he'd like to go on a date, thinking apps *were* still just a way of vetting who in your life already was available and interested.

"Oh, sorry!" he responded. "My girlfriend lets me swipe on here for fun, but I'm not single."

How fun for me.

A few days after my date with Anna, I was rehearsing for a sketch show. The director had asked me to participate, and I didn't really know most of the other cast members, but pretending to be someone who can't stop farting for a sketch quickly makes you friends with your scene partners.

The tech run-through was going along at the usual achingly slow pace, music stopping and starting, the lights lowering then coming on too bright in the eyes of people onstage. I was wearing a long white nightgown covered in fake blood. I was playing Bloody Mary, summoned to a little girl's sleepover. The guy playing the kid's dad, Charles, was an actual dad. We didn't know each other well, though I did know he was divorced. I watched him pacing farther downstage, dressed imprecisely like Bruce Springsteen for the next sketch. Sensing my perusal he turned around, lowered his prop sunglasses, and pointed right at me.

Despite having "done comedy" for many years, I'd never really dated a comedian. That one person I'd slept with in the middle of my six-year dry streak was a guy who worked at the theater I performed at most. Having to see him afterward had ruined the allure of shitting where I eat. But Charles was a very different guy, and I wasn't the same person I'd been then. When the show was over, I asked him out.

First, I texted the director, who was one of Charles's good friends, to ask if he was single, which felt like a real throwback after all the swiping.

OooOOOoohhh, let me find out for sure.

I don't know what she texted him, but she soon responded that he was and passed on Charles's number. Very retro. Dating apps have eliminated the wingman. Or woman. Charles must have been expecting my message, because when I asked if he'd like to go out some time he responded, *Sure!* without expressing any confusion.

I was confused by the way he took things in hand. Despite having leisure time to perform in comedy sketch shows with Sunday-morning tech rehearsals, he was a pretty together dude. Once he'd agreed to a date, he made all the decisions.

What about this movie? he said, sending me a link to something playing at a small indie theater. It was a dark comedy, and there'd be a talk-back with the director and cast afterward.

Oh, yes! I wrote. *That looks great, I'm excited.*

It's a date.

Charles was late to the theater. My inner clock had always been more precisely set than most other people's. I didn't believe this to be a virtue; punctuality mostly annoys folks who aren't employing you. It never felt like a choice for me. I couldn't help it. I was always early to things. If I deliberately attempted to be late, I would arrive exactly on time. It made meeting people a challenge, because waiting around for someone never gets things off on the right foot, even if it's your own damn fault.

When he did arrive, Charles looked a little on edge, which made me less tense. We were both adults. We'd shown up when we were supposed to, more or less. We could do this. Then, he revealed that he'd already bought tickets.

"No, no, no," I objected. "I asked you out. You didn't need to do that."

He shrugged, "I wanted to."

"Can I buy you a beer, at least?" I demanded and he wisely agreed. Once we had settled into the deep buckets of our seats with beer and candy, it felt a lot like being out with a friend. I didn't know Charles well, but we knew a lot of the same people. We shared a pack of Sour Patch Kids and gossiped, creating a little zone of familiarity.

The conversation was so effortless. As the lights went down, I considered whether this was how dating was supposed to feel. Yeah, that was it—dating is supposed to be slowly getting to know someone you feel at ease with until the idea of making out with them becomes appealing.

Then I remembered: sexual chemistry. There was none. Charles was definitely good-looking, but it was like being on a date with my cousin. And not the super hot one. I'd forgotten how mysterious attraction can be, like a combination lock that just won't click. I wanted to be attracted to him and wondered if I could somehow make myself feel it over time. How in control are we of our desires?

The sensation of loneliness is rooted in biology, a chemical reaction directing us to return to the safety of other people. Desire is another chemical reaction. By extension, so is love, even though many people don't like to think about it that way. In her paper "Lust, Attraction, and Attachment in Mammalian Reproduction," American anthropologist Helen Fisher explains the various chemical responses happening in our brain and body when we're falling in love or out of it. Fisher and her team of scientists at Rutgers University believe that there are three categories of romantic love: lust, attraction, and attachment.

Lust is a basic desire for sexual gratification. Attraction is differentiated from lust because it means your desire encompasses the entire person. Attachment is the bond that develops over time. The chemicals controlling each of the three are different. Lust involves testosterone and estrogen; the human body needs both to feel a sexual impulse, whether or not that body has testes or ovaries. A region of the brain called the hypothalamus triggers a release of both hormones, with testosterone playing a heavier role in stimulating the libido. Lust, at the most basic level, is our evolutionary drive to mate, no matter how thoroughly we've channeled that energy away from reproduction.

Attraction is related, but it involves reward-focused chemicals, such as dopamine, norepinephrine, and serotonin. Dopamine is released whenever we do something that feels good to us, and when you feel an attraction to someone, you're getting high doses of this delicious internal drug. You'll feel euphoric. You may even be unable to eat or sleep, a common complaint of the newly in love. The amount of serotonin in the brain decreases during attraction to levels similar to that of someone who suffers from obsessive-compulsive disorder.

Finally, if you survive the ups and downs of lust and attraction, you will theoretically arrive at attachment. Attachment isn't only the purview of romantic love. It's also present in friendships, family relationships, even regular acquaintanceships you have good associations with. The hormones involved here are oxytocin and vasopressin. Oxytocin is generally released during bonding activities, like sexy cuddling, spending time having deep conversations, breastfeeding.

Why one person and not another? It's not really something that can be entirely explained with brain scans and blood levels. As Fisher writes:

"In humans, attraction is mediated by a host of cultural stimuli. *When* an individual falls in love, *where* they fall in love, with *whom* they fall in love, *how* they court, even *whether* they choose to act on their bodily sensations of attraction can be expected to be influenced by childhood experiences, by myriad other cultural forces, and by individual volition." *Individual volition* can get a lot of pushback as a motivator for love, because it means "social conditioning." When in the grips of romantic attraction, it can feel like you have absolutely no choice in the matter, but people's responses aren't magic; they're triggered by all sorts of complicated psychological needs, and reactions to the familiar or unfamiliar. It can be about what you're told love looks like and what the dominant culture considers attractive. Who you love has as much to do with your external influences as the impulses of your own heart.

Before I was a writer, I worked at a small Brooklyn venue that catered on-site parties. The majority of the events were weddings. I served at three or four of them a week, sometimes two a day. In my black uniform, I passed the prosecco, poured red wine into emptying glasses, offered plates of gnocchi and the less popular broccoli rabe. During the wedding ceremonies, I'd stand discreetly in the background, watching for the moment the bride and groom kissed, a cue to get the crostini plates ready. If it wasn't a wedding, it was a rehearsal dinner filled with the closest friends of the future committed couple. They used our rudimentary AV setup to present slideshows of the two honorees as children, as young adults, and then (finally) as a pair. At every event, interminable speeches were broadcast from a microphone; there was nowhere to go where you couldn't hear about how these two had searched for each other, and how each of them had finally found The One.

Their lover, their equal, their best friend. Love becomes very banal when you hear the same old chestnuts expressed again and again.

That didn't mean the love being expressed was hollow, though there were some couples who gave off future-divorce energy. The repetition made me think that most people will express their love in the way they've been told to, because that's what makes it feel real or important. That was what they knew, so it was what they were going to do, even on *their* special day.

A wedding was nowhere in my immediate future. It was hard to think of what I might say during those vows. What would make me want someone? What would motivate my brain to release the necessary chemicals for love? What made love valid to me? Or triggered sexual interest? I certainly felt lust, even if it wasn't currently directed at anyone in particular, the same way you might crave fried foods out of nowhere. I just wasn't feeling it about Charles.

The movie was very dark on the scale of dark comedy, and it was about relationships, to a degree. Mostly, it was about men who never grow up and how threatening they can be to other people in their perpetual boyishness. When the lights gradually came on, the audience shifted like they were being woken from a trance. Charles looked at me, blinking his eyes rapidly.

"Whoo boy!"

That about summed it up. We sat through the talk-back, then went to get a drink at a bar nearby. He showed me pictures of his daughter on his phone. We started to talk about dating apps, and he said when he'd tried them, he'd found a lot of women didn't want to date a father or presumed it was a strain for him to do so much single parenting. He'd deleted them all quickly.

"I don't want to date someone who thinks my daughter is a burden," he said. "She's awesome, and I feel so lucky to spend time with her."

As I'd gotten older, I'd joked that I'd catch a partner on their second round. At some point, half the couples who married in their twenties would split. They'd be moving a little slower, be a little more pragmatic, ready to try something new. It was a joke that was more true than funny, because so many people I knew really were paired off. It certainly did seem like I'd missed the boat. I would have to wait for the next launch!

If I pictured it at all, I imagined potential older partners with kids in only the most perfunctory way. Charles was hardly suggesting I come be his daughter's stepmom. We had had a few beers, and it seemed like he felt open enough to be honest, that's all. It made me consider the complications of fitting into someone else's life when there were already so many key parts to it in place.

We said goodnight with a friendly hug. I felt like I wouldn't mind seeing Charles around in my community at all, even if I didn't want to go on another date. That was reassuring. So reassuring that I started to mentally go through all the people I knew in real life who I found attractive and who might be available. The number was minute, I realized, and none of them were people I'd necessarily trust to meet in company again if we had a bad date.

When I got home, I opened all my apps once more, setting my parameters even wider, increasing the age range, extending the circumference of my search. It might be hard to find someone I sparked with, but there were plenty of people to meet if I let the algorithm take me further and further afield. I'd follow wherever it wanted me to go.

CHAPTER 6

What Is Dating?

On a perfect afternoon in June, I sat fuming in a chair outside a bar around the corner from my apartment, a place called the Georgiana. I was waiting for a date named John who was almost an hour late. He claimed in his messages to be stuck in traffic, wheeling closer and closer to me by the moment from somewhere else in Brooklyn. It may even have been true, but I was pissed that this unknown entity was eating up my time with poor planning. The seconds felt like they were crawling over me, each one wasted on a person I probably wouldn't even like. I couldn't like anyone who would leave me waiting for an hour.

I kept picking up my water glass and running my fingers through its rings of sweat, forming cats, stars, hearts, then rubbing them out again and wishing I'd brought a book. The waiter would step outside periodically, take a look at me frowning at the tabletop, then step back in.

I'd developed a new system after a few dates had gone haywire in ways that felt correctable. I'd learned never to travel longer than twenty-five minutes on the train to meet someone.

I decided this after someone canceled on me while I was already on the train there. If the other person was willing to travel my direction, that was their business. Over and over, I'd ask matches, "Have you heard of the Georgiana?" They were usually willing to try it out. My ass would have worn a groove in a chair there if I hadn't mixed things up. Sometimes I sat at the slightly sticky bar, sometimes under the projector screen showing old movies or soccer; sometimes I sat in the window seat, watching the neighborhood pass by until my date arrived. On nice days and nights, I sat at one of their sidewalk tables, leaning out of my fellow patrons' cigarette smoke.

There was no one else outside yet, because it was just at the beginning of happy hour. I started and stopped work early. John was a school administrator. Meeting as soon as drinking was considered socially acceptable had seemed like a good bet for both of us. He had not stuck to the plan. As it occurred to me that I could head home and tell him to let me know if he ever made it to the bar, he arrived, dressed in a hoodie and carrying himself with surprising self-assurance, considering the delay. He projected both an awareness of how he was incredibly late and a certainty that I'd come around.

He was right in the sense that I was still there. At least this date would count toward my two for the week, I thought as we greeted each other. If I was going to stay, berating him wouldn't lead to a pleasant hour. John did apologize as he sat, and the waiter happily appeared to take his order. After we both had half-priced IPAs in front of us, we started a lazy conversation.

John was a few years older than I. He had a calm demeanor that was probably necessary for someone who spent a lot of time working with kids and bureaucracy. He slumped into his beer as we talked. He'd grown up in Flatbush and gone to a magnet high school in Manhattan. We tried to see if we knew any of the same people from school, but the ages were off. I kept trying to figure out who John reminded me of before realizing it was myself. He was trying a little. Mostly he seemed to be going through the motions.

"What are some of your hobbies?" he asked, another uninspired conversational volley. I hesitated, then made a decision.

"Dating," I said, and he laughed in the first real way since we'd sat down together.

"Yeah, I guess that's one of my hobbies, too," he admitted. "Lately I've been wondering if I'm doing too much."

"In what way?" I asked. He seemed to make a decision, too, then said:

"I dunno. I guess, how do you know when it's time to stop? There are so many people out there. . . . I've just gotten into some situations where I wonder what I'm doing. Like, there's a girl I see sometimes when she's in town."

He glanced at me and I nodded, to show that this wasn't alarming info.

"Well, she was visiting, and she left me a voicemail saying she'd be at such and such a bar at such and such a time," he continued. "But I didn't get her message. I *did* go to that bar— with another date. The first girl saw me walk in and thought I was there to meet her."

I hid my face in my hands, destroyed by secondhand embarrassment. I identified more with the girl who foolishly thought someone had shown up to meet her than with John, even though I'd not (yet) been in her situation. It was more the notion of allowing oneself excited expectations and then finding you're getting gut punched instead.

We laughed together, in an agonized way.

"Well, I don't worry about doing something like that," I said. Not enough people were excited about me to start mixing them up. Most of the people who had expressed interest hadn't been folks I'd been interested in, or they'd wanted to just hook up before I was really ready, or they'd disappeared after a few promising meetups. John seemed jaded by success. I was becoming jaded by failure.

I'd initially started dating regularly as a way to steel myself against exactly that lack of success, and it had kind of worked. After a month or so of my program, I didn't feel it that deeply when something fizzled out. But this middling apathy didn't have much to recommend it either.

I still had no idea what success would look like. There was no reference point in my head as to what dating was for, aside from developing resilience to bad dates. In January, I'd been motivated to change by the external pressure of so many people saying I should, by internal curiosity about whether I could, and by the need to know if changing myself would change how I related to other people. It was now halfway through the year, and in a way, I'd done it. I was dating after six years of not dating. In itself, that was kind of amazing.

It did not, however, feel like it had actually changed anything about the future. I could very easily still end up alone, and all these dates hadn't made me feel less lonely. If anything, going through the motions had turned dating into another something to squeeze in with my exercise and work and family time. I would say that going on lots of first dates will make you much, much better at meeting new people; it doesn't do more than that.

Before long, my internal clock was timing out my first and second drink to pace the conversation, measuring how long to stay before I could graciously end it. Dating is passing the time, I'd think. Dating is hoping for the alleviation of loneliness, I'd think. Dating is developing immunity to disappointment, perhaps. Then, after finishing my drink, I'd go, unmoved by what had transpired. I'd sometimes be a little bluer, but that was it.

In some ways, this was definitely a personal problem, perhaps a lack of imagination or positive role models. In other ways, it seemed much more universal.

For some time, what dating means to modern society has been completely up in the air. This is partly because the semi-official understanding hasn't been around very long at all, though many don't realize it. In her book *Labor of Love: The Invention of Dating*, Moira Weigel explains that, historically, most heterosexual people met and married through community; their families arranged their meeting, they crossed paths in church, they had prearranged ties settled while they were in the cradle. For upper-class white people in the West, the richer you were, the more people would get involved in your romantic future. Anyone who tried to set up or plan a date for themselves as an individual looking for love would have been considered completely looney tunes.

In a way, we've come full circle. Actual dates have become increasingly rare. A few weeks after meeting John, I tried to set up a date with someone who balked at the very word. It sounded "too serious."

"Then what would you call it?" I asked, baffled.

"A meeting. A hangout, maybe," he offered. I had to go on a date to find out if I was on a date? I passed.

According to Weigel, dating as we recognize it now began around the late nineteenth century, as more and more young people moved away from their small rural communities into big cities. Once upon a time, a young man would court a woman by "calling" on her at her house, with chaperones watching for any sign of premarital no-no behavior. This kind of courtship was approved by the elders of the family, likely with their guidance or even arrangement.

That changed when young people started going out instead, into public spaces. They had income and free time, and there were fewer prying eyes regulating their behavior. Stepping out required money, and men generally had a lot more of it than women. To go out and enjoy a dinner, a fair, or a show required some extra cash, and most ladies didn't have anything extra. It was understood that a young man taking out a young woman would "treat" her, or pay for her evening. This trend was initially shocking to the general populace, and vice squads were formed to police daters. Many women were even arrested as sex workers, though there was, and remains, a legal distinction between accepting cash and accepting an all-expenses-paid evening out.

For my happy hour with John, I paid for myself. I usually did, because despite the many decades since the development of these rituals, it was hard not to feel that pull of obligation. Of owing someone something for two ounces of hard alcohol and a mixer or a glass of wine. I always wanted to be able to get up and leave. Even though I was a confrontational person in so many ways, that drink was like a weight on me, keeping me in my seat.

John and I finished our drinks and stood to leave. I stretched my back, which was sore from sitting too long.

"If you'd like to hang out again, that would be fun," John said. "I'd be into something casual."

Obviously.

Hooking up with someone kinda charming and congenial wasn't completely unappealing, but I was betting he never showed up to assignations on time. Perhaps not even alone. I hugged him goodbye, knowing he didn't really care one way or the other, and walked around the corner to my home. The evening had cooled a bit and there was an earthy smell to the air.

Dating had quickly become so stale for me, it was funny to imagine what a revolutionary thing it once was. The advent of dating made explicit the unspoken reality that women were economically dependent on love. That troubled the wealthier, calling classes, because it threatened to undermine all of their systems, even patriarchy.

"The old-fashioned practices of chaperoned courtship and calling had drawn clear lines between the worlds of men and women," Weigel writes. "Dating undid them. It took court-ship out of the private sphere and into public places. It trans-ferred control over the process from the older generation to the younger generation, from the group to the individual, and from women to men." It doesn't seem entirely accurate to say that women waiting in sitting rooms for men to visit them were necessarily in control of the process, especially since those visitors were likely carefully vetted by their families. It is true that the direction in which invitations were extended had switched. By the late nineteenth century, women waited to be asked out rather than waiting for an invited guest to show up. The separate spheres of men and women in the late nineteenth century maintained the illusion that women kept to their homes because they were naturally loving, domestic, and pure in their willingness to sustain a household with their labor, not because economic opportunities were incredibly limited for their gender. Women who went out on dates, perhaps so they could see the newest play, were exchanging their time and company much more explicitly for gain, and the calling class found this distasteful.

The transactional nature of heterosexual dating is often a source of repulsion even now. I'd see a lot of profiles by men who stated in their bio that they weren't interested in "gold diggers," even that they'd refuse to pay for drinks, wanting to "go Dutch." Many women I knew also complained, often about the expectations men had after buying a single vodka tonic at a bar, if they offered that much. The idea that a guy would ever pay for a woman's entire meal on an evening out seemed like a dream from another generation, like a steady union job with full health and dental benefits versus freelance.

The day after my date with John, I walked to my mother's house after work. I was going to take her out to dinner at her favorite Japanese restaurant. When I arrived, her two cats, Jimmy and Lloyd, greeted me with desperate cries, competing for who would get a pet first. The front door of her apartment opened into her living room–kitchen, the bedroom was down a short hallway to my left. She walked out of it in a long T-shirt covered in coffee stains, wearing a pair of glasses with a lens missing.

"Ah!" she shrieked. "You're here!"

She planted her feet and shook her arms over her head like my presence was an electric shock. She wanted more attention than the cats. My mother was from the generation that expected guys not only to pay for dinner, but to make the plans for an evening out well in advance. What luxury. She often noted how expectations for dates had changed throughout her time as a single woman.

"The only thing men took away from the feminist movement was that we would split the bill," she'd joke. "I'd tell them, 'Look, if I thought paying for dinner made us equal, I'd do it.'"

So she never did, because it certainly didn't. We sat on her couch and my mom told me about her day, which had involved a lot of emailing and a trip to the small local health food store. The couch was also her bed. Her boyfriend slept in the bedroom. The situation was not something I entirely understood, and it was another warning: the longer you're with someone the more inseparably your daily life becomes linked, until it's easier to sleep on a pull-out couch than leave. Were they happy? I didn't think so, but inertia is so powerful, perhaps more so as people age and understand how much work goes into building any kind of life. Starting over gets much less appealing.

My mother lived mostly on SSI and small artist grants. Her apartment was owned by her boyfriend's parents, whom I considered to be my grandparents. This made it much easier for my mom and her boyfriend to live their chaotic lives. I knew she dreamt of a better situation, even though she loved her familiar neighborhood. A two-bedroom wasn't something I could afford. Should I let my mom live in my own living room? Move with her somewhere more affordable and far out and dedicate my life to managing her needs? She'd aged, her physical difficulties aggravated by MS, but she certainly had all her faculties. She was still an autonomous person, making art, putting on shows, running through her own daily patterns that were none of my business. The balance of responsible support versus interference had not yet tipped.

My mom knew all about my recent dating life. She always wanted more gossip. I told her a little bit about John, including the story about his awkward mistake at the bar with two women, which she found very funny.

"It feels like everyone is just switching off partners all the time, always hoping to find someone better," I said. "Even if I met someone I liked, I can't imagine them sticking around long enough to know me."

"Well, if you really want a man," she replied, "This is all you have to do. Figure out how they want to see themselves and then pretend that's who they really are."

I was scandalized, and my mom giggled. "I know you would never do that!" She patted my hand. The thing was, I believed that this strategy had worked for her, a beautiful young woman in New York City in the seventies, getting all her drinks paid for and making every one of the men doing it feel like the most important person she'd ever met. My mom was right, I'd probably be crummy at it.

Dating is just pretending to be someone you're not, I thought, so the right person will like you.

But how could someone be the right person if you have to pretend? My mother was willing to pretend because she needed to. At first because it was culturally expected at the time, and then because she was raising a daughter pretty much by herself. There was no immediate economic imperative to fill my date book, though. If anything, going out on a date with someone cost me. If that date was a man, the amount of cash we both put into dating probably set me at a deficit. The maintenance fee for being considered groomed and attractive is far higher for a woman, and we are still paid less on average than our male peers.

Which meant that for me, at least, and probably lots of women like me, the real hope of return was emotional. Once, years ago, after dating began to be seen as the norm rather than a deviance from decent courting rituals, it was easily incorporated into the primary directive that people meet, marry, and mate, preferably with someone they could combine resources with to mutual material advantage. This is simply no longer true. Dating can lead to permanent partnership, but as the rise of singleness and diminishing birth rates attest, that isn't a reliable outcome. If feelings are now the real investment, many of us aren't really getting much return on our portfolios. Why, then, are we doing it?

"What even is dating?" I asked myself yet again, eating a tub of ice cream in bed a few nights later, after another lackluster meetup. One pattern to dating I soon identified was the frequency with which I ended up in bed afterward, eating junk food and contemplating what it all even meant.

On a Saturday afternoon, I facetimed my friend Dylan, who was making lunch across the country in Los Angeles. It had been three or four years since we'd lived in the same state. Despite the distance, or because of it, Dylan and I had maintained our friendship, flying to visit each other, texting, sending memes (the highest form of communication), or facetiming. On his drive to L.A., he met the woman he would eventually marry. I'd seen the ups and down of that relationship, yet he still frequently dared to offer me dating advice. Especially when I foolishly asked for it.

I leaned my phone against the wall over my kitchen countertop and started cleaning the grout around my sink. I watched him very inefficiently cut garlic with an impractically tiny knife as I scrubbed away, and let my complaints about dating pour out. I explained that I'd basically accomplished what I'd set out to do. I'd learned to go out again, to meet people again, and it wasn't enough.

Then I hesitated before admitting, "The people I find attractive don't seem super interested in me. The ones I'm not that into always want to go out again."

"You just don't understand your value on the sexual marketplace yet," he replied calmly, throwing a spoonful of butter into a pan.

When Dylan and I met, I had just broken up with Morgan. Dylan was very much enjoying his value in the sexual marketplace. Dylan was very handsome, and he was especially handsome when he was twenty-three. He had the kind of looks that made people pay attention to him when he walked into a room. Then they'd ask if he was an actor. Then if he was single. That was something that other women would generally ask me when we went out together, guessing correctly that Dylan was not interested in my body. It was a confusing dynamic, all these beautiful girls trying to befriend me to get to this beautiful man, and it chipped away at my own perception of myself. There was no one I felt less attractive around than Dylan, and also few people with whom I felt quite so certain of myself. I never doubted that he liked me for me, because he definitely wasn't interested in having sex.

Having reached thirty and settled in a marriage, Dylan had softened somewhat. In this statement, however, I heard all the entitlement of his younger self who had once acquired phone numbers just by breathing. I was tempted to ask what exactly he thought my value in the sexual marketplace was. He probably would have directly told me which physical attributes he thought were holding me back, which wasn't information I particularly wanted.

"Sexual marketplace?" I repeated instead. "How harsh."

"Everyone is evaluating where they are on the market and seeing if they can get more," he answered. "From what I remember from being single, everyone is chasing someone who is chasing someone else. And then at the top is Jake Gyllenhaal."

We laughed at the running joke we had about the power of Jake Gyllenhaal. I thought about the last time Dylan was single; he had just broken up with the woman who would one day be his wife. He spent the next year in an existential funk, alternating Tinder rampages with crying about wanting true intimacy. The story hadn't unfolded with the cold calculation he was describing now. And if he did think of love as an act of bargaining, who did he think got the better deal in his marriage?

"I don't want to see people that way," I said, meaning I didn't want to see myself that way: as a bunch of composite parts that someone would be either settling for or showing off.

Dating is grabbing the best you can get, I thought, like a fire sale.

That didn't seem quite right either, though Dylan's unpleasant outlook did get distressingly close to my own observations. Not just that I was being judged, but that potential dates were assessing what they could get from me and how little they would have to invest to get it. Sexually, of course, but also romantically or emotionally. How needy they could be in texts, how much attention they could expect, how willing they were to respond to *my* neediness. The sexual marketplace wasn't just about your personal value; it was about how much someone could extract from you, like in a mining operation.

The term "emotional labor" has come to mean the extra mental and emotional effort, mostly made by women, that is often unacknowledged and unpaid but is necessary to keep things running. Things like managing household duties, remembering family birthdays, keeping track of what needs to be done to make a functional life for other people. The term was coined by sociologist Arlie Hochschild in her 1983 book, *The Managed Heart*, and the way it's used now has gotten away from her original intention.

She told writer Julie Beck in an interview for *The Atlantic* in 2018 that she saw that much of what was being described as emotional labor, like chores, is actual labor. Her original intent was to draw attention to jobs like flight attendant or nurse or childcare worker, which demand people moderate and perform their emotions in a certain way.

"The point is that while you may also be doing physical labor and mental labor, you are crucially being hired and monitored for your capacity to manage and produce a feeling," said Hochschild. I could understand why this definition creep had set in over the last four decades. So many women feel the work they do is unacknowledged, especially in relation to cishet men, and this was a way to describe the unseen internal work of family life. It was part of a larger trend of monetizing the demand for unpaid emotional labor that became bigger and bigger after the 2016 election.

At first, posting a Venmo or CashApp "for emotional labor" was something I noticed activists doing, usually Black women who were being asked to donate their time and expertise for free to the public, and even to private institutions with the budget to pay them. This was an entirely reasonable response to white people's thirst for education and information and their reluctance to shell out money in exchange for it.

Then, in March of 2017, I remember seeing a friend, another white woman, post that every man should Venmo a woman for International Women's Day. For some reason, it bothered me. While it's always fun to get money, reading her half-joking tweet, I realized what I wanted far more was for a man to read a book by a feminist author, support an artist who didn't share his gender, show up and be kind. Five dollars for a coffee wouldn't offer the meaningful changes to my life that men understanding misogyny would.

Over the next several years, the idea that all relationships and interactions are essentially transactional took up more and more space, extending beyond dropping a Venmo handle. Listening to a friend in crisis, talking to your roommate about chores, planning a bachelorette party all became some form of emotional labor that was owed compensation. A term that had been intended as an anticapitalist analysis of actual work-loads had instead turned interpersonal relationships into a capitalist system, where you could pay someone rather than be a decent person to them. Like a corporation paying for the right to pollute the environment.

These acts used to be considered part of being in a community; critical examination of who is doing the most work for the least payback in a community is always necessary, but this change in language had turned community-building into something that could only happen within capitalist parameters. To borrow that framework, it struck me as a net loss.

I will say that coming home from a bad date did make me feel that even the most speculative encounters came at a cost, though not necessarily one that could be paid back in United States dollars.

But in terms of literal money, I had thought a lot about the costs of dating during my experiment. I tallied up what I spent on drinks or food, what I spent on making myself look good, or on clothes. It cost plenty, and this was just the preview. If I did ever meet someone I wanted to commit to, they could potentially determine my lifelong quality of life. I didn't mean in just the emotional sense, though that was relevant—another of my mother's sayings was "marry a rich man and you'll pay and pay and pay."

Yet, if my mother hadn't had a partner with a home, she would be in a much tougher spot than the living room. It was sincerely scary to think that I might end up with somebody who could bring me down financially, or to whom I could become a liability. The divorce and custody battle my mom had gone through with my dad had been devastatingly costly, leading to one of the most desperate times of my childhood. Economic survival is still as much a part of couplehood as anything else, even if we pretend it's not.

The greatest liability to future me could be remaining single, and eventually growing to an age where there weren't family members left to turn to in an emergency. My income had been high for about a year. I didn't know for sure whether it would last. I suspected it wouldn't. Having grown up with very little money, thinking about making plans or opening a savings account turned my mind blank with anxiety. I knew I would owe a lot in taxes, and I wasn't remotely prepared. I was approaching my midthirties with absolutely no plan for how I'd pay to live into old age.

Dating is a retirement plan? If so, I had to admit I was a bad economic bet for anybody looking for a 401(k) partner. I didn't have much economic value, and if Dylan's assessment was correct, my value on the sexual marketplace wasn't where it needed to be if I wanted to get anywhere close to Jake Gyllenhaal. But I couldn't think about these dates as a means to a secure future or as a business negotiation over the assets of my humanity. That left only the immediate pleasures or displeasures of the process.

Late in June, I met a woman named Katherine at a party. Because I had been talking about dating a lot, lots of people had been talking about dating to me. It's sort of like when you learn a new word and then start hearing it everywhere.

"I go on a date almost every night," Katherine told me, after we discovered our mutual pastime, then smiled like that was a superb thing. She had a very rich voice, full of enigmatic delight, like the narrator of a fairy tale.

"That's wild," I trumpeted in my own unmodulated bray. "How do you do it?"

I'd felt somewhat proud of my measly two dates a week and Katherine had so easily shown me up. I wanted to at least commiserate on the horribleness of it all, to prove I'd been down in the trenches, too, by offering some negative observations about mating rituals. Instead of saying how gross it was, she smiled.

"I just love it!" she crooned. "I love meeting new people, learning about them, connecting over something. There's always something to learn from everybody, I think, even if you're not interested in them romantically. I'm always excited to talk to a new person."

I believed her. Some people do have that capacity for human engagement. I was no introvert, but this level of excitement for everyone who crossed her path made Katherine a powerful dater.

Dating is being excited about meeting new people, I thought, and tried to apply that perspective. Even when I grinned and laughed and tried to approach every interaction with the enthusiasm of a thousand burning Katherines, I wasn't really answering the question of what it was for.

"Dating is . . ." I'd think, walking to meet another Dan/ Matt, trying to fill in the blank.

Dating is a way to pass the time.

Dating is a social call.

Dating is to get laid.

Dating is patriarchy.

Dating is feminism!

Dating is a wish your heart makes.

Dating is . . .

I didn't know, and I understood that I didn't know what dating was because I wasn't sure what I wanted the outcome to be. It was like hammering together a frame without knowing if you're building a house or a rocking chair. Dating was pleasurable to Katherine because it seemed like an end in itself. I'd started from a similar place. I'd forced myself to tell other people in my life that I was trying to date. Did I dare admit that I wanted more? Having achieved one goal, I wanted to set another one: to find an actual relationship. Whatever that meant.

CHAPTER 7

. . . .

Expectations

Sometime in July, I was sitting on the side of a hill in Fort Greene Park, listening to a man talk. It was about that time in the summer when all the fresh, pale shoots of the spring have thickened into mature green leaves. The tough grass had had its slim points ground down by hundreds of feet passing over it. Things hadn't yet begun to shrivel, they just looked tired. A recent rainstorm had coated everything in mud, which was now turning to dust as the moisture steamed away. It was too hot. The man talked, and I kept shifting into the shade as the sun moved over us; he followed me, an orbiting body.

This hillside had been a part of my life for many years. I'd climbed up and down and all around it. I'd ridden a garbage bag wrapped around a cardboard box down its slope when it was coated in snow. I'd drunk wine from water bottles with friends as twilight descended, watched soccer games, eaten picnics, petted many adventurous dogs, and observed the trees blossom, turn gold, then shed their outerwear.

Dating had given the hillside an added dimension. Now I could map one spot to another: there's where I'd walked with the Egyptian tech developer, that's where I'd lain with the woman recently arrived from San Diego who brought a blanket and homemade kombucha, there's where I'd made out with a guy who messaged me later to ask if my pussy was clean. I told him I regularly dipped it in a bucket of ammonia, then blocked his number.

The spots created a surveyor's map that lay over the hill's topography, and here we were, adding another point. I'd call this point the Very Interesting Man, because he was. He'd just moved to the United States from India about ten months before, and he'd spent most of those months traveling around to different states, many of them places I'd never been and wondered if I ever would. Traveling seemed like something one did with a partner, and I didn't know how to drive. Initially, this man's stories made him more appealing, like he could be somebody I would travel with.

He had ended up in New York for grad school, working on a fascinating project that would, as far as I could understand it, definitely benefit all of humanity. He also hadn't asked me a single question about myself, no matter how I hinted that I, too, might have some thoughts to share. The appeal of his interesting life faded quickly.

It was common for men to not ask me any questions. Sometimes I'd feel half in love with a woman just because we were having an actual conversation rather than a series of monologues interrupted by brief moments where my date was thinking about what they'd get to say once I stopped talking. Not everyone was like this, of course, but it was bad enough that if I suspected a guy was that type, I'd start to test how long he would go without needing any information about me. This man had been stream-of-consciousnessing for a good forty minutes and I no longer had any urge to interrupt, having been lulled to a complacent drowsiness. My neck had started to ache from turning toward him, so I'd just stopped, instead staring at a distant tree. He hadn't seemed to notice.

I'd tried to talk to my friend Marian about the imbalance I'd observed between men's and women's expectations of mutual understanding on dates. She'd admonished me.

"Well, you have a tendency to focus on other people," Marian said. "Like, it's great you ask a lot of questions; you seem genuinely interested. But it's a way of hiding a little."

This was a fair point, and it reminded me of my first date in the spring, the one that had inspired the whole experiment, where I'd tried to maintain some anonymity by focusing on him. I didn't want to share myself with people I didn't like, and I ended up guiding those dates like a therapist, gently probing one of their answers after another without revealing anything.

But Marian undermined her point a little when she added, "And all men are like that, anyway. You have to interject."

It's not that useful to draw binaries around behavior based on gender, and I felt a little guilty doing it. Anyone can act any way at any time. Who knows what oblivious thing I was doing on all these dates that never went anywhere? Perhaps I was annoying people with something they blamed on my gender that actually had to do with my awful personality. Plus, to be fair, the Very Interesting Man genuinely had a lot to share, even if he didn't read any of my cues, and it was possible he didn't know what else to do. Right after we grabbed coffee, he'd admitted that this was his very first date on Tinder.

"Welcome!" I'd said. "I hope it's fun for you."

That was about the last thing I'd said. People willing to meet me spur of the moment, or sometimes at all, were often new to apps or new to New York City. They were enthusiastic about the experiment of online dating or making connections. This guy was both, and he could have just gotten carried away. When my coffee was done, I wanted to politely part, but then he sat down firmly on the hill. I'd felt pressured to join him.

There was a pause in the flow of words, and I glanced at him, wondering if I'd missed something. A question, finally? He was looking out over the field below, as I had so many times. Its bare, sandy center was expanding as more and more people used it for sports or a dog toilet.

The silence became awkward. My mouth was dry, like when you wake up in the morning and pry your lips apart to gasp in the first breath of consciousness. I had no idea what he'd last said, and my own thoughts were far away.

"What are your parents like?" I coughed.

"Very conservative," he said. "They care about what their neighbors think, what everyone in their community thinks, but they're very unhappy."

See? He was interesting. Then silence again.

"Do they approve of you?" I asked, since he had no curiosity about my family.

"No, we're very different. I have a much more liberal mind. Since I've become more successful, they have fewer complaints and it's easier being far away."

He told me his folks had their marriage arranged by their families, and I wondered aloud what they'd think of Tinder.

"They'd hate it!" he chuckled. Based on his parents' attachment to community perception, I gleaned that a lot of people he'd grown up around had ended up in arranged marriages. The only person I'd grown up with who had expected that arrangement, that I knew of, was a girl in my sixth-grade class whose parents were from Albania. One day she came into the gym crying because her family had told her they'd picked out her future husband.

My best friend, Billie, and I had gathered around her, confused and upset by the news, since the three of us made a little trio. The situation was beyond our limited understanding, but it *seemed* wrong. Plus, she was crying, so she couldn't have felt good about it, according to my twelve-year-old logic. We lost touch after middle school, then eventually followed each other on Instagram. She was married, though I couldn't tell if it was to the man her parents had picked out for her. They appeared very happy and had a few children. One of them was a little girl who could have been a clone of my childhood friend. I wondered at times if her mom would make the same choices for her.

At twelve years old, knowing what adulthood would look like in such a specific way was inconceivable to me. Did the knowledge reconcile my friend to the circumstance? Did it pressure her to accept something she didn't want? Was it a relief to not have to think about those matters in college or young adulthood? Would it have been worse to do it like I was doing now, in older adulthood? There was a part of me now that thought an arranged marriage didn't seem like a lamentable fate if what you wanted was simply *marriage*. But that would be a heterosexual marriage, of course, and just that was enough for me to dismiss the idea entirely.

"Choice" in relationships is a murky concept. Family structures always inform how people go about seeking a partner, or how they refuse to. Reactive rejection of the status quo is its own form of behavioral control. Billie grew up in a household that centered family above all else. Within five years of our friend's arranged engagement, she met the man she would marry. By our early thirties, Billie had a growing family with the guy she'd started dating at seventeen. I did often think that she'd been too young to close that window of possibility, and that it had changed and shaped her when she became part of a pair so soon.

The things she had acquired, however, were far more obvious and certainly more culturally valuable than whatever self-exploration I'd managed to do in the same amount of time.

"Would you want an arranged marriage?" I asked my date.

"No, I can't imagine doing that now," he said, with a significant look at me. The implication that he was imagining something more serious than a coffee date was enough to make me finally stand up, my knees creaking.

"Well, I gotta get home," I said. "Let me walk you to the train station."

As we went, he talked more about his graduate-degree project, which filled the time. There I bid him adieu, saying, "I hope this has been a decent first Tinder experience."

"It's been amazing!" he said, which puzzled me. We shared a brief hug and he went on his way. Later, he messaged me to say what a great time he'd had, and I realized he hadn't seen anything questionable about how we'd interacted at all. I responded in a way that communicated I would never go out with him again, something like *Good luck with the rest of your life!* but nicer.

Though my date had seemed extraordinarily confident in himself, there's no way it had been easy for him to move to a new country and reconsider everything he'd once thought about how his adult life would look. I didn't think I'd be brave enough. I was living a pretty commonplace life, at least based on my own parents' history. Being unmarried and childless in my thirties didn't feel like a very radical thing where I was raised.

Yet, every day, more and more people my age were falling into mainstream patterns, those of traditional nuclear family structures. Even the queer people I knew were pairing up and having babies and buying property somewhere far outside the city. My life was looking weirder and weirder in comparison, though I hadn't made any drastic choices about going against that model. Inevitably, there comes a point when you cease to be conventional by default, by not participating. I had never wanted kids. I do remember many occasions when I was told my "clock" would suddenly start ticking and I'd be desperate to feel that sacred weight in my womb. The only internal clock I'd ever heard was the one telling me when to order a burrito in time for lunch, a sacred weight of a different kind.

Billie is proof that opposites attract. I could remember a time in high school when I noticed her looking teary-eyed as we played a videogame where people chuck grenades at each other. I asked what was wrong. "I was just thinking about how sad I would be if I couldn't have kids," she replied, and after a silent moment we both started to giggle. Eventually, she had two, though she waited until her thirties before starting her family.

Like mine, Billie's parents were theater artists, except they'd stuck together. She'd grown up with her brother and parents in a rent-controlled one-bedroom on Avenue A, as my mother and I moved from apartment to apartment around the East Village grid. Even when we eventually went to different junior highs, I'd call up to Billie's window in the morning to take the MTA bus across town together, pissing off the neighbors, because her buzzer was perpetually broken.

Sophomore year she dated Owen before passing him on to me, and then she dated her future husband. End of list. How would Billie's life have been different if she'd had more time to experiment, grow, and explore without him? Her development became so deeply entangled with his—a danger for any young person settling down right out of their parent's house. She even moved in with him sophomore year of college instead of finding a place with me, as had been the plan.

And she'd become an incredibly accomplished person, working for years in a nonprofit and eventually getting her graduate degree to teach. She'd also become a wife and mother, the center of her family, and to all appearances, she was pretty happy. She could even drive. I had just continued to be me, stunted in so many ways by comparison.

The only confrontation we'd ever had as adults about our differing "lifestyles" happened that summer, and it was memorable mostly for being so cliché. As I began dating again, Billie was well into her second pregnancy. She was exhausted from caring for a three-year-old while growing another human being in her torso. Her husband had agreed to take their kid on some sort of shopping adventure so she could have a day of rest and relaxation with me. We got pedicures at a "chemical-free" salon she'd found on Yelp that smelled like every other nail salon I'd ever been in, then went to a quiet restaurant near her apartment. She sighed multiple times, saying how nice it was, how good the food, how much she'd needed this day. Billie couldn't remember if she'd felt this strained during her first pregnancy. She was really at the end of her rope. She complained that her husband had been having back troubles, which made it harder for him to help with their daughter; that household work was piling up, and she felt so behind with things to do in preparation for the new baby.

I was probably the perfect person to complain to if you wanted someone to say "That sounds like it sucks" about childcare. Twenty minutes of babysitting always wrung me out like a rag for the rest of the day, even in my perky teens—an age when all young women are pushed toward caring for other people's kids for cash at some point. So I said "that sucks" a few times and she relaxed further.

As we finished our dumplings, I asked what she was planning for the rest of her afternoon. Billie fretted about some furniture from Ikea that needed to be assembled, but admitted she'd probably sleep for as long as everyone was out of the house. She then asked me what I'd do.

Thoughtlessly, I replied, "I don't know, I might walk in the park or get a massage."

What can I say? It was a Saturday.

"It must be nice to have so much free time," she snapped, a sharp edge of genuine irritation in her voice. It was jarring to feel judged by someone I'd known so, so long, someone I considered my sister. Like a sister, I was angry. The impulse to snap, "Well, you have a *family!*" was strong.

I wanted to shout about how she'd been able to split the rent everywhere she lived since college without Craigslist roommates, that she had her husband's health insurance, that she'd traveled all over with someone who helped shoulder the cost, and cared for her when she was sick, and helped her move, and they only ever had to buy one present combined for parties (which is bullshit), and that one day I'd be all alone and she'd be surrounded by grandkids. I deserved a damn spa day before my cats ate my face!

And on her end, she was likely imagining all the sleepless nights, mounting bills, troubles with daycare, and shrinking space in her own mind as all these other people took over, demanding more and more of her, including me. She could have shouted right back.

Instead, there was an awkward moment as we both recovered our tempers; we finished our lunch and bade each other farewell. With the distance of a few hours and a truly excellent hour-long massage, my anger dissipated. Between the two of us, Billie has by far the calmer, kinder, less sarcastic disposition. To talk to me like that, she must have been feeling truly frayed.

But I didn't try to bring it up with her again, and I never asked her directly if she thought less of me because I hadn't lived the way she had. That small altercation let me glimpse what Billie must sometimes think about my life, and I was sure I sometimes did the same to her, mostly unconsciously.

Despite the difficulties of parenting, especially if you expect to find someone romantically compatible to coparent with, there is considerable stigma against childless people. In a study from Indiana University in 2017, undergraduates were asked to assess the potential happiness of their school's alumni based on their profiles. All were married; some had children, some didn't. According to the study, the child-free alums were "perceived to be significantly less psychologically fulfilled" than their counterparts with children.

This isn't shocking to anyone who has soared past the average fertility years without making a baby. Even my dearest friend saw me, on some level, as a pig rolling in a shit pile of free time. What was I doing with my life besides going from brunch to pedicure to massage? That's how it sometimes felt with family, too. Though it could technically happen, my grandparents considered me a lost cause as far as producing another generation. I was lucky to have parents who had never pressured me one way or the other, though their lack of interest in my replicating their DNA sometimes felt accusatory, too.

Married with no children is suspicious enough. Being single is sinister. In an editorial for *The Washington Post*, author Bella DePaulo criticized the conflation of being single with being alone, saying that using the terms synonymously paints single people as isolated and self-centered. DePaulo writes that actually single people are more likely "to support, visit, advise and stay in touch with their parents and siblings" than those who are married and those who have been married. Marriage seems to make you more selfish, not less, even when it's over. According to a study from the *Journal of Marriage and Family*, people in marriages often become more insular, and it is generally single people who step up when parents are sick and ailing.

Another study from the *Journal of Family Issues* suggests that single people test higher when it comes to personal growth, autonomy, and self-determination, all of which grow feelings of positivity in the swinging single person. Conversely, a sense of autonomy breeds negative feelings in people who are married, perhaps driving a wedge between codependent couples.

In her book *Singled Out: How Singles Are Stereotyped, Stigmatized, and Ignored and Still Live Happily Ever After*, DePaulo focuses in particular on the myth that America is always teetering on the edge of the total end of marriage. In her opinion, Americans are far more attached to marriage than they admit, or than the numbers imply. "America, in its own fantasies, is a nation of rugged individualists and daring adventurers," she writes. "In reality, though, countless adults are so stuck on coupling that they seem reluctant to venture into safe and comfortable places, such as restaurants and movie theaters, unless they have another human at their side. Preferably one of the opposite sex.

"According to its own ideals, America is also a nation of nuclear families. When couples have children, they often settle into the comfort and privacy of their own home. They might slip out now and then for a baseball game or a pizza, but like the cliché says, the home is their castle. With a moat around it. They practice what I see as intensive nuclearity." In DePaulo's opinion, marriage isolates people far more than singleness. So why is it that marriage is so rewarded with social acceptance and singleness is not? If the reality is that married people are more lonely than single people, and that single people have a deeper interest in their extended family and neighbors, then we should be pillars in our communities, celebrated for our sacrifice. Or at least get a tax break.

I had a married friend, Tessa, who was very vocal about never wanting to be a parent. Similar to me, she had a childhood best friend with one kid who was considering having another.

"Okay, I can understand, if you feel you must, having one kid," Tessa said to me one afternoon over coffee. "But *two*? It's like you'd rather make an entirely new person than invest in relationships you already have in your life."

We laughed like she'd just told an off-color joke, knowing this is the kind of thing childless people can never, ever express to parents. Of course, Tessa would love her best friend's second baby, if it ever came into being, just like I loved Billie's little girl (and eventual son). It was just a relief to share understanding with someone else who had found themselves edged out of decades-long friendships by entirely new people, literally, and discovered that lamenting that distance was socially unacceptable. We were obviously supposed to have our own kids to fill the gap and retreat into that nuclear family, setting our love for our friends on the pile of childish things.

Sasha Roseneil is a co-author on the book *The Tenacity of the Couple-Norm,* a sociological study of changing relationship structure in four different regions of Europe. In a 2020 op-ed for *The Guardian,* Roseneil writes that though there have been weighty changes in obligatory heterosexual partnership from a cultural and political standpoint, they are not nearly as far-reaching as people think. As gender and sexuality have gone through mind-bending revolutions, the norm of couplehood has tenaciously remained, and become even more important, because so many of our other intimate connections have become weaker.

"The couple norm mandates that the intimate/sexual dyad is the basic unit of social life," Roseneil writes. "It operates through laws and policies that assume and privilege coupledom, with myriad economic impacts in terms of access to welfare benefits, pensions, inheritance and housing. It works through the injunctions, expectations and informal social sanctions of family, friends and colleagues who encourage and cajole the uncoupled towards coupledom. And it is perpetuated through cultural representations of the good life as the coupled life that makes it hard to imagine the possibility of contentment beyond the conventional pairing."

She goes on to say that this external pressure inevitably becomes internalized, leading to a sense of "shame, guilt, disappointment and anxiety for uncoupled people" even though there's nothing atypical about it.

"This can impel a desperate quest to rectify the situation as people seek the comfort and social inclusion they believe is to be found with a partner," she adds. Hmm, wouldn't know anything about that . . .

Nominally, singles can do what they wish, which hasn't always been true for people who had no urge to marry. But laws and social norms still indicate that what they *should* want is to be in a couple. When you become part of couple, you haven't just met a compatible person to share your life with. You've acquired the cultural acceptance that comes with conformity to these well-established expectations.

I sometimes felt like a freak around coupled people because

they didn't perceive their relationship as some sort of submission to the relief and safety of the couple norm. Rather, it was a sign of their superiority, a sign they were worthy of love and acceptance, and that meant there had to be something wrong with me. Roseneil says that coupledom becomes so important because many other forms of connection are choked off so efficiently. That means couples are lonely, too, which I sympathized with when I read her op-ed. If thinking something is wrong with people like me helps them through that, I get it. I just wasn't sure I had to think something was wrong with me, too.

That summer, as I went on more and more first dates and felt further and further from submitting to protocol myself, these became the most sour thoughts I'd ever had about coupled people. Their bitterness was like a warning of what the flavor of my future would be if I didn't either beat them or join them. There seemed to be very little reward for resisting, besides knowing you lived your life differently. What would everyone on the outside know about my life besides that it was lonely? It was much harder to be brave when I considered what others saw when they looked at me.

CHAPTER 8

Deep in the Heart
of Summer

Soon after the date with the Very Interesting Man, I met up with a woman named Vanessa. She was tall, was growing her auburn hair out, and had a personality that might be called radically honest.

"I'm unemployed," she announced on our first date at a coffee shop. She'd recently graduated from a master's program, where she studied economics, and was now looking for a job in her field. I wasn't sure how I kept ending up on dates with all these brainiacs. When she commented that the app we'd matched on, Her, was clearly just mining users for data, it was like a lightbulb went off over my head. Of course it's all a data mine, just like the apps that pop up every few months to show you what you'd look like as an old person or an anime character or a painting from a museum. Except dating apps let you picture yourself in love.

Vanessa's earning potential over her lifetime was probably higher than mine, but as an older person with a job I felt obligated to buy her a coffee. She drank it and told me about her girlfriend—Vanessa was poly—and her housing commune that apparently hosted regular sex parties, though they sounded a lot less formal than the one Anna described to me. I had a twinge of nostalgia for being young and vital in the way only an unemployed person in their midtwenties having lots of sex can be. Vanessa started to look around the café, distracted.

"I'm not feeling well," she said suddenly, and I wondered if she was just trying to get out of our date. "I think I need to eat something."

"If you need to go home, that's totally okay, we can meet up some other time," I said, trying to give her a graceful exit.

"No!" she insisted. "I think I just need some bread."

We walked to the bagel shop and she ordered an everything with cream cheese. We ended up in the park, sitting on a bench, slightly off the main drag. She methodically devoured the life-saving carbs and I observed a squirrel run up and down a tree trunk in silence. Watching other people eat when I am not doing so grosses me out.

"Can I hold your hand?" Vanessa asked, out of nowhere. I shook my head in disbelief. The whole date had already been such a roller coaster.

"Okay," I said. Like, whatever. I took her hand. She continued to eat her bagel with the other.

We sat quietly, hands clasped. Hers was warm and a little damp, and mine probably was, too. Birds chirped, the earth continued to turn on its axis. It was awkward. It didn't bring up any immediate sense of intimacy. But when you're holding hands, it is harder to look at your phone. The discomfort passed, as it often does when you stop and sit with it.

Vanessa finished her bagel, releasing my hand to roll the paper bag into a ball.

"That's better," she sighed. "How was that for you?"

I surmised she didn't mean the bagel and answered, "It was nice."

We got up and walked without holding hands to the top of the park, which featured a phallic monument to prisoners of war who died on ships during the American Revolution, erected on a square connected to a long, wide staircase that runners were trotting up and down. Kids with skateboards tried to flip them a few feet away, making an arrhythmic clatter to punctuate our conversation. I realized I wanted to see her again. There was something about her open approach, saying and doing whatever it occurred to her to say or do, that was very refreshing. Could we all just say and do exactly what we really wanted with another person on a date, within reason? I'd been managing my dates, accommodating their interests and following their leads—or taking the lead in the easiest direction when they wouldn't. I could just be whoever I was, too, and they could take it or leave it.

I wanted to go home and consider this revelation in privacy, so I was also hoping the date would be over soon. It was like trying to have a conversation when you feel a migraine coming on, except the migraine was an idea.

"Why did you want to hold hands?" I finally asked her. I am an affectionate person. I like hugs and cuddling and sitting on the couch, legs entwined. I like it with friends. But I hadn't been able to picture those simple gestures with the people I went on dates with, even if I could picture us having sex. I suspected most of them felt the same, until Vanessa.

She rolled her shoulders expressively.

"Just wondered what it would feel like," she answered. "Wanted to jump-start things."

That I understood. From what I'd seen, queer people are often willing to experiment with connection, with forms of intimacy and sex that heterosexual people are not. There is a very well-worn narrative for heterosexual romance: dating, marriage, babies. Until recently, none of those things were simple for LGBTQ+ people, and often they're still not, even if they're legal. There are plenty of clear and serious downsides to this. There is also an openness to possibility, creativity, humor, compassion, and risk-taking that comes from walking a difficult path, expressed in both large and small ways.

The heat was beating down on the square, and I was noticing the moistness of my palms more acutely. There was sweat behind my knees and under my hair. It didn't seem like she felt it. She was edging closer to me. I started to be a little worried she'd ask to kiss me, and I didn't want to in the heat and smell of bagel and coffee, when I was feeling like an old, wet sponge. I said I had to go to the bathroom, and we walked back down the hill.

When I got home, I took a cool shower. I wanted to see Vanessa again and thought she probably would, too. Even though it had been a date that was both mentally and physically unpleasant to a degree, she was cooler than anyone else I'd met.

I decided that second dates counted toward my weekly minimum. For ours, she asked me to meet her at a wine bar that was mostly empty when I arrived. She lived across the street. I was early and she was late.

"I told my roommates you're a masochist," she said, after getting a drink from the bar and sitting across from me in the booth. The bar was on the second story of the building, offering an elevated view of the empty Bushwick sidewalk. Our seats were cracked and repaired with duct tape. I'd been feeling very chill. This comment raised my hackles.

"Why is that?"

"Well, I told them about all your dates," she answered. I had admitted to Vanessa that I was dating as a sort of experiment—that I wanted to get *good* at it, for lack of a better word. The more complicated explanation was that I wanted to learn how to accept rejection without turning my back on trying again, but that would only lead to more questions. Vanessa had seemed like the kind of person who would get experimenting. She already had a girlfriend, after all, so she at least understood alternative types of relationships. Hearing her interpretation of what I'd said about my two-dates-a-week commitment concerned me. I didn't like being called a masochist. It reminded me what a loathsome reputation dating has. Really, anything that requires us to do something uncomfortable has a bad reputation, especially slow things. Even more pleasurable stuff like developing friendships or acquiring a new skill are harder to start because they demand so much time and care. Adrenaline junkies might do something scary or painful, but not enough people want to come out of their shells for smaller, more nuanced joys when the process can be tedious. It was puzzling to me that Vanessa, hand-holder, didn't intuitively understand that.

Whenever I talked to people about loneliness, they would almost instantly bring up technology. I agreed with most of what people said—yes, it's isolating to feel like the search for love has been reduced to a videogame. Yeah, social media does make people feel bad about themselves. It's true, people do look at their phones instead of talking to one another. Something I had noticed that few people talked about was how the convenience of technology made people so unwilling to engage with inconvenience. It was luxurious to be able to swipe on dates from home, form initial impressions without leaving my couch, and delete anyone who bothered me. It was convenient. It was comfortable. Prioritizing convenience and comfort is the death of deep connection.

Convenience is the justification for so many of the apps that shred human interaction, because, let's face it, interacting with other people is often extremely difficult. It can feel completely justifiable to cut some of the less necessary interactions out of your life.

I could remember debating with friends about who would call a restaurant to order take out. Now there are a half dozen apps that make it unnecessary to talk to anyone to get borscht delivered to your house, except the delivery person, who doesn't really want to talk to you either. Often, these apps utilize a network of contract workers, so it may not even be a familiar delivery person bringing you midnight snacks every Friday—someone who recognizes you when you open the door.

Some of the streamlining effects of these platforms might seem innocuous. They're not. Many of them drain money off the businesses, in addition to charging fees to the people ordering through them. Restaurants risk falling off the map if they're not on Seamless or Postmates. The development of wide-reaching apps that insert middlemen into every human interaction has spread far beyond the service industry. A friend of mine who worked as a therapist started doing freelance sessions with an online app, which paid her substantially less than she would make in a private practice.

"It's very much the kind of thing that a group of Silicon Valley types must have reverse engineered," she told me. "Like they thought, 'Okay, what's a service that just requires a computer and talking and not much infrastructure? Oh! Therapy!' And then they built the app."

Deciding to participate in these structures may seem like a personal choice. I did believe people had agency, to a degree; but I also thought part of why tech middlemen were so insidious was that refusing to participate could make you irrelevant. Without dating apps, who would I have met? It was more common to meet someone from Bumble than in real life at this point, especially at the pace I was going. I could choose not to use them and that would most likely become a choice to stop dating.

On dating apps, the ease of disconnecting dictated all kinds of behaviors. There were a few people whom I went on first dates with where it seemed we liked each other and it might be worthwhile to go out again. Then something would come up and I'd cancel; then they'd cancel next, and that was it. We'd be done. Or I'd be out with someone and a disagreement would arise and I'd think, "I'm disconnecting from this person as soon as I walk out the door." And I'd be able to literally delete them from my life.

Some of them—like the guy who looked me up and commented on every one of my public Facebook posts before we met, or the guy who *insisted* I hug him goodbye—deserved the disconnect. I was glad for the sake of my safety that I was able to do so. At other times, it just felt like we were both willing to give up immediately, picturing that endless line of prospects standing right behind the person in front of us. The next person would be *more* congenial, casual, a better fit, easy-peasy. It seemed like we were conditioned to do this—not just by dating apps, but by all tech that demeans human interactions, turning people into product-delivery systems to be used, rated, then forgotten.

Discomfort, boredom, exhaustion are not the same thing as pain. Trying to eliminate all of those things from our lives has a cost, because along with them go so many wonders.

For Vanessa, I knew what she was saying wasn't that deep; it was just a joke. I still felt defensive.

"I'm not a masochist," I replied, after taking a long sip of my drink to collect myself. I thought of Katherine, the woman who relished the dating life. "There are a lot of nice things about meeting new people."

I took Vanessa's hand and ran my thumb along her wrist.

We went across the street to her apartment, a built-out loft. I watched her get undressed in front of her vanity, admiring her own reflection in a lacy black bra. Her expression looking at her own body was endearing. I was on the heaviest day of my period and had no intention of taking my pants off, so I kissed her and helped her with the bra instead.

I had promised to meet friends in the city later, but we lay in bed and talked about nothing, the way you do when you're in bed with someone you've been kissing. Finally, I said goodbye, put on my shoes, and headed out of her bedroom. Two of her roommates were sitting at their kitchen table, wearing only aprons, jolted to see me in their home. The woman hid her face. I waved and sped away.

Did you see my roommates naked?! Vanessa texted me, moments later.

Yes, I replied. *They seem very shy for people who throw sex parties.*

Hahahahah, she wrote.

I wondered what she would tell them about me. An apartment full of sex-positive queers obviously made Vanessa feel supported in her explorations. The way I'd lived with roommates over the years had informed my dating life quite a lot, and influenced how I looked at the inflexible boundaries that seemed to be such a huge part of monogamous sex and love.

Just after college, I lived with a close friend, and we did everything together. We went on road trips, went out dancing, visited each other's families, and generally acted as each other's support system as we set up our first home outside of school life.

Then things started to change. She began dropping plans with me to do things with whomever she was seeing instead— always a man, of course. I didn't get it. Why would hanging out with some guy she barely knew be more important than plans with me?

To her, disregarding my feelings to promote romantic ones with someone else was a totally fine thing to do. When I got mad at her for spontaneously going with a guy she'd been dating for two weeks to a local farm that we had talked about visiting for ages, she told me matter-of-factly, "I was raised to look for the person who I am going to share my life with and that's my priority."

Through that friendship I discovered that as people age, deeply close nonsexual relationships are not as acceptable as romantic ones, even when the people in them share a gender and are ostensibly straight. When we were in college and freshly out of it, my roommate was happy to go on road trips and cohost epic parties at our house. The more she got to a place of being ready to settle down, though, the less important our friendship became. Close friendships between two women after they found partners was *queer*, and not in a positive way.

On the night before my roommate was supposed to come to Easter dinner at my grandparents' house, we had a blowout fight at a bar in front of a very alarmed bartender. I don't remember anymore what I said to start it. I'm sure it had something to do with how we'd been spending less time together since she'd met the Italian architect she was dating.

"It's like you th-think," she stuttered, as though it was almost too unspeakable to say out loud, "It's like you think you're my boyfriend or something!"

Shame silenced me like a jab in the neck, and we walked home separately. We made up the next morning in time for dinner, but the feeling of being somehow wrong or grasping stuck with me until I moved into a queer co-op a year or so later. There, the idea of how relationships should proceed and who could be included in what and what gestures of friendship looked like were much more fluid, more carefully considered, and nothing about my perspective felt aberrant at all.

The importance of same-sex relationships has fluctuated over time, along with how they're perceived from the outside. In *Marriage, a History: How Love Conquered Marriage*, Stephanie Coontz writes about the decline of the acceptable same-sex friendship. Until the late nineteenth and early twentieth centuries, the nuclear family was not the common family unit. People's attachments to their other kin took too much precedence. It wasn't an expectation that marital intimacy would bring "happiness" per se; the emphasis was on economic stability and producing children. As Coontz explains, it was hard to think of personal happiness as the goal of marriage when so many women simply did it to survive.

Under those conditions, very close friendships between women were common. The Enlightenment-influenced view that reigned supreme during the nineteenth century was that love was based on "admiration, respect, and appreciation of someone's good character," even in a romantic relationship. People didn't really discuss sex, so expressions of love with regard to friends and lovers sounded remarkably similar.

That changed when the taboo of speaking openly about sexual intimacy in marriage began to break down. A healthy sex life soon became a priority, and a somewhat sudden obligation for wives, who in the Victorian era were consigned to being angels on a pedestal in their domestic sphere. As the separation between men and women crumbled, those angels were expected to participate very differently in earthly delights.

"Deep marital intimacy had been difficult to achieve in the nineteenth century," Coontz writes, "in the face of separate spheres for men and women, sexual repressiveness, and the strong cultural, practical, and moral limits on a couple's autonomy. Now it seemed attainable. And because the progress of industrialization and democratization had weakened the political and economic constraints forcing people to get and stay married, such deep intimacy was now seen as the best hope of stability in marriage."

Laws that made it more possible for women to survive outside of matrimony made romantic and sexual love the new focus of marriage, putting new pressure on the couple's bond. To bolster this change, all other loves had to be diminished—or demonized. Coontz writes:

> The pressure for couples to put marriage first and foremost in their lives led many women to become *more* dependent on their relationships with men. Proponents of "modern" sexuality and marriage were deeply suspicious of close ties between women. By the 1920s the heartfelt female friendships that had been such an important part of nineteenth-century female culture were under attack. . . . By that time intense relationships between women were considered childish infatuations that girls were encouraged to outgrow. At worst, they raised the specter of "abnormal" sexual or emotional development that could make heterosexuality unsatisfactory and marriage unstable.

Some of these same-sex relationships were definitely between two queer people, and I'm certain that many of them were not. The understanding of coded queerness in history has changed, and so has the standard for how close two people can be before it's considered too close for "just friends." Soon after friendships between women came to be seen as deviant, close relationships between men became suspect, too. Homosexuality was outlawed in many Western cultures, but two men sleeping in a bed together or showing other physical inti-macies didn't necessarily read as homosexual until the 1920s, according to Coontz. This shift didn't just affect friendships; it dissolved intimate relationships within extended families, too.

"The new emphasis on heterosexual bonding," she writes, "also called into question the veneration of mothers and the close sibling ties that had made it hard for nineteenth-century married couples to retreat into their own private world. . . . This was another way those of the new generation turned their backs on whatever stood in the way of achieving marital intimacy."

All of this led to the "growing primacy of the couple in people's range of commitments," meaning the age of mar-riage for men and women fell during the first decades of the twentieth century, and marriage rates increased everywhere. Whatever people had once found in all sorts of dynamic, im-portant relationships they were now only allowed to find within marriage. And so they started committing to it sooner and harder.

That doesn't mean people don't enjoy this relatively new order. For many, there is a great deal of diversion in making marital love the center of their lives and they're happy to leave behind friends and other family ties in pursuit of that. But how much of that happiness is attached to an idea of a "tradi-tion" that is only about a hundred years old?

I assumed Vanessa had thought about some of these things: she had told me about her home like it was a meaningful place to her; she had a girlfriend with whom she had an open rela-tionship; she seemed like someone who was trying to expand her life by including as many people as possible in it rather than whittling it down to only one special somebody.

It soon became evident that Vanessa was trying to recruit me into all that, and quickly, though that might have been partially related to having a lot of free time. She contacted me almost every day, asking how I was doing, what I was up to. It was friendly and I liked the attention, but it was irregular compared to everyone else I'd dated that summer. Was it healthy? Was it expected? Was it just different communication styles? I couldn't tell.

Soon after we met, there was a heat wave. I tolerated it for a few days, then finally broke down and hauled the inefficient old AC on my floor up into the window. It might be okay to roast myself, but the cats had started hiding behind the toilet to keep cool, and that couldn't be sanitary. I struggled to lift the AC unit and hold it in place, thinking that this one chore would definitely be easier with a partner. When I finally got the unit in place and cranked it up, I fell onto the couch. I was an airless balloon, shriveled and sticking to itself in a balled-up mess. Vanessa and I had plans for a third date that night, but I texted her asking if we could reschedule. She agreed, then tried to nail down a day immediately. Tuesday? Next Monday?

I told her I'd text tomorrow. In the morning I felt ghastly. My throat was sore and I was aching all over. I was getting sick, which seemed rude for the weather. It was much too hot to eat soup, though when I texted Vanessa that I was ill, she offered to bring some. *No, thank you, that's so nice,* I replied. It *was* nice, and I couldn't imagine trying to entertain or talk to anyone bringing me food. Being alone was all I wanted, to not have to perform or pretend or meet demands or make plans. I needed to rest. It sounds despicable, but if she had ignored me for a bit, I probably would have recovered and messaged her. Instead, she kept checking in and asking when we could see each other. Having not been accountable to anyone for a long time, I was overwhelmed by this level of attentiveness from someone I'd been on two dates with.

I'm sorry, I wrote to her on the third day of this. *I like you a lot, I'm just too busy to really date, I've realized. It's been wonderful getting to know you.*

After a little bit she answered, *I understand. I hope you feel better soon. It was nice getting to know you, too!*

This kindness made me feel even worse, like I was some sort of goblin who couldn't respond to affection. I'd tried so hard to learn to accept rejection that I hadn't yet learned how to accept connection. At that moment, it seemed like I never would.

The heat and the guilt and feeling sick had made me insufferably cranky. I wanted to stay away from everyone until I recovered some equilibrium. I ate ice pops on the couch and watched movies. Most of them were action flicks I didn't need to pay attention to as I simultaneously scrolled through my phone. For no good reason, I ended up watching the 2012 film *Seeking a Friend for the End of the World.*

The movie is about an alternate version of earth where a humanity-destroying asteroid is about to hit the planet. Everyone knows it will happen, all attempts to prevent disaster have failed, and people everywhere are doing whatever they need to do in the last month they have left to live. It's supposed to be a comedy, starring Steve Carrell and Kiera Knightley, so almost until the very end I expected this asteroid to somehow be circumvented. Surely, it wouldn't end with the two lovers, brought together by exceptional circumstances, being exterminated.

It did. As the credits rolled, I was engulfed in a wave of existential terror unlike anything I'd ever experienced. I don't know if it was because it was unexpected or because I'd never really pictured a cataclysmic annihilation event, but it made me literally nauseous. I had to get up and pace around the small square-footage of my apartment as my fever spiked. I'd been confronted with death many times in my life. The thought of my own death often filled me with dread. This was different. I didn't know until then how much consolation I took in the idea of life going on even when mine would be over.

Whenever I left this existence, I wanted it to be with the faith that somewhere people were sitting in the park, filling their bird feeders, applying eyeliner, spitting, being tired, being excited, knocking on doors, taking the training wheels off bikes, dressing up to go to a birthday party, starting the coffee maker, gossiping, having their bones set, getting knocked down by ocean breakers, crying on the phone, high-fiving ironically, high-fiving sincerely, checking the weather report, forgetting to bring out the recycling, running to catch a train, blowing on steaming cups of tea, smacking mosquitoes, celebrating, getting woken up by the neighbors, being ugly, or kind, or funny, or just nothing, because life has no necessity except to repeat itself in all of its tiny, insistent declarations. If it all ceased to be, there was no point in being right now, and that was unbearable.

These sorts of breakdowns can't be sustained for long if your brain is functioning appropriately. I cried irrationally for a minute and then took a nap. When I woke up, I was feeling semi-normal, having managed to compartmentalize the terror of being. I stood at the window without the AC in it, and Bert hopped up to join me. I scratched his soft head. Communing with my cat, I was sensitive to all the thin threads of connection tying me to the people below, a thousand filaments of care, interest, commitment, that made living extend so much further than the borders of a single life. So many people have only one anchor holding them down. What a waste, I thought, when there was so much else out there. Soon that softness faded as well. Within a few days, that open acceptance had closed and I was just a girl alone in her apartment again, looking for a date.

CHAPTER 9

Let's Party

The bar my date had chosen looked like an unpopular gaming lounge. Piles of giant Jenga pieces and table-sized Connect 4 sets served as centerpieces for small groups of rowdy young people. Its size muted their exclamations and flirtations. The tone was very "birthday party right before everyone shows up and you're nervous they won't."

My date, Tal, was already there. I recognized him immediately because he actually looked like his photos, broad-shouldered and lean. It was those photos that had lured me from my usual haunts to Williamsburg. There was also a party nearby, making it a two-for-one train trip. If the date was bad, I'd have a consolation-prize event.

After Vanessa, I didn't want to quit dating, even though I'd hit a limitation for interaction I didn't know I had. I wasn't sure how to get around it. It seemed as though I'd learned most of what I could from going on so many first dates. There was no way to "practice" interpersonal relationships on a deeper level without finding someone compatible, and that still seemed to largely be an issue of luck. Additionally, was it fair to work out your issues on someone in such a prolonged and intimate way? Your partners shouldn't be therapists you get to have sex with, in my opinion. This is what I wondered about, instead of why getting closer to someone had felt more draining than fulfilling.

I decided to stick to my dating intentions, and there were still a few weeks of summer left. I picked Tal because he looked relaxed and handsome and wrote that he was in the arts and new to Bumble. When he saw me, he stood up, looking relieved. We hugged.

"I chose this place because they supposedly make great cocktails," he said, pushing the moisture-warped menu toward me. Having worked in bars throughout my life, I find that cocktails hold very little mystique. I've seen too many of them shaken and stirred and spilled and snuck behind the bar to value them at their price point anymore. Leaning over the list, a hundred different nights of serving tables flitted through my head and I had to seal my lips to keep from babbling something inane about bar culture. When I finally ordered a paloma, the bartender seemed mad about it.

"It's not a very well-balanced drink," she warned me, planting her hands on the surface of the bar as though daring me to go through with it.

"That's okay, I'll still have one," I said, confused about why she didn't just make it better, in that case. Her posture radiated pique as she turned away to make Tal and me our drinks. He had ordered the same thing out of solidarity, and it did create a sense of familiarity between us. Banding together against someone else over something as stupid as a cocktail choice was enough to make us a unit. How enticing the feeling of being in a unit is, even when it's based more on rejecting others than on finding internal commonalities.

When she plopped them down, I took a sip. It tasted tart. I preferred that to something sugary, so it all worked out.

Tal sipped, swallowed, grimaced, then asked, "So, what do you do?"

Happy to get back to basics, I told him I was a writer, where I'd grown up, that I had no siblings, that blah blah blah. He was good at going back and forth, telling me about himself, asking me questions. He was an artist, one with some success. He showed me photos of his large-scale paintings. After the second paloma, I caught myself fantasizing about what it would be like to date a guy who traveled the country to install art at big-name galleries. I realized I was attracted to him beyond his good looks. Lots of people are good-looking. Getting along with someone is much rarer.

Even though I was having a good time with a hot guy, I wanted to go to my party. It was already on the late side. Tal said he actually had to go home because he was traveling in the morning. I took that to mean he wasn't interested. Disappointing. It had been a nice evening. Outside, I leaned in to give him a hug goodbye, feeling warm due to the tequila. As my arms went around him, he tried to kiss me, missing my mouth. I stood back and we laughed.

"Can we try that again?" I asked.

"Yes, of course!"

We moved toward each other more slowly and started making out on the street, which I'm sure everyone passing by, as well as the bartender watching from inside, appreciated.

Tal leaned back and whispered huskily, "Are you sure you have to go to your party?"

"Yes," I replied, smiling. It felt like something was flaring between us, which was exciting. There was a hesitation, too. I'd felt something similar about Vanessa and ended up pulling away. Or the hesitation could even have been from the reminder of the spring, and the first man I'd kissed in years disappearing right after. It can be so hard to take a person as they are without being haunted by all the dynamics you had with other people from your past. If only we could just start over fresh with every person we try to know. This is what people call "baggage," or even trauma—the suspicion that all relationship patterns just repeat and repeat, and you'll never get to have something better than what's already come. It can be hard to remember the other person has their own shit they're carrying around. You're each unique snowflakes of hurt feelings and bad memories.

As I left, there was also a part of me that was cocky, certain there would be other chances to meet. I thought he liked me and would want to make that happen. There was time.

I found my way to the bar where my friends were waiting. "Waiting" wasn't quite the right word, because when I walked into the rager taking place in the bar, I knew no one would have noticed if I'd never shown up. A smoke machine was pumping regular fresh layers of fog across the dance floor, and a disco ball reflected back a rainbow of lights shooting out of an LED display. Most of the people there were friends from my comedy life, including the DJ. Even though they wouldn't have missed my presence, they were happy to see me, cheering over the blasting of the music.

There was nothing hesitant or slow about the dancing. Things had already cranked up to a ten. The bad palomas had loosened me up, as had the kissing. A wave of energy seemed to be connecting everyone; groups formed circles, splitting apart and re-forming, everyone consumed by a mad summer fever that made unified movement a psychic directive. I was absolutely off my head within twenty minutes, triumphant, streaming sweat, and jumping up and down.

"I'm having so much fun!" I literally screamed in my friend Patrick's face. He took my hands and we jumped up and down together. The night spun on, and I was so joyously glad that I'd gone to be with this group of people instead of home with a man, though the promise of meeting that man again gave the dancing an added sheen.

The next morning, the cats' demands woke me. I felt like a grapefruit someone had stepped on, split and leaking juice. I stumbled to the sink for a glass of water, opening my mouth and coughing a little fog smoke out. I wasn't exactly hungover; it was more that my entire body was aching, particularly my neck and the soles of my poor feet. Too much head banging and stomping. After some eggs and coffee, I felt almost functional, and impressed with myself; I was inside a strong, powerful body that could process palomas all night and still get up before noon the next day. I spent so much time alone with my job, it sometimes seemed like I didn't know anyone at all. That illusion had recently been propped up by so many dates with people I was meeting for the first time. At that party, I remembered there were lots of people who had known me for years and who knew one another.

If that kind of feverous unity was something I could participate in every weekend, or via some other community activity, indefinitely, I would have abandoned dating completely for the rest of my life. Nights like that made me understand church better. It was sort of a similar feeling to the two Dolly Parton concerts I'd been to, during both of which I'd openly wept. I rode the dance-party high for a couple of days before reaching out to Tal to see if he wanted to hang out.

He did. We made plans. He canceled. He was going out of town. I never heard from him again.

This time I wasn't upset about being rejected. I was sexually frustrated. Complaints about dating apps are often accompanied by a secondary complaint about hookup culture—that people sleep with each other too easily, too often. Why hadn't I managed to get laid? There are many definitions of sex, and I was flexible about what sex could mean. By my personal standard, nothing I'd done had really satisfied that craving.

Remembering my reaction to Vanessa's texting, I left Tal alone. My high from a weekend of excess and excitement dissipated, and a more typical weekend followed, with another lukewarm date or two.

The thing about my friends from comedy was that they were as close as I had found to a self-replenishing community. My casual high school or college friends and I had grown apart. My closest friends had mostly all married, and many had children. I could visit their lives, though it seemed we rarely went out to do new things in life together. Most of my other hobbies were solitary ones. Despite my love for Dolly Parton, I wasn't following her around the country in a little caravan of obsessives. Comedy people came and went, sure, but there was always a core of people I could reliably find things to do with. That kept me coming back even when making and watching comedy wasn't as satisfying as it had been when I'd started.

Every year there were new people in that community, and most of them were younger. Older people filtered out, called away by the same changes my peers elsewhere had been. People tried to be inclusive. At a certain point, I didn't know that I would still feel right dancing on weekends with people who were younger and younger than me. Or that I would even want to.

How many comparable groups were there where people could join together in a friendly way on a regular basis, and that weren't arranged around a family dynamic? Church? Unfortunately, most popular Western religions are all about a patriarchal family dynamic, too, even if all are theoretically welcome at service. Robert Putnam's *Bowling Alone* was published in 2000, over twenty years ago, when there was already a noticeable decline in group activities. Putnam's overall thesis is that the quality of civic engagement, which he calls social capital, is degrading as people are separated by the technology of the Internet or television. The variety of choices available to us in entertainment splits people in so many directions that we can't focus on the health of the communities we live in, and the country at large. Though he has none of DePaulo's beliefs about wanting to destroy traditional family structures, he does seem to share her opinion that people have become too reclusive, withdrawing into their homes rather than seeking out town squares in their free time.

Bowling Alone was published four years before the advent of Facebook, and it reads partly as a premonition of how humanity would become so politically divided via a curated news feed, and subsequently isolated from alternate perspectives. Putnam talks about the limitations of time, too, and how people have become far too busy to sustain community ties. He wanted to see more civic engagement and suggested that it was largely a difference of generational attitude that had led to the deterioration of organizations that bolster community.

In the two decades since the publication of Putnam's book, technology has only become more niche, filtering interests into ever more specific subsets. The political landscape became even more divisive. Putnam's warnings about the desperate need for face-to-face interactions were not inaccurate, but the structures he had faith in as unifying groups (Boy Scouts, rotary clubs, the NRA) were not exactly neutral meeting grounds. Trying to drag people backward, to a simpler time with three TV channels, one big game on a Saturday night, and essentially one point of view, was not possible.

Personalized technology can separate people. At the same time, the cost of a phone is marginal compared to the cost of joining clubs, finding free time to participate in group hobbies, or the emotional investment required for sustaining community ties. Many of the improv and sketch classes I took were paid for in exchange for working at the theater, but not all of them. I recognize that I paid for my friend group as much as any sorority or fraternity or other exclusive club member.

Removing tech or television from your life might simplify some things, but it won't address these financial barriers to community building. Couplehood and a shared Netflix account might be the easiest, most affordable alternative to complete isolation for many people, especially as they age and don't have the energy or free time for other hobbies.

Another suspicious thing I'd noticed about hobbies is how rarely people are allowed to do anything for enjoyment without being asked to make money off it. An artist, a poet, or someone who knits or makes quilts will often be asked if they have an Etsy shop; they themselves may even be thinking about how to turn the thing they started doing to relax and enjoy into another job. The pressure to monetize every moment of our days, every output or bit of fun, makes hobbies that include other people seem like a waste of time—unless it's a networking opportunity.

Comedy, of course, was no escape from that. Most of my friends were trying to be successful as actors or writers, or just famous on Twitter. I still thought I was incredibly lucky to have the outlets I did, even with their limitations. The weekend after my date with Tal, though, there was no dance party, nor the one after that. There are many moments to fill in between the ecstatic highs of life, so I turned back to my routine, eventually feeling regret about not jumping on the opportunity for finally fornicating when I had the chance.

New York is mostly penned in crossways between towering concrete rectangles. Nonetheless, the city's residents are quite aware of the changes in nature. In winter, cold winds shoot through the corridors created by the skyscrapers as icy slush fills the gutters. A New York winter, even a mild one, seems to last an eternity. There is no giddier place than the city on the first warm day of spring. Summer is parties and concerts in the park and wilting miserably under a fan in a box of an apartment. These cycles were as embedded in me as the growth of the field is for a generational farmer. That's why I recognized the moment when the summer began to turn. One night after the sun went down, a coolness crept in, replacing the oppressive humidity that hangs in the air on early August nights. Then the 99-cent stores hung up new backpacks and pushed the Mead notebooks to the front. Fall was arriving.

As excited as folks were for the beginning of summer, they were just as excited to begin donning the widow's weeds of fall. There is some internal calendar built inside anyone who has been forced to attend U.S. public school. Beach and sexy fun are over after Labor Day. Let's move on to talking about Halloween and foliage trips upstate.

Giving up on the rest of the month was an appealing idea, especially as I doggedly tried to complete my mission of going on two dates every week. The giddy slew of connections I'd been making in early June had slowed to a trickle. I could not get a freaking match! As for actual dates, they were flakes, fakers, and no-shows. Everything was experiencing a slowdown, including libidos.

On a muggy evening, I lay on my couch in my underwear, watching *Taken 2* and swiping morosely. Bert walked gracefully toward me, let out a disturbed cry, then tiptoed away, message delivered. The place where my back touched the gray faux suede was soaked, and my front was slightly chilly from the light AC blowing through. I'd thought the restlessness that had first driven me into dating again, and into my little project, would be assuaged by now, either because my curiosity would be sated or because I'd actually meet someone to go with on one of those foliage trips. Instead, I was more restless than ever. The searching for answers had left me dissatisfied, hankering for more. It seemed hopeless, and yet I couldn't stop trying. I'd promised myself just a few more weeks of torment before officially giving up.

That's why I was up at 11:45 on a weeknight, messaging *Hey*s to the few options on my match list. A man on Bumble had a picture of himself with a small tortoiseshell-patterned cat. Sometimes I swiped right on people with animals I wanted to get to know.

I wrote to him, *I love your cat*, and he instantly replied.

Thank you, he said. *Look, I don't want to beat around the bush, so I'll just say I am leaving town tomorrow afternoon, but I'll be back in October.*

October. I could be dead by then.

Oh well, I wrote, sighing over another match going nowhere. *If you don't meet right away, you never will. Feel free to message me in October.*

Well, why don't we meet right away? he asked.

Now, many people who swipe on dudes could tell you about the sheer number of *U up?* messages they receive on a nightly basis from thirsty men they've connected with on dating apps. The fact that it happens so often must mean that it works sometimes. I'd occasionally been tempted. Here's how those dudes would usually blow it:

1. Demanding some assurance that if they come to meet me, I would absolutely have sex with them. I personally can't trust myself with someone who doesn't seem capable of taking no for an answer.

2. Messaging me at 3 A.M., when I was already asleep.

This guy was aware of these two important hurdles. He'd caught me at an alert moment and pressed that advantage.

How about I come to meet you at a bar, I'll get in a car right now, and there's absolutely no pressure to do anything, he wrote.

Staring at the phone in my hand, I pondered whether or not to say yes to meeting some passing wacko after midnight when I had work in the morning. I looked at Bert, who blinked at me slowly. Then, suddenly, I felt the brisk wind of the dying season howl over me. Summer was ending. Life was fleeting. Chances for kissing a cute man were passing me by. Would I meet the winter of my life without having run through the green fields?

Okay, I wrote. *But if you're not in a car by 12:30, forget it.*

I gave him the address for the Georgiana, cleaned the kitty litter, took out the garbage, and even managed to put on pants before running downstairs. I arrived right behind him, recognizing his hair as he stepped out of a cab in front of the bar. We turned toward each other in the doorway and embraced as we evaluated the reality against the pictures. Then we entered, conspicuous in the almost empty establishment, clearly there for a hookup. He had very lovely skin, showing the heat in his cheeks, the slight film of sweat at his temples. He had nice arms, pretty eyes, and a heavy gold ring on his pointer finger, a flamboyant adornment incongruous to his simple hipster aesthetic. I decided right away that unless he said something absolutely incriminating in the next five minutes, it was going to happen.

I watched him drink whiskey on ice as we tried to cover whatever needed to be said before making a final decision. He was an actor, in town to discuss producing some project or other. Having grown up among artists with media ambitions, I recognized someone trying to seem more successful and important than they actually are, which was fine. I was not as successful or important as I wished I was either, and it ultimately didn't matter very much to me who he would be tomorrow, when he returned wherever he had come from.

I had always been very attracted to the superficial charm of people who perform for a living. Their work demands a certain ability to observe others and respond well, to re-create a simulacrum of a human person that disguises their actual vulnerabilities. Something in me loved to search for and touch the spots where the real person showed through. I wanted to split their shells like I was shucking an oyster, throwing defenses aside and looking at the wriggling pink matter within.

Or I just knew an actor, a good one, would fake whatever you wanted or needed in the moment, which is useful when you're trying to have a pleasant one-time encounter. It was also great that this man would be leaving my city in less than twelve hours. There'd be no opportunity to try to chase after him or feel rejection, as I had with that first attempted hookup so many months ago. Though there'd been some make-outs and heavy pettings since then, this would be it: I was gonna go *all the way*. If there were emotional aftershocks to that decision, this guy would be too far away to feel them.

At the bottom of his drink, my date asked, "Should I get another round?"

"No," I said, and we walked around the corner to my place.

When I was very young, I was shy about my body. When I was with Morgan, I even preferred to have sex with my shirt on most of the time, especially in the daylight. That state of mind had become harder to relate to as I aged, even as that body had probably gotten "worse" over time, according to magazine standards. It was now heavier, hairier, more marked by various small injuries, subject to the pressures of gravity. My mind was also older, and being modest didn't occur to it. We kissed in the light of my living room lamp, and then I pulled my shirt over my head.

He extended his hands out to cup my breasts, very slowly, in a way that reminded me of someone reaching toward a baby deer wandering on the lawn. I leaned forward to make it easier on him and realized I was really the one playing a part. Someone for whom this was expected, someone who could take the lead. The role made the next step easier, and the next, and then it was over in almost less time than we'd taken to talk at the bar.

We lay for a minute in my bed, breathing, and I savored the feeling of having a secret. I'd done it. Now I'd feel the satisfaction of having accomplished what dating is for: mating. The idea amused me, because I could already tell it wasn't true. Sex sure made me feel alive. It made me feel like I was participating in adulthood, which six years of seclusion had not. Even moments afterward, though, the satisfaction of having finally done it was already fading. Sex was just sex. It wasn't an answer to loneliness any more than doing a triathlon was. A physical act can connect to our emotions; it can't hold them all.

"Wow," he said, interrupting my train of thought. "That was fun. But, man . . . I could have been anybody."

If this were a horror story, that conversation opener would probably be the buildup to my murder.

"Like, meeting someone for this is such a risk for women, obviously!" he continued, his rising voice implying a huge epiphany.

"It can be scary," I answered after a moment of pregnant silence. "I want to live my life."

His reminder of the risk embedded in sexual gratification for women was unwelcome. I understood it far better, having weighed the dangers of all sorts of things he likely didn't think much about. Meeting up with a man, having sex with a man, accepting a drink from a man I didn't see get made, getting into a cab driven by a man, walking home alone at night in a world full of men. In the world of women, I was relatively safe. Cis, white, heteronormative-looking, and with enough money to fund my luxuries. If something violent did happen to me during a consensual sex romp, I knew the narrative would still be that I had been asking for it.

I stretched and said, "I should get to sleep soon."

He took his cue to leave, gathering his clothes as I drank a glass of water. After he left, it no longer seemed like a monumental moment at all. Things were exactly the same as before we met. Nothing dire happened to me during our encounter. I checked myself, running through the sensations in my body, exploring the potential for revelations. Nothing bad, no. Nothing transformative had taken place either. The coldness of the future stole over me once more.

PART TWO

CHAPTER 10

Total Eclipse of the Heart

I met the person I'd fall in love with on a steamy night a few days before a total solar eclipse. I was sitting in the window of the Georgiana, wearing cutoffs and a white V-neck shirt. My legs were up on a barstool and I was sipping on a flute of sparkling rosé. I was in one of the worst moods I'd been all summer, hungover, bloated, and miserable.

That week, an infrequent astronomical event had stolen everyone's imagination, even people who ordinarily barely glanced at the sky. There were only certain places where the full effects of the complete solar eclipse could be seen. Dylan and I had been planning to meet in Los Angeles, then drive together to Wyoming to stay with a friend of his at his family home, which happened to be parked right in one of those visibility corridors. Dylan's wife would be there, of course, but as we planned, we mostly talked about what we would see—the mountains, the blue lakes, the classic roadside Americana. I imagined finally talking to him in person for hours, sitting shotgun as the highway sped underneath us and the sun set up ahead.

Except I wouldn't be sitting shotgun to Dylan. I'd be in the back seat, his wife in front. That reality would flash into my road trip plans occasionally, but I'd switch back to my pre-ferred mental programming. As the date approached, it was harder to turn off. Dylan had invited a few other friends to come along, too, so I reassured myself that we'd be a group, two carloads of eclipse chasers at least. Not just a couple and their third wheel. There was no way that could happen.

One by one, the prospective company dropped out. Less than a week before my plane was set to take off, I sat on my couch, heavy with foreboding. How had I put myself in this position? How could I get out of it?

My text to Dylan was long and carefully crafted. I was as close to honest as I could be, explaining such a long road trip with a couple wasn't a great idea for a vacation for me. I didn't say it, but I was especially reluctant to go because his wife didn't particularly like me, and I knew they'd been bickering a lot. I'd already been the kid with parents going through a di-vorce. I didn't need to re-create that scenario in my thirties, especially in a sedan.

The parameters of the trip had deteriorated, too; Dylan had initially thought we would have time for sightseeing and he'd recently realized he couldn't leave work when he'd thought, meaning we would probably have to book it from L.A. That meant day after day in the car, just to camp at a large family gathering of people I didn't know to watch the sun disappear behind the moon. I'd left the camping plans up to Dylan, and based on how things were going, I was nervous about what the tent arrangements would end up being.

My cancellation didn't cost them anything, except some

help with the gas money, but Dylan protested. He tried to negotiate, suggesting we spend one night in a specific national
park and take one scenic route along the way. Whatever I
wanted. It wasn't until he started to argue with me that I lost
it. I called my mother, trying to parse my roiling feelings.

"He uses you emotionally, as a buffer," she said. "It's not
fair to you."

I objected, insisting that was what friendship was: emotional support. Inside, I knew she was right. Not about Dylan,
really, just that it wasn't fair. I wasn't being fair to myself. It
was wrong to have put myself in the position of feeling like a
beggar at the table of someone else's love. I deserved my own
adventure, and spending days trapped in a car with a couple
would only make me unhappy.

The determination that carried me through the cancellation process exited my body right afterward, leaving me hollow. All my talk of independence meant very little when I
looked at the future and wondered if every trip I ever took
from here on out would be alone, or as part of some dissatisfying compromise. What had seemed like wise self-protection
one moment looked like cowardice the next.

I was hungover because I'd spent the night before this evening at the Georgiana with a group of girlfriends, trying to
rally them into planning a trip smaller in scope together. The
discussion had been lively—where we would go and when and
who we would stay with and *isn't it so beautiful there in summer*
and *I can get us this house* and *we would have so, so much fun* but *I
can't do this week* but *I can't make spring* but *I am planning a trip
with family then.* The plans soared and crashed in the space of
a few hours. Fragmented hopes flitted around the room and

settled in darkened corners, forgotten the next morning as we ground on through another day of waning vacation opportunities. I'd awoken with a killer headache and covered in cat hair. My apartment was filthy. My expensive single-woman cat hotel was filthy. I felt so, so low.

In the late afternoon, I got a message on Bumble from a guy named Adrian who had flaked on me a few weekends earlier. We had matched when I was visiting my aunt and uncle out in Montauk. He told me he was working at a Long Island restaurant for the summer. He visited the city on Saturdays off. He wanted to know what I was doing tonight.

My impression of Adrian when he walked into the bar to find me remains vividly fresh. There is a pause when you're meeting up with someone from a dating app, a nanosecond where your formulated idea of what they look like aligns with what they actually look like. There is then a second pause when you recognize whether or not you're immediately attracted to them.

When I close my eyes, I'm looking at a perfectly clear playback of those moments. I know memory is not always reliable. Since I'm aware of what would happen over the next few years with this man, I am suspicious of mine. My mind has likely gone back, tweaking, adjusting, changing the meaning of all our shared moments to suit my narrative about us and even about love. I can only say that I clearly recall the sensation of our eyes meeting, a little shiver that started at the top of my skull and zipped down my spine, and a smile. It seemed like we were smiling the same aware smile of interest, creating a parallel. I can see his eyes sliding away and then back to me, as though to take a moment to recover as he lifted his shoulder bag over his head, then joined me in the window.

That said, I was not sure about Adrian during that date at all. I was still tired, on the tail end of my period, aware that my house was the only place for us to go and that it was mostly cat hair. Adrian also had the habit of asking few questions and talking endlessly about himself. He was a writer, and I heard all about his published novel, his literary influences, and his current project before he thought to ask me what I did. When I told him I was a writer, too, he laughed. So did I.

It didn't matter. The current of attraction was there. We finished our drinks and got another round. At the end of that one, he asked what I wanted to do.

"Let's try a kiss," I said. He obliged, and the kiss was bad. He came in tongue first, reminding me of a parrot reaching delicately for a grape. When he leaned back, I stroked his face to delay a second kiss and he let me, leaning into my hands. He had a neatly kept black beard, sparkling with silver, a mustache trimmed carefully over a wide mouth. My fingers ran up through his curling, peppery hair, and his light green eyes closed, enjoying the touch. I liked that.

"Let's get one more drink and see," I said. There was a pause. If he'd said no, urged me to take him home, I would have said goodbye and never thought about him again.

Later, he would tell me he'd been messaging with another girl on Tinder that night, someone who was "guaranteed." How different this story would be if he'd left to meet a sure thing. He stayed. We had one more drink and then I took him back to my apartment, climbing the long creaking staircase with him at my back. We reached the top, and I waited for him to catch his breath.

When we entered, I left the lights off and led him to the window, showing him the night view of Manhattan. He agreed it was an amazing sight, then leaned into my ear.

"I'm going to fuck you over that window ledge," he said.

It was just sex. Much better sex than our lackluster kiss at the bar had led me to expect, and the kissing soon caught up as we found a meeting place in style. It was still just sex, and afterward I sent him home, not wanting to sleep next to a stranger. He told me he'd be back in town soon, because he was flying out to where he actually lived: Los Angeles. That seemed to be where everyone was or was from these days, and it felt like the city was waving to me and calling me over through yet another ambassador. Would I ever go?

I gave him my number, and though we'd had fun, it was unexpected when he texted me.

Our next date was on the eclipse, just a few days later. In New York, it was only a partial eclipse, but entrancing enough to the people standing stock-still in the street looking through special glasses or homemade box viewers. He'd asked me out to dinner. Again, I can see Adrian perfectly, waiting for me outside the restaurant with his arms crossed, holding still until I leaned in to kiss him. It was like we were playacting being a couple for the night. Why not? He was leaving the next day. I didn't eat. Instead, I drank a glass of orange wine and watched him munch a Caesar salad, thinking that he didn't care much about how his breath would smell for me.

To distract my unnecessarily critical thoughts, I started covering the crunchy rhythm of his chewing with a story about an old friend I'd used to come to this restaurant with, how we'd grown apart and how I thought about that friend often and wished I could talk to them again. In some ways, it had been more painful than the loss of a romantic relationship, with none of the emotional support of when a romantic relationship ends. Lost in this reverie, I started when Adrian reached across the table and stroked my arm. It was the sort of empathetic gesture you might make with someone you knew very well.

We bought a bottle of rosé at the wine shop next door. As we stood at the counter to pay for it, that same hand ran across my thigh, across my backside. I sensed the posture of his body change when he realized I wasn't wearing underwear beneath my long sundress. We took our wine to the park and drank it.

"You're fun," he said, in between kisses, as though surprised. I was fun, I thought. I was young and fun and summer wasn't quite over yet. His fingers ran up my legs as twilight turned to dark.

Much later, we sat naked on my couch in a now well-vacuumed apartment, sitting turned in toward each other like the two fish of the Pisces symbol, swimming in opposite directions.

"I looked you up on Twitter and read your essay about loneliness," he began. I groaned, then admitted, "It's what I'm most famous for."

I didn't add that if it wasn't for the relative success of that essay and the subsequent pressures it invited, I wouldn't be sitting across from him right now. Every step I'd taken from the day it was published until now had brought me here, naked against my temporary lover. He was about my height,

lean and muscular, hair lightly covering the center of his chest
and legs, sprinkled with glittering gray like the beard on his
face. I'd ask him one day what he did for exercise to create the
sculptural stomach, the slight but defined curve of pectorals
and he'd say, "Nothing. Isn't that unfair?"

That night, about my declaration of loneliness, he only
said, "I liked it." He added, "Romantic love is mutual delusion. I'm not doing the relationship thing anymore."

It was probably intended as a warning. Most people will
warn you about themselves if you listen, knowing you won't
heed them. I didn't hear what he was saying, because I thought
I didn't need to. This was a brief fling that would be over very
soon. Whether or not he'd be willing to offer the relationship
thing to someone in the future didn't seem really relevant to us.

I'd started dating in early April, and it was now late August.
In less than six months, I'd become very secure with dating
again, even with sex, though he was only the second person
I'd slept with. These were huge adjustments. In many ways, I
was a different person from the one who had sat at that dinner
party. I'd gotten through some barriers that had seemed im-
penetrable. On the other hand, my experimental dating habits
hadn't convinced me yet that love really was inevitable. I still
wasn't convinced that being alone was an issue of my own
limitations.

Did that mean love was a mutual delusion? No. Only that
it was rare, far rarer than the number of couples out there
implies. There are so many difficulties in striking out on your
own path away from couplehood, so few safe harbors outside
of it. The models of couplehood I saw most were more about

practicality, survival, and compromise than anything else. It was tempting to grab someone who could promise some stability and care in my future. I wasn't there yet. If I were to undertake it, it certainly wouldn't be with someone who lived across the country.

Adrian got up and wandered around my small square footage, stopping to pet Bert, who sat flicking his tail on the window ledge. Adrian paid gentle homage to his fluffy toes. He looked over my desk piled with papers, then stopped at my bookshelf. A photo album was propped up, facing out, the front featuring a photo of me sitting on my mother's kitchen sink eating cake decorated with Xena the Warrior Princess's icing portrait, wearing pajamas and heart-shaped glasses. Above the picture, an engraved inscription read, "Aimée's Sweet Sixteen Party." It had been a special gift from my aunt. It was filled with little notes written on an old typewriter by my friends at the big co-ed sleepover my mom had indulgently allowed for the occasion in our one-bedroom apartment.

I felt more shy watching him look at my teen self than I had taking off my clothes. He smiled at the me in the picture, and the me beside him felt it. I'd been a difficult sixteen-year-old. At twice that age, I wasn't sure I'd become much easier. He put my picture down, then grabbed my knee.

"Too bad I'm leaving," Adrian said. "What fun we could have had."

Then, a day or two after his departure, I got a text. He was returning for one more week of work up in the Hamptons, and should he stop by after his flight landed? He spent the night this time, and I barely slept because it was so unfamiliar to share a bed. Plus, we stayed up late talking about dating and apps. He said he'd been out with a woman in L.A. in the past week. They'd had "great text chemistry," then when they met up it was just so-so. He explained that she seemed to want him to be the pursuer, to court her, and he wasn't that kind of guy.

I'd been on a date with someone that week as well, a former co-worker who I had asked out. It had been very nice to spend time with someone I knew again, somehow inherently more romantic. We'd ended up walking along the Hudson River, kissing and looking out at the water. He'd had a dazed expression, like someone discovering something, but it hadn't gone further. I told Adrian about how my date had kissed me goodbye at the subway stop. He didn't respond.

"I just thought it was nice," I said, meaning courtship. "I don't know if it's really my speed."

"Yeah, it's all bullshit," he said, running his hand down my side.

I turned away and looked up at the ceiling, thinking about the last time I'd been in love, many years ago. Not Morgan or Owen, but the roommate in my communal home, someone who had never been my boyfriend. It had been insufferable in a lot of ways, but it hadn't felt like bullshit. It felt like my being was divided, one side observing with cool clarity that my roommate lover was lying, cheating, and leading me on, the other side possessed with a heated madness for him that often led to us crying in each other's arms. It was a level of feeling I didn't think I was capable of at this point in my life.

"I know how it feels to want to possess and to want to be possessed," I said. "Maybe I'll want it again someday. Not right now."

I threw in that last part so he'd know my sights weren't set on him for any kind of possession. The next morning, he left on the bus after suggesting I try to visit him in the Hamptons, saying we could stay at his boss's summer home. It sounded like a great idea to me.

"If I weren't coming and going so much, all these meetups would be borderline rude," he joked.

"Yeah, I've been wondering if you've been fabricating all these goodbyes for the sex," I said, and he laughed.

It was very surreal to be making these plans with someone I'd essentially been on three dates with, so I looked at it as my adventure, the one I'd wanted when I'd canceled my trip to Wyoming. I had to go on it.

That weekend, I got off the bus in a small town close to the beach, jittery and a little suspicious. With the remove of almost a week apart, I had begun to feel silly. Who was Adrian, anyway? And who was I, traveling to meet someone I barely knew out in the middle of nowhere? Then, when I saw him getting out of the car, it was all right. He was so graceful, so sure, his face bright with excitement. It made something inside me that had been still for a long time quiver unexpectedly, causing a ripple effect; other nerves lit up in response. I was almost vibrating when we met on the grass and kissed.

His breath smelled like garlic, and I was briefly irritated that eating pungent food before making out seemed to be a pattern of his. Then he told me he'd rented the car because I'd told him I'd never had sex in one. It was so dorky and stupid, and I loved it.

Happiness feels like the beginning of the rest of your life every time. There were so many moments during that brief trip when I felt like *This is it.* I've found happiness and now it is mine to keep and tap into whenever I need. All my growth, my effort, my loneliness, had taken me to this, and now the universe of love and connection would be open for me, always.

Every moment we shared was a bead I strung on a line, points of crystalized memory to wear like a rosary, which I'd later pray over. There was the moment when we tried to have sex against the side of the car, under the stars, only to see headlights in the distance begin to light up the trees brighter than Broadway. We threw ourselves into the back seat, ducking down and giggling until we couldn't breathe. There was the moment when I leaned over him on a towel by the ocean and he brushed the wet hair out of my face, saying, "I like to look at your eyes." There was the moment he lifted my hand out of my lap as we drove through shimmering fields of grass and brought it to his lips. In the end, it was the tenderness that got me, not the sex, though that threw its net around me, too.

Adrian dropped me off at the bus stop late the next day. I was taking it farther east to visit family in Montauk again for the rest of the weekend. I told him I had a bit of a headache, probably from the late night and wine on the beach. He drove off to return the car, and I walked to a coffee shop across the street to cure myself with caffeine. Then I sat on the bench to wait, mentally replaying the hallucinatory fun of the past twenty-four hours.

Suddenly, he appeared on foot. He'd walked back with a pack of Tylenol for me.

"Thank you," I said, slipping it into my pocket as a memento.

The late afternoon light made his green eyes glimmer, almost gold. I was wondering if I could possibly be as beautiful to him as he looked to me when he reached out to cup my face. Then he waved goodbye, crossed the street to walk back to work, looking over his shoulder at me.

Adrian left for L.A. a week later, after visiting me one more time in Brooklyn. We had another evening out. It was Labor Day and the end of summer. At dinner that night, the topic turned to dating again. Adrian brought up my loneliness essay once more.

"You shouldn't worry," he reassured me about my future dating prospects. "You're attractive and even fun to hang out with."

This assessment was jarring, like he was trying to pat me on the head when I'd been making him see stars the past few weeks. Of course, for all I knew I'd been one in a rotation of Long Island bikini queens, though I didn't think so. Whatever he thought of my prospects, I obviously was no longer the person who had written that essay. I was doing things she couldn't have done, like have sex. And now I had this all-access pass to happiness! It didn't matter that he was leaving, I told myself. My time with Adrian had unlocked what it was about dating and sex and connection that was so great, and now my experiment was over. The conveyor belt of possibility was up and running, and I planned to shove enjoyment into every orifice, Lucille Ball–style. I'd done the work and now I'd reap the rewards, and he would leave on his own journey. Yes, it was a little regrettable to see him go, but we didn't really know each other that well, when I considered it.

We celebrated his final departure the next morning by

fucking one more time. Caught up in the moment, I asked Adrian to say my name. It sounds odd, but he rarely said my name when we were together. We'd met on an app. . . . When he hesitated, I wondered if he knew how to pronounce it. Then he did.

The sound of my name had an unexpected effect on me. My throat tightened and my eyes welled. I hid my face and breathed heavily to disguise the incipient tears. After all the things we'd done, the sound of my name on his lips as he moved inside me made me the most vulnerable. To expose the cravings of my body to Adrian was nothing next to exposing the longings of my heart—to keep him, this person, and let him see all of who I was and would become. To say, "Let's try to be together, somehow."

I composed myself as we finished, returning from that boundless inner landscape to the far shorter longitudes of my body. Once again, we were just two people meeting briefly, in the middle of other things.

As Adrian got ready to go, it was difficult to strike the right parting tone. He started to mention something we could do in the future before drifting off, silently acknowledging there was no future.

"Had we but world enough and time," he started again, quoting the Andrew Marvell poem "To His Coy Mistress." A bit inappropriate, as I had certainly not guarded my virtue.

"The grave's a fine and private place, but none, I think, do there embrace," I answered, then wondered aloud if it was the same poem at the confused look he gave me.

"No, I don't think so," he said. How ghoulish of me to bring up graves just before we said goodbye.

I checked after he left and found I was correct. In his poem, Marvell is trying to convince a woman to give up the "prize" of her virginity, promising nothing except that death will eventually come for us all anyway. I couldn't help noticing that the risk is really all hers, though Marvell certainly makes that risk sound delicious.

> Let us roll all our strength and all
> Our sweetness up into one ball;
> And tear our pleasures with rough strife
> Through the iron gates of life!
> Thus, though we cannot make our sun
> Stand still, yet we will make him run.

Everything good about what Adrian and I shared had pretty much already happened. He continued to text me upon his return to L.A. After undergoing a minor surgery, he sent me daily texts from his recovery bed, half-kiddingly suggesting I fly to L.A. to care for him.

I kept dating, though I considered my two-dates-a-week project to be at an end. I dated now out of habit, and with the dawning realization that those feelings I'd enjoyed with Adrian weren't so easy to re-create. I did wonder how many other girls Adrian was texting for tea and sympathy, who he had "great text chemistry" with, who just happened to be reading the same book of Pablo Neruda poems as he (a real detail he mentioned with regard to a past date). We'd made no promises to each other, and texts were just texts.

Then one night, he texted me that he was looking at tickets to New York. Wednesday to Wednesday was cheapest.

I was out on a date in the West Village. The guy I was with was fun and we were having a nice time and I had zero interest. I looked at my phone as we walked to a diner to get french fries. I wanted so much to say yes to Adrian, but instead I said, *That's a long time for us to be together. Would that be okay?*

It had been so long since someone had made it so clear they wanted to see me, not since Morgan and I had broken up all those years ago. I was worried we'd get sick of each other, that he'd arrive and the magic we'd shared would disintegrate. I wanted him to reassure me by having no doubts of his own.

Is it? he replied, echoing my uncertainty instead.

I tried to course correct and say I'd still love to have him, but he replied, *Let me think about it and let you know tomorrow.*

It was hard later not to remember that moment and wonder, What if I'd been brave? What if I'd said, "Book it"? What if that slight hesitation ruined my chance at a happily ever after? Forgetting that I didn't believe in happily ever after anymore and also not getting that no one who really wants to be with you is so easily dissuaded from finding their way closer.

Adrian didn't let me know the next day, or the one after that. He eventually texted to say he was worried about money. His texts began to taper off. They started again when I mentioned I'd be in Los Angeles at the end of October to visit Dylan and a few other friends. On Halloween, I flew to LAX. The next day Adrian picked me up at Dylan's apartment in another rental car, this one paid for by me, because I couldn't drive and he offered to be my chauffeur.

We spent the next few days together, driving around L.A., having sex, going to shows. We stood on Venice Beach, and he wrapped his arms around me, joking about putting a baby inside my stomach. I screamed in actual distress, and he hugged me tighter. As we walked down the street hand in hand, he said I should move here, so we could do this all the time. I had told him about my longstanding plan to move to L.A. some-day. There was now an even more compelling reason to do so, perhaps.

"I'm going to when my lease is up in June," I reminded him, though I hadn't really committed to a date. It suddenly seemed feasible to take the leap. He didn't say anything more.

We went out with Dylan, sharing fried rice dishes at Jitlada, and Dylan told us about the solar eclipse I'd missed. He ad-mitted it had been a grueling trip. It was funny to be sitting with Dylan and a man I was "seeing," since it had so often been me with him and his dates. We talked about when I would have to catch my flight back.

"The last time I was here, you told me to get there an hour before takeoff and I almost missed my flight," I accused Dylan. "I had to beg people to let me pass so I could get through se-curity."

"Oh, that's what I do every time," he admitted, then grinned arrogantly at our disgust.

The night I left, we ate with a friend of mine at a restau-rant in Los Feliz. She took our picture together, and Adrian kissed my cheek for it. Afterward, I looked at that picture a lot, not comprehending the meaning of the gesture. Adrian still wasn't my boyfriend. He still wasn't my anything. We'd made no promises, no plans. A car came to pick up me and my friend, and she walked ahead to it, giving us privacy. He and I pretended to dance down the sloping street. It was feeble play-acting; I still wanted it to go on longer.

"I should have just stayed later and done a Dylan," I said.

"No! Don't do a Dylan!" he chuckled, spinning me one last time.

I could sense from how he held me that it was goodbye. I waved to him from the car as we turned the corner, the shadow figure dressed in black, his liquid eyes reflecting the lights.

My flight was a hellish red-eye that I spent face down on the pullout tray. New York was cold and ramping up for the holidays. Adrian sent me a few short texts in November. The more he withdrew, the more I wanted to cling to our fleeting time together. It hadn't taken many uninspiring dates with other people or nights alone to understand that happiness isn't a switch you turn on. I became pretty sure my happiness was actually something Adrian had, and that he could give it back to me by just answering my texts or making plans to see me.

It had been so good, and it didn't seem like there was any reason it couldn't keep being good if we just reached out toward each other a little. I knew I was reaching out further and further toward someone who was probably looking the opposite direction. Finally, I offered to pay for him to visit me in New York. He didn't say yes.

Can I let you know? he asked.

Sure, I replied, knowing that was a no. *But can you do me a favor? Can you tell me by mid-December and not make me ask?*

Of course, he said. Thanksgiving passed, and then my requested deadline. I checked in with him about the wildfires in California, and he assured me he was safe without mentioning my offer.

Dylan came to visit me between Christmas and New Year's, stopping in the city after visiting his family upstate. We ended up at a fancy bar in Union Square, hung with garlands and holly, and ordered overpriced manhattans. It had been a year since I had written my essay, and a lot had changed, except one pretty big thing. I still didn't think I'd meet anyone I could keep.

Adrian was just a delirious interlude. It sucked that it ended on the sour note of his disappearance, that he'd never kept his promise and told me definitively he wasn't coming. The silence was clear, it just seemed like what we'd shared deserved slightly more respectful communication. Perhaps saying nothing was the most efficient way for him to dump me. On my end, it had involved weeks of waiting and hoping. That new terrain of joyful possibility I'd briefly glimpsed had been passing scenery.

I told Dylan all that as he thoughtfully nodded, sipping his cocktail.

"The worst part is, I worked so damn hard, you know?" I'd been dry-eyed discussing my disappointment with Adrian, but this complaint made me emotional. "I went on all these dates and met so many people, and then at the very end I met this one special person, and we had such an insane, magical time. And it felt like all my searching and growth—"

"The trials and tribulations," he interjected.

"Yes, the trials and tribulations! It felt like they'd paid off. Because the story is that someone goes through their self-improvement journey, and at the end they get a reward."

"But really, there is no reward," Dylan reminded me. "There's no one way anything is supposed to happen. No one deserves anything in particular, they just get what they get."

"I'd hoped there was, deep down, which is embarrassing,"

I said, mournfully. "And the motivation to keep trying, to do it all over again, is now much harder to keep up."

"Well, the thing about stories is that they have an end so their conclusion seems meaningful," he philosophized, clinking the giant ice cube in his empty glass. "Your story is still going."

"So nothing seems meaningful at all!"

"Exactly."

We laughed and ordered another round.

Dylan flew home in time to escort his wife to his company's extravagant New Year's Eve celebration featuring a performance by Drake, and I went to a house party in Bushwick. There, I saw a guy I'd kissed at midnight at another New Year's Eve party many years ago. I approached him and asked in a half-hearted attempt at flirting, "Remember when we kissed on New Year's?"

"No, we didn't," he replied.

Astounded, I stupidly answered, "Yes, we absolutely did."

I started to describe the party and the bar. He interrupted.

"I totally remember the night you're talking about, and we didn't kiss, because I was interested in this other girl, Tammy, and she and I started dating soon afterward," he explained.

For some reason, this enraged me. This guy in particular didn't matter, nor did our kiss. I just knew it had happened, and having it denied made me wild.

"You couldn't have liked her that much, because you kissed me!" I spat.

"I find this super interesting," he said, much more calmly. "Did you know almost all of our memories are fake, because we reconstruct them over and over again until we're remembering something completely different than what actually happened?"

"Why is your memory of that night real and mine is a re-constructed lie?" I asked.

"I just remember Tammy—"

We argued back and forth about shared reality, until I walked away in aggravation. If he didn't remember, there wasn't much I could do about that. It was the discussion of memories that really bothered me. I was thinking about Adrian, and the treasure trove of moments I'd been sifting through in my mind to sustain that spark of hope, long past when it should have been extinguished. Even after it was super clear he'd moved on, I'd continued replaying them for myself, all the way back to that first hint of connection, the look in his eyes when he walked through the door to see me sipping pink champagne.

How was he remembering it? How could something so special for me be so easy to give up for him? In his mind, had any of it happened at all?

On January 15th, I received a text from him.

Hey, sorry I didn't message you before. Hope you and the cats are well.

CHAPTER 11

. . . .

The Great Escape

I hadn't heard from Adrian in two months. Instead of playing it cool for a day or two, I responded within the hour, saying the cats and I were fine. I asked him if he was well.

Yup, all good! he answered. That was it. All I would get. A few days later I wrote him an email, trying not to sound like That Girl, like someone he could dismiss as crazy because she'd expressed how she honestly felt. People joke that if a man says a woman is crazy you should ask what he did to her. Adrian hadn't done anything except ignore me, so I wondered if I had a right to complain. The trope of the woman scorned was inextricably bound up with what we might owe each other in relationships—respect, communication, clear boundaries, compassion—and a culture that teaches us it's everyone for themselves.

Or my email was crazy and I should have just considerately faded away, like the first wife consigned to the attic in a Brontë novel. I wrote to him that it actually wasn't all right that he left me hanging, that I'd really liked him, and I rarely liked anybody, and it was unkind to make me wait and wonder so long. I still wished him the best, though!!!

Unsurprisingly, he never answered.

There is no quick cure for heartbreak. I had complained the previous year about how getting your heart broken at least makes you feel alive. It's more accurate to say it feels like you're trying to survive. One day would be fine and another would bring a wave of intense sensorial memories that put me right back at that beach with him. Like I had told Dylan, it wasn't just the end of something that had barely started, it was the amount of work I'd put in to get even that far. I'd tried through praxis to make myself immune to hurt and simultaneously open to love, and it turned out those two agendas are fundamentally incompatible. This agony of shame and regret was the final result of my adventure, and it made the whole year of work seem not remotely worth it.

I didn't know exactly how to recover, but instead of giving myself time, I opened up my apps again. It had been over a year since I'd begun the physical transformation that metamorphosed into a continuing-education course in dating. I'd found some happiness, and here I was, finding some sorrow. Adrian had been only the second person I'd really slept with on my adventure. Now, all bets were off. If I couldn't have love, I could have some solace in sex.

I met a man named Tommy for coffee one afternoon for a first date near the park. His Tinder profile read that he was engaged and in an open relationship. Something anyone on a dating app in the last few years could tell you is that almost no one on them is single. We're not talking liars and cheaters, though there are probably the same mix of those on there, too. We're talking polyamory. No longer taboo, the lifestyle has become so ubiquitous that it is often more surprising to encounter an attractive bio that doesn't finish with the phrase "ethically nonmonogamous."

I might have found it maddening, but the longer I went without a long-term relationship, the more curious I became about how people managed to maintain them. I wanted to talk to folks who considered their relationships committed yet open, because it intrigued me. People who were open often seemed to have the most complicated perspectives on love, why it does and doesn't last. Making nonmonogamy work requires a lot of processing. They'd talked and talked and talked about the boundaries of their relationships, unlike people who committed to monogamy without much consideration. Monogamy was just the thing to do for a lot of couples. Polyamory was a much more active choice.

In her book *Mating in Captivity: Reconciling the Erotic and the Domestic*, psychotherapist Esther Perel explicitly states that monogamous couples have a hard time finding everything they need in each other, and not just with regard to sexual variety. "Today, we turn to one person to provide what an entire village once did: a sense of grounding, meaning, and continuity. At the same time, we expect our committed relationships to be romantic as well as emotionally and sexually fulfilling. Is it any wonder that so many relationships crumble under the weight of it all?" she writes.

Sex holds a unique place in this litany of needs. It's culturally acceptable to admit that sexual monogamy is hard, though most still claim to maintain it or choose to blow up their relationships when promises are broken. Sex is also one of the first things many people begin negotiating when their couplehood starts to show cracks. Opening a relationship has a reputation for being the last stop before Splitsville, for good reason. It seems like many ill-fated couples embark on their ethically nonmonogamous journeys when they should be resolving other issues.

How do these other issues accumulate, and why do they get boiled down to sex? Perhaps it's because the waxing and waning of sexual interest is easier to grapple with than the waxing and waning of love. Sex can *be spiced up*. There's spontaneity, role play, lingerie, toys, porn, and in extremis, other people. What do we say if someone admits that they love their partner a little less today than they did yesterday? A statement like that calls far more into question than admitting to not being in the mood. Love is supposed to be an everlasting constant, despite all evidence that it is not. Through all personal growth, across space and time, no matter the external circumstances, Love must remain steady if it's to be considered real. It can never take a break, because a breather from Love is its death. Like a shark, it must keep swimming.

Under the pressure of maintaining a façade of perfect companionship, few people would admit the ways they outsource nonsexual love, like with a best friend they can *really* laugh with, a crush who always notices when they change their hair, a cousin who will listen to them talk any time of day, an entire softball team who makes them feel included and important on game day. People find what they need outside their monogamous relationships all the time, and rarely do these emotional secondaries get the credit they deserve for keeping a couple afloat. In a way, most monogamous couples are practicing an emotional polyamory that makes their couplehood stronger. That didn't seem gross to me, so why would making a relationship stronger by having sex with other people feel like a jump too far?

It was easy to be this unbiased about free love when I wasn't in a relationship. The idea of sharing a person is very manageable when there's no one you feel passionate about. A few times I did imagine Adrian being with another woman, and it didn't feel great, and he was about the furthest thing from a boyfriend you could get. He wasn't even an ex-boyfriend. On the other hand, I'd often functioned as a listening ear or a fun party buddy for friends who needed a break from their partners. I was used to being a "secondary partner" in relationships in a lot of ways, and sex was just one more thing to add to the list.

As a visitor in these open relationships, negotiating jealous impulses and complicated feelings wasn't really my problem, anyway. That was for the couple to work out. All I wanted was to have a nice time without violating anyone's set boundaries. Most open relationships do have a lot of boundaries, I discovered. True polyamory usually admits to the fact that we have the capacity to love many people at once, and allows for the possibility of nonhierarchical relationships between many people. Sounds nice. In practice, I found that people's definition of what it means to be ethical outside of monogamy varies widely. This wasn't too surprising; I doubted there were as many truly ethical people on earth as there were folks trying to get "ethically" laid on Tinder.

When Tommy showed up, he reminded me of every stereotype of the poly man. Though he was handsome, his personal style was in complete opposition to what I find attractive. It looked like he was going to a steampunk conference. He had a mustache that had been grown out and curled at the edges. He resembled a rakish young Mr. Monopoly, which was not nearly as hot as that sounds. Alcohol might have diluted the effect of his matching vest, tie, and sleeve garters, but we were stuck with coffee.

We walked across the dusty fields of Fort Greene Park. It was a scary warm day for late January. We'd traveled about thirty feet before I decided to ask some tactful questions about his relationship. I was curious: How had he met someone who was so perfectly willing to commit yet not commit?

"How did you meet your fiancée?" I asked. "Were you friends for a long time?"

He chuckled to himself, hesitated, then appeared to make the choice to reveal all.

"No, we actually met doing The Stranger," he answered.

"What is The Stranger?" was my wary reply, sensing that what I was about to hear would set the vibe for the rest of our date. Since that afternoon, I've told many people about The Stranger and have found that whether or not they've heard of it is a pretty good indication of their kink level. If they have, they definitely have some other tantalizing stories.

The Stranger, as Tommy did it with his wife-to-be, meant that she left her door open for him at a time they picked together on OKCupid. He arrived and found her waiting in her bedroom naked "with the condoms all arranged" and then he "had his way with her."

"People say I'm good at making them feel comfortable via messaging," he added.

"So it would seem," I said, shaken. There was nothing about The Stranger that was really so very shocking . . . people have anonymous sex all the time. Yet this sounded like the sort of preplanned sex appointment story I'd only ever heard third hand or read in some Penthouse-style letter. But here in front of me was a real man who had not only convinced someone to do this with him, she'd become the love of his life. As I considered the series of events that had drawn them together, he told me that for their second date, they'd gone to a sex party.

"That seems like a de-escalation from The Stranger," I exclaimed, still floored. It wasn't even the potential danger of The Stranger that stunned me, it was the fact that you were having sex with someone without testing them out first. What if they didn't smell good or had an obnoxious laugh or wore an ugly hat? Some turnoffs can't be discerned through a few photos and a messenger app. Presumably, the erotic appeal of doing The Stranger outweighed those qualms, or perhaps the potential unpleasantness was part of it. Plenty of people get off on having sex with someone they find repellent. These two crazy kids hadn't been repelled at all. They'd found someone uniquely suited to their needs. I looked at Tommy and wondered how he might suit my needs.

We sat on the barren hillside where Adrian and I had kissed on verdant grasses not too long ago, and I learned more about my date. Sensing my prurient interest, he told me a little more about his personal history, maintaining a neutral tone. Had he gotten suggestive or made personal remarks about my face or body, it would have put me off. It was more like being given a tour of someone's personal museum of sex by an enthusiastic yet professional docent.

Tommy had worked in adult entertainment in his twenties, as both a performer and an administrator. He gave me his stage name so I could look him up later. Of course, I did, and watched some of the wackiest plastic pornography I'd ever seen. By plastic I mean that the woman involved was wearing a latex corset and plastic gloves, and the entire group (yes, group) was standing in a field of bubble wrap.

He enjoyed threesomes with two men and one woman, and he knew a few fellas in my neighborhood who might be interested in meeting me. He showed me some artsy, graphically erotic photos after asking my permission, saying he was planning to blow them up and frame them for his studio. None of this touched on what we might do together. It was only as we parted that he asked if he could come over and use my restroom. I pointed him in the direction of the park's facilities, knowing what that was code for: The Stranger Lite. Though intrigued, I wasn't sure I was at Tommy's level, at least not that afternoon. He'd given me a lot to think about, and I saved his number.

Tommy wasn't the first person, nor the last, whom I went out with who was pretty flexible about the terms of traditional courtship. I met and dated people who had just opened their relationships; those who had begun with the understanding that their relationships would always be open; there were the ones who were just dating around and hoping to find someone with whom they could enjoy the polyamorous scene. There were people who allowed for the idea that they might meet someone they really liked, to date alongside their primary partners, and those who were just looking for casual hookups on the side with people who knew the score.

The enjoyment in these encounters was fairly dependent on the person I was out with, as with all dates. Overall, I'd say people who already had partners were far better about communicating their needs and expectations than, say, someone who just wanted to meet for a drink. They were used to discussing what was allowed with their lovers and what wasn't. They were honest about the fact that some needs can't be met within a single romantic partnership. Again, I wondered if it would be possible for me to allow a serious, beloved partner that level of freedom. It was hard to conceptualize loving so many people when I couldn't even find one I wanted to commit to and who wanted to commit to me.

Tommy and his fiancée seemed to maintain their commitment by letting go of the myth that one person is all we need. I admired that. I wasn't sure I wanted to participate in their arrangement, though, until a night I got drunk as a skunk at a work party featuring a free gin-based novelty cocktail. After two of those, I started texting Tommy in the ladies' room, asking exactly what we might do together.

I want you to sit on your couch in just a T-shirt, he wrote back immediately. *You'll be drinking a glass of wine. I'll come into your apartment and kneel in front of you and eat your pussy as you relax.*

It was a compelling offer, and he delivered as promised soon after. Tommy and I saw each other every few weeks. Though the sex was as technically good as it had been with Adrian—probably better, as Tommy was basically a professional—it never came to mean anything more. I kept thinking it would, that one day I'd be overcome with jealousy at the thought of him leaving to meet his fiancée or that I'd desperately wish for his company on a lonely night. My obsession with Adrian had made me wonder if I was just hardwired to fall for anyone who made me orgasm over and over. It never happened with Tommy.

We had little to talk about and even less in common. We almost never laughed together. Sometimes he would mention his fiancée, and I never felt envy. From what he said, she was working hard to make a difference as an activist and volunteer, finding personal fulfillment in her life through a sense of duty to others. Despite their unorthodox sex lives, they had the same worries as most couples. It seemed like for Tommy, our time together was a break from the challenges of caring for his ailing dad, starting a business, and navigating all the other stresses of life that a fun night with someone you have no commitments to can help you forget.

Tommy's approach to nonmonogamy was informed by his sexual history and development, which had been far more varied than average. He was also a few years older than me and as settled as someone with his lifestyle was likely to get. The emotional parameters of our relationship were very different from what I experienced dating someone younger, a woman named Jane, in her midtwenties.

Often, when I would match with women in open relationships, they were looking for a third. I was a gift to their boyfriend, a gift they almost never followed through on giving.

People discuss insecurities and awkward dynamics with regard to group sex. They never discuss what an absolute pain in the ass it is to schedule. Three busy people, in one room, all in the mood at once? And no one is on their period? Rarer than a total eclipse.

When Jane and I connected, I expected a message about meeting her and her boyfriend for drinks, as she was clearly one half of a couple. When she asked me out, I followed up to see if her boyfriend was coming. From the pics, I knew he wasn't my type.

No, she wrote. She just wanted to meet me.

Jane was the sort of person who made me want to be a better human being from almost the first moment I met her. To describe someone as sweet makes them sound treacly or phony. Jane was simply *sweet*, a person who emanated generosity of spirit. Her blue-green eyes were framed by thick dark brows and a fringe; her face was luminous. When had I ever looked so young?

And why was she here with me? I couldn't understand Jane's attraction, though she clearly was attracted. If I looked at her too directly, she'd blush and glance down. On our first date, we sat at a bar she chose, discussing nonmonogamy and life. I drank sparkling water, since I was recovering from a cold, and she slowly sipped a mojito. She had lovely hands, fingers covered in delicate rings.

Jane and her boyfriend had recently opened their relationship, and it had been going well. They were incredibly sure of each other. She was one of those folks who refer to their partner as "my person," and it sounded true. Yet, she wanted more. She especially wanted to be with a woman.

The first time we had sex, we lay in bed afterward and she drizzled compliments over me like syrup. Men would sometimes make admiring comments after sex about my body, always things that could never come close to being interpreted as romantic. Jane had no such compunction.

"Your hands are so beautiful, I can see how words come out of them," she said. "Your hair looks like it's made of fire."

My impulse was to laugh, but I didn't dare. She was so earnest in her attempts to make me feel appreciated. I was the freak who found that funny.

Jane leaned over me, waiting. Wanting to give something back, I shocked myself by blurting out, "I love you," then quickly added, "You're the sweetest!" to try to dilute those words. Graciously, she didn't comment on my insane escalation. Cheeks burning, I went to the bathroom to splash water on my face.

I didn't love her. It just seemed like anyone who would be so nice to me deserved something grand. Grander than I could offer. After a few dates, she told me she'd deleted the app we met on, saying simply that she had enough people in her life that she liked, which included me. I couldn't say the same.

The thing about dating people who already have partners is that you still end up having a lot of time on your hands. My lovers and I didn't go out to dinner or sleep in on weekends. I didn't have to attend weddings as their plus-one, or go to coworkers' birthday parties, or any of the other time-sucking duties of serious relationships. Instead, I was the exciting new thing they used their free time to explore.

It was flattering and distracting and still not quite enough.

While I liked my independence, I also wanted someone I could do the time-sucking stuff with, and that would never happen with Tommy or Jane. Since finding them both, I hadn't been quite as active on the apps. I pictured ramping up the search again, even repeating my two-dates-a-week system, and that's what made me question polyamory and nonmonogamy the most. Imagine finding someone I really wanted to commit to, having them commit to me, and then still searching for more? That would be so much work!

When do we get to relax? I asked myself, imagining keeping up this carousel of dates while in a committed relationship. Inviting in all the same highs and lows, the unrequited interest, the disappointments, the jerks, the potential for danger. That was the excitement, I supposed; it just sounded so tiring. On the other hand, if you had a bad date, you had someone at home to eat the post-date recovery junk food with. And then fuck.

Tommy and I made plans to see each other on an afternoon we both happened to be free, and I realized after confirming that it was going to be Valentine's Day. That amused me. Before he came over, I decided to treat myself for the holiday and ordered nachos from my favorite Mexican place in the area. Sex and nachos, a single girl's dream come true.

He arrived, and we kissed in the doorway. As he tried to pick me up, sloshing the contents of my digesting stomach, I thought, *Next year, I'm going to do this in the opposite order.*

We worked around my gut and got down to business. Eventually, I was naked and on my back, looking down at the top of Tommy's head. I closed my eyes and focused on having an orgasm, something that sometimes required more concentration than I would like. It hit me, along with a curious feeling I'd never had before during sex. I burst into loud sobs.

This cry was far more violent than the pensive sadness that had risen up when Adrian whispered my name to me. They were nothing that could be disguised or even stopped. I *had* to cry. Tommy stood up as I covered my head with my crossed arms. He offered to get me a glass of water.

"Thank you," I cried. "I don't know why I'm doing this. It has nothing to do with you."

"I know," he said, walking, casually naked, to the kitchen. What polite lovers I had.

I appreciated that Tommy gave me space to collect myself, because any attempt to soothe me would have been humiliating. Despite his consideration, I wanted him to keep walking right out the door so I could continue crying. It felt like a true release, much deeper than an orgasm, full of desolation and exultation all at once. I wiped my face and drank the water Tommy handed me a few minutes later. After he left, I tried to get started again, to wring out all my anguish, and I couldn't.

The crying and impulsive declarations of love worried me. The boundaries that had protected me before sex and love and dating had come back into my life were crumbling. Boundaries that, in some cases, I didn't know I had. Why couldn't I let someone tell me I was beautiful? Why did I feel frightened to let someone see me cry? And why couldn't I hide anything anymore?

One day, Jane invited me to the apartment that she shared with her boyfriend. I'd never met him, and he wasn't there; she wanted to introduce me to her cats. I took off my sunglasses inside and she giggled timidly.

"You're so pretty," she said.

I wanted to ask if she was yanking my chain. I kissed her instead. Why not? Why not believe someone liked me and thought I was pretty? It was unseasonably hot, again, so we took a couple of IPAs in bags to the park, throwing down one of Jane's new towels. She had taste in a way I did not, and she explained that she'd recently replaced all her terry cloth towels with Turkish cotton ones she'd found on Etsy.

"I'm so appalled by my apartment compared to yours," I said. "My place looks like a college bachelor lives there."

"You just need a few things to pull it together," she said. "On our second date, I thought about bringing you a rug. But then I thought . . . it's too soon to give gifts."

Even though I hate rugs, I was touched.

"You don't need to give me anything," I said, lying back down on the thin towel. "And yes, it would definitely be too soon for a rug. Anything big enough to disguise a booby trap is inappropriate on a second date."

"I want to!" she protested, then asked, "Can I take your picture?"

"Sure," I said, looking up at her iPhone and smiling. We had been discussing whether or not to follow each other on Instagram. I thought my Instagram made me look like even more of a maniac than I was and had it set to private. Plus, the last time I had really dated someone long-term, Instagram didn't exist. Facebook pictures of my exes had been enough torment. Now everybody's curated brand was being injected into my eyes every time I opened an app.

In Jane's case, I wasn't sure I wanted to see her everyday

life—hanging out with her boyfriend, visiting his family, playing with their cats.

She looked at her phone screen thoughtfully, and I asked, "Are you gonna post that?"

"No, it's just for me."

Jane's boyfriend was public material, and I was for private perusal. I knew Jane dated other people, men mostly, and they weren't making appearances on her timeline either. Yes, I'd checked. She wasn't set to private.

It's hard enough to negotiate your relationship when it's open, juggling everyone's needs and expectations. When you tell people who aren't direct players in your love life that you're nonmonogamous, it seems to invite all sorts of judgments that complicate things even further. I could understand why Jane didn't want to make it a part of her public feed quite yet.

Jane and I had been seeing each other for close to two months when I texted her to see if she wanted to hang out. In response, she said that she and her boyfriend were discussing their boundaries and needed a break from dating other people. Entirely reasonable, but when she asked me out again a bit after that, I didn't like how it made me feel. The problem with being someone's third—or fourth, or fifth—is that you're never their number-one priority. You also don't get an equal vote in the relationship; a man I'd never met had the power to end mine with Jane whenever he wanted to.

Monogamy has certain expectations. Though many, many couples fall far short of them, there is a general social understanding of what someone expects when they expect monogamy. There's a general understanding of what the betrayal of a monogamous relationship means. A broken promise, a lie, a fracture in love. Though it's become far more popular and less taboo, nonmonogamy doesn't have the same culturally agreed-on parameters. It's so different for everyone, as are the arrangements between all the people involved. There's not much sympathy extended to someone like me getting burned by a partnered partner. Other people in the poly lifestyle might understand why it's painful to suddenly be shut out of someone else's relationship. Everyone else would probably see me as a deviant who got what she asked for.

Opening Up, by Tristan Taormino, is considered the Bible for people exploring open relationships, but even their definition of what being open means centers the couple: "Open marriage thus can be defined as a relationship in which the partners are committed to their own and to each other's growth. It is an honest and open relationship of intimacy and self-disclosure based on the equal freedom and identity of both partners." Since the book is full of practical advice for managing jealousy and breaking out of the strictures of monogamy, that makes sense. As Taormino writes, "The truth is, many people do not consciously choose monogamy; society chooses it for them, and it becomes the default."

With that in mind, couples exploring nonmonogamy need all the gentle guidance they can get about how to respect each other's feelings and communicate honestly and kindly. And some of that guidance is about communicating with the other people you're dating, valuing and caring for them. I just couldn't help but see that free love, the lifestyle, polyamory, nonmonogamy, whatever it's called, still generally prioritized two people together, with everyone else on the outside, shoring them up. I know there are polyamorous people who would vehemently disagree with that, saying some variation of "then they're doing it wrong!"

You could say two people in an awful monogamous relationship are doing it wrong, and it would still be considered monogamy. All relationship structures are only as functional as the people in them. I was skeptical that anyone I'd met so far was capable of living up to the standards of the ideal poly relationship. I had found that I wasn't either. My energy was depleted. It felt like I was helping other people get what they needed so that their primary relationships could continue to function, and there hadn't been enough return. I texted Jane back a response to unpausing our relationship.

I need to take a break from dating, I told her. *I think we have a really nice friendship, too, and I hope we can keep it.*

It seemed like I was taking a big chance by ending something that was still better than most of the other options on the table. No one was offering to be my one and only, and Jane was pretty great. Before I could regret-text a retraction, she responded that she understood and she'd love to be friends.

Tommy didn't require any special marker for the end of our time together. I simply never asked him over again and he didn't ask if he could come over. It suited us both.

Nonmonogamy can work. It had worked for me for a few months, even as an outside-of-a-couple participant, longer than any other type of sexual or romantic relationship I'd experienced in years. The problem with all this dating and drama wasn't the nonmonogamy, it was that it had become my whole life, absorbing my thoughts, sucking up my mental space. I wanted to get back to being someone besides The Woman Who Dates.

The lease was coming up on my apartment. I remembered my long-ago assurance to Adrian, as we walked by the beach, that I'd move to Los Angeles in June. I looked out over the Manhattan skyline, scratching my cat's ears. I looked at my desk, where I spent most of my waking hours scrolling through Twitter and slamming out eight hundred words of aggregated content every forty-five minutes. There didn't seem to be much point to leaving the life I'd created, even if it wasn't exactly the life I wanted. No one was waiting for me across the country. It was time to throw in the towel and sink back into my static, solitary life.

I signed my lease and put it in the mail, along with several postdated checks to my landlord, and settled in for another year in the apartment I could barely afford.

About two weeks later, I checked my bank account. I owed a ginormous amount in taxes as a self-employed person. So much that I could barely consider it without a full-body shudder. There was a chunk set away that would take a big dent out of the final tally. When I logged in to my account with the intention of funneling some to the IRS, something was seriously wrong.

Ten thousand dollars was missing. Gone. Poof. Before the emotional upset fully encompassed me, the more impartial part of my brain started to calculate what that meant in terms of blog posts. How many words I'd written, how many hours spent in front of a computer, vacations I never took, and sick days when I'd stayed upright typing. Just gone. Then I started to hyperventilate.

After some time on the phone with the bank and my landlord, I figured out that the lease and checks had been intercepted. My landlord blamed me for not sending them in via certified mail. He was right. I was still pissed off about the whole thing, not knowing if it had happened in his busy office, on the street, or at the hands of a postal worker.

The bank replaced my money, which truly felt like a miracle, and I used it to pay my taxes. Some of them. Not enough. My landlord gave me until the end of the week to decide if I wanted to renew for the end of the month, since the lease had been lost, too. In that week, I got an email from one of my bosses saying they were going in a different direction. They would give me four more weeks of work, then that was it.

With my income suddenly cut in half, it made no sense to renew my lease. I simply couldn't afford it. The unfortunate series of events had severed so many of my responsibilities it left me free to go in any direction I liked. I read the signs and interpreted them in the way I most wanted to. I decided to move to Los Angeles.

CHAPTER 12
. . . .

The Road More Traveled

My house didn't burn down, no one died, and my body was still functioning as usual; in terms of destabilizing events, losing my job was sort of low on the totem pole. The problem was that my identity was wrapped up in my work, and now that identity had a big hole blown right through it.

After college, I'd worked in restaurants for most of my twenties. When I'd managed to find a way to support myself through writing, it felt like a knee-saving miracle. But the media industry, my naïve self soon learned, was incredibly temperamental. I had worked for the place that let me go five days a week for almost three years, but they never offered to hire me officially full-time. I could have pressured the union to insist I get hired or let go after two years—it was strongly implied by the union member who advised me that I'd be let go. Then it happened anyway.

I was mad, but it still didn't seem anomalous. Anyone who has been dependent on the gig economy knows how it feels to be holding your life together one contract at a time, or dependent on sharing platforms for access to clients, where the percentage those platforms take off your earnings can fluctuate without warning. It had become very customary to have no recourse when your employers suddenly decided to let you go with no severance, and potentially no unemployment benefits. Worker protections have been chipped away so steadily and blatantly, even the union members most publicly vocal about these issues seemed to ignore the permalancing writers at the very same company helping to keep things afloat. Everyone had to watch their own backs.

I'd been working remotely, too, so though my co-workers were certainly aware of me, we weren't really friends. There was no one I said hi to in the morning over the coffee machine, no one I said bye to as I gathered my stuff at the end of the day. Most of them didn't even realize it was my last shift until I said farewell on Slack. It was sort of like my entire work history there just melted away as soon as I logged out for the last time. During the pandemic, this out-of-office culture became the new mode of work for a lot of people, but with video calls and surveillance built into their Zoom life. When I lost my job, it felt like a more uniquely isolating moment.

If my family hadn't been living in New York, there would have been nothing keeping me grounded at all. I had some part-time gigs blogging, but those felt fragile as well. How long would these jobs last? The security I'd once felt as a good employee had turned to ash. Your employer is not your friend, even if you personally like them or seek their approval and validation. An employer is not family, and co-workers are not necessarily community, even if working conditions demand that they be the people you interact with the most on a daily basis.

I'd forgotten that. I was almost as angry and confused as I would have been in the case of a much more intimate betrayal. Without that workplace identification, I shuffled around, not sure how to explain who I was anymore. I had been someone with a job at a really well-known publication, my work circulated to thousands if not hundreds of thousands of readers. I'd been someone who lived alone in a beautiful, unaffordable apartment, a solitary queen up in her roost, and now I was moving to sleep on a pallet in my mom's one-bedroom apartment. I was someone who had proudly lived their entire life in New York, and now I wanted to get away from my city as quickly as possible. There are a lot of things you can do when the life you've been building for yourself suddenly makes no sense. Fleeing felt right.

I purged most of my belongings, throwing out pieces of furniture that I'd acquired for free over the years and moved from place to place to place as if they were valuable. My overactive imagination saw them begin to crumble as soon as they hit the sidewalk—the bookshelves collapsing, the couch sagging until it caved, my stained mattress fogging inside its plastic cover like it was filled with trapped poltergeists. Sex ghosts, I thought. When I went upstairs to sweep, I saw the small collection of discarded condom wrappers that had accumulated under the frame and closed my eyes, thinking of the movers uncovering them.

When I left for Los Angeles, I didn't really admit I was moving. It took me about a month to get all my stuff together and acclimate Bert and George to their new home with my cat-obsessed mother until I could safely retrieve them. Mostly,

I told people I was planning to go on a trip, then stay in L.A. a bit and see how I liked it. Inside, I knew.

Billie picked me up in her car at the crack of dawn to go out for a goodbye breakfast. We ate omelets and pancakes and talked about my itinerary, which was as amorphous as my plans. The first stop was Montreal, and that was about all I could definitively say. She drove me back to my mom's house, then we sat in her car, not done talking even after thirty years.

"You'll be back in September?" she asked.

"I don't think I'm coming back," I admitted. "I'm not sure."

"What?" she exclaimed. "You're *leaving* leaving?"

"I think so."

It was weak to not be able to confirm, one way or the other. Part of the problem was how I was coming apart at the edges. I'd written about how single people or lonely people have few anchoring points in their life after a certain age. Now I was really feeling it. Who could say what I would do, or what I'd find, or even who I was? Not me. Who was "me," anyway? I got on the train to Canada and left, unraveling as I went.

Books about women with identity issues traveling for the purpose of self-discovery make up an entire literary genre. Elizabeth Gilbert's iconic *Eat Pray Love* is probably the best-known example of "priv-lit," or a story about a woman, almost always white, who manages to find some form of spiritual peace through tourism. This trip generally requires a lot of money from an ambiguous source, meaning self-actualization is once again only available to those who can afford it.

I'd saved some cash in the month before my departure by

sleeping on the floor at Mom's, and I was still working part-time. The very day I left, I was blogging as the view of the Hudson sped past my train car window. I'd managed to find a few places to stay for free, with friends, family, and friends of my family. Over the next month, I zigzagged, connecting a train to a plane to a bus, letting ticket prices and housing options make my plans for me. Even so, I knew I was doing something many women my age don't get to do. My lack of connections freed me, and my ability to work from anywhere put the money I needed in my pocket. Can a trip qualify as a real adventure when you have such a safety net?

Gilbert started traveling after a difficult divorce and famously married a man she met on her journey. She later left him to be with a woman, who'd started as a friend until Gilbert realized she'd fallen in love with her. No journey is ever done until the very end, even when the conclusion you choose makes the perfect ending for a book. *Eat Pray Love* became a bestseller in part because of the vision it offered. Through practice and prayer, Gilbert seemed to have earned her grand finale, at least to women who could imagine themselves in her place. In the years since its release, the book has received plenty of criticism for Gilbert's seeming obliviousness to her own privilege. That hadn't stopped her story from becoming a film starring Julia Roberts. The single woman traveling alone is an image that persists for a reason: it's still seen as a way to fix whatever is wrong with you that makes you feel lonely—especially when it ends in a love affair.

In an article for *Boston Review* in 2015, Jessa Crispin writes about how she was warned by friends, "Just don't be an Elizabeth Gilbert," as she undertook a trip alone abroad. It led

Crispin to consider what it was about Gilbert's persona that was both so divisive and enticing. In her estimation, the delight of the priv-lit genre is found in the way it is generally read as subversive. It presents women travelers as fighting the status quo.

"The authors of these narratives talk a lot about how they shouldn't be on the road because good girls stay at home," writes Crispin. She points out that many of them reflect mainly on their internal perspective, with varying degrees of description of what they actually see outside themselves, like Cheryl Strayed remembering her mother in *Wild* rather than detailing the flora and fauna on the Pacific Crest Trail. In her opinion, a man would instead tell you exactly how many gophers he saw and how he acted upon them during his adventures, drop-kicking those rodents right out of his path.

"But these books are not so much transgressive as regressive," she says. "After all, they obey their gender codes: men go on adventures, women on journeys of self-discovery."

Most of the historical writers Crispin reflects on are white westerners who rely on colonial tropes in their storytelling regardless of gender; they regard people foreign to them either with a certain level of contempt or as semi-mystical founts of insight and guidance. Both perspectives are dehumanizing and still found in a lot of current travel writing. Crispin argues that the really subversive act is to eradicate these tendencies, since gender and travel is too well trod a subject to be meaningful.

I didn't consider myself a travel writer, and I hadn't deliberately planned a journey of self-discovery. It was almost like I'd fallen into the narrative for single women at a loss without meaning to because that path *is* so well trod. Crispin's essay and other criticism of priv-lit touched my conscience from a different angle, because when she talked about using people and places to learn more about oneself, it reminded me of my many months of dating for the same purpose. And I was still doing it.

Everywhere I went, I used dating apps. Everywhere I landed, I found men and a few women willing to meet up for the night. In New York, I hated being a tourist guide for people on apps, so I reasoned that by stating how long I'd be in town explicitly on my profile, I was letting those who felt differently about it choose me.

My guilt wasn't about wasting their time. Some likely thought I was a good prospect for a one-night stand. Some of them were right about that. Some probably just felt like meeting a new person or showing off their town or having a random interlude. There are certain things you can only say to a stranger, and I'm an easy stranger to talk to. Dating as I traveled didn't seem to be hurting anyone, but it did end up making a more explicit connection in my mind to the emotional tourism I'd been indulging in back in New York.

I'd been dating people as a way to better understand myself rather than trying to better understand others. The fact that I hadn't actually learned much didn't really excuse it. How well can we know another person or truly care about them if we're only treating them as a mirror? It reminded me of my mother saying that most of the men she'd met had treated her as one, and she'd learned how to reflect what they wanted back for her own reasons, some necessary, some selfish. This observation intersected with the sense that without someone in my life, I was unseen—that I was supposed to have one special witness to my life in order for it to be valid. Though, if so many people were just looking at each other to see what they wanted to be, that was impossible. It created a hall of distorted replicas, everyone twisted and reflecting for infinity in an effort to be legitimate, instead of being truly together.

These were the kinds of thoughts I was having: nihilistic and borderline nonsensical. They made me feel both ashamed and doomed.

Eventually, I managed to dismiss that sense of culpability, believing that in most cases, I'd been used as well. Mostly in ways that weren't particularly harmful, and perhaps even mutually beneficial. In some cases, though, it had been bad for me. Adrian had acted as though he wanted a relationship with me in a way that had fooled me and left me wounded. He'd made plans with me, made it seem like if I was there in his city, we'd be together. When it came down to it, he didn't want to do the work of keeping a connection between us alive. He didn't even want to go through the difficulty of being straightforward about his intentions and directly saying he wasn't interested. That's how it's supposed to be, I thought. Fun was the best you could really expect from anyone and the most you could offer in return. I moved on to the next town, and the next date, and the next town. I went from Detroit to Chicago to Austin, and then on a soupy Florida night I met a man at a fancy hotel bar on Miami Beach.

Miami was the point in my trip where I really began to

wonder what the hell I was doing. Everywhere I'd visited had been hot. The heat in Florida was primal. Air conditioning had always been a slightly unpleasant sensation to me, except when absolutely necessary. Air conditioning was absolutely necessary at all times in Florida. My room on Miami Beach was on the lower-rent end of the island, which was still expensive. My plan after Miami was to go to a Florida town not too far away for a few days to stay with a friend for free, which helped justify the cost. My hotel's hallways were lined with bins overflowing with sheets and towels, and it stank of chlorine. There didn't seem to be a pool. The room was outfitted with a microwave and a bed that looked like it was designed to be a pod on a spaceship before anyone had been to space. Much of the area had this same dated sci-fi feel, probably related to the historical art deco buildings lining the streets. It was like the film *Metropolis,* except colored in pastels, and the women all wore thongs instead of an armored shell.

I worked in the mornings. Sitting in my bra with the blinds drawn, I could still hear the party that raged incessantly in the street. Everywhere you went, people were having the time of their lives. Drinking, dancing, driving erotically shaped sports cars and revving the motors. At one point, I watched two people kick a bag of weed as big as a bread loaf back and forth to each other on the sidewalk. This was in the middle of the afternoon.

I went to the beach when my blogging was done. My hotel room included an umbrella and folding chair, but I felt out of place next to the other beachgoers. Entire families were camped out with giant coolers of beer, tents as big as a living room, and stereo setups powerful enough to DJ a small wedding. It was like I was crashing someone else's big vacation, soaking up their energy and jams from my tiny towel.

I'd buy a cold Corona from enterprising men selling them to anyone who forgot to bring their own. The sand in that area was a little rough, and there were a lot of pigeons for a beach, but the sky was astonishing. The humidity created cloud formations that belonged on the ceiling of a cathedral. Drinking my beer, I'd let the hours spent locked in a dark hotel room go, gazing out at the water. It was filled with as many people as the shore.

The trip had taken on a hallucinatory quality. After a couple Coronas, I'd wander out into the ocean. The water was shallow and calm so far out, it was more like walking in heavy gravity than swimming. Looking around at the people standing in groups here and there, with buckets of booze bobbing in floaties, I'd think about how I was probably mostly standing in piss. I thought about how I was alone in Miami and accountable to no one. I thought about how easy it would be to just slip under the surface and slide away on the almost nonexistent current.

I was so lonely, and in an unfamiliar way. It seemed as though I was connected to no one, to nothing. No one knew where I was or what I was doing. It's obvious that traveling alone disconnects you from the familiar, it just wasn't quite like I'd expected. Rather than feeling myself growing from being immersed in new places and sensations, I felt my presence in the country shrinking. Someone who could go down the wrong street or fall down a staircase or get swept away by a wave, down through the cracks of reality into blackness, then out of range entirely.

No one was waiting for me back in my hotel room. I suspected that if I didn't log in to work one morning, my bosses would just shrug and move on. My mother would worry, bless her. She most likely wouldn't have the resources to locate me. This sounds as though I was considering disappearing myself on purpose; it was more about how easy it is to become invisible on the map of what matters to others. I had mostly chosen my invisibility, so boo-hoo for me, who cares.

I was perfectly fine. I was drinking a beer in the ocean. I was alive and had money for dinner. The difference between me and nothingness felt as thin as the wing of a moth.

After a couple of days of this ennui, I became less dreamy and distracted. Boredom forced me to engage again. There was still an opportunity to shake things up before I moved on. Miami deserved more effort. What would be next in the script if my life were a movie? What if I *were* Julia Roberts? I probably wouldn't be drinking cheap beer in piss water. There would be some intrigue. A night of romance with a delicious hunk. After several solitary evenings in my icy closet, I decided I wanted to meet up with someone who could get me into a really, really nice hotel.

The man I matched with was in an open marriage, and his profile was goofily discreet. I could see he had hazel eyes and a nice body. He did admit where he was staying and invited me to meet him on the rooftop bar there. Googling revealed it was right on the beach, on the swankier end of the island. Excellent. We would both get what we wanted.

I felt unusually nervy, like I was headed into an audition, which is a common feeling around dates. It was the first time

I'd felt that way in ages. It was this sense of trying to fit into a part: freewheeling woman who meets lothario at upscale hotel.

One of the benefits of meeting people in the same local bar over and over is that your plans for escape are streamlined. If I wanted to bail, I knew exactly when to duck to the bathroom, then go secretly settle my tab. I knew how long of a trip it was back to my apartment if I wanted to escape my date. Or take them with me. More importantly, people knew me. The bartender, the guy who worked at the deli across the street. If I screamed, they would most likely intervene.

No one at this fine hotel knew me, not even the man I was coming to meet. The prospect of the unknown woke me from my traveling stupor a little bit more. The yawning lobby was decorated in luxurious white leather couches, carefully lit by a professional. Sculptural objects matching the décor, not burdening viewers with any greater artistic significance, were scattered about on pedestals. A waterfall rippled down a freestanding wall, the other side hung with local plant life.

My date messaged me that he would be late. He was in a meeting. His job was to redesign this hotel, to decide what material the next round of couches would be upholstered in and whether the lighting would be recessed. Or it was his job to pick the color of the bedding in the rooms upstairs. Whatever he did, it was decision-making far above my pay grade. He was important. He was married. We were at his hotel. Who was I in all that? Nobody. I got even smaller.

When he arrived, he was more or less exactly what I had mentally pieced together, based on his mosaic of pictures. Shorter than me, as many men are. Handsome. He was dressed to match his hotel, in an effortlessly wealthy way: linen shirt, a gold watch. I didn't know much about watches, but it looked expensive. He hugged me hello.

I was wearing a seven-dollar dress I'd bought at a thrift store in Toronto and a pair of beaten, sand-filled sneakers, my big toe poking out the tip of the left shoe. This probably would have been the night to dress up as a worldly woman of mystery. Regrettably, I'd been traveling light.

My date made smooth introductory chitchat as we walked onto a roof that offered a fabulous vista. To one side, the contoured roofs gleamed, crowned as always with voluptuous cumulus clouds. On the other side was the sea, stretching out in a graying panorama as the sky darkened, smudging the line of the horizon.

We ordered drinks and sat on the long, white canvas–covered lounges. People with various parts of their anatomy tanned or bleached were scattered around, enjoying the sunset, though most seemed to be frowning.

After a generous glass of sauvignon blanc, my nerves were forgotten. It was no longer an audition. I'd booked. It was The Scene.

"My wife and I opened up our marriage about eight years ago," he told me. "We'd been together since high school, and we read this book—"

"Was it *Opening Up*?" I asked, with a knowing smile, advertising my poly education.

"Yes!" he exclaimed. "But it is a great book, actually. . . ."

My date went to a lot of sex parties in New York, where he usually lived. Most of them were at an apartment complex that was a kind of intentional commune for people who loved orgies. As he described the founders, I realized I'd matched with one of them on Tinder at some point. We'd never met, probably because I'd had more sexual shyness at the time than he was clearly used to.

"He's a bit odd," my date admitted. "But the venue is amazing and a really wonderful group of people."

He related that there had recently been one conflict. A woman had said she'd been taken advantage of; my date said she'd arrived too high or drunk to really participate. Noting my reaction, he quickly backtracked, expressing dismay with the whole situation.

"Things like that shouldn't happen anywhere," he assured me.

My date was remarkably adjustable, playing his own role in a slightly robotic manner. Not that he was cold or stiff. He moved so easily from one moment to another, it felt like the machinations of an algorithmic man. His conversation wasn't so much rehearsed as it was used, an old program he'd run through a million times during a million conquests. All I had to do was follow along, and I'd make it to the end of the installation. If you know what I mean.

He told me the story of his business development, insisting he still had no money, because he had to pay all his employees so much. Imagine having an employee! Multiple employees! He claimed that before starting his current business he had worked with rock and roll bands, name-checking a group that happens to include someone I know; I asked that friend about it later, and he had never heard of my paramour.

I asked him if he always brought every girl back to a fancy hotel room, and he paused.

"Well, the very first time I did it, something happened," he said. "There was a renovation going on, and I took her upstairs to show her the new space. She ducked into the bathroom, and when she came out, she was completely zonked. Higher than you can believe. And she walked toward me two steps, then fell right on her face. I thought she was dead. And I was like, 'My life is over.'"

The end of the story was that the woman recovered enough to tell him her address, so he hustled her into a cab and sent her home, relatively lucid.

The words "My life is over" reverberated in my head. I could imagine the fear that your marital secrets would be exposed, the fear that your career could come crashing down after a woman overdosed in your workplace.

I could imagine dying in front of someone while they thought, "My life is over."

This frightening glimpse at the fundamental selfishness of my date's psyche didn't deter me. There was plenty of selfishness to go around, and I selfishly wanted to continue my bizarre evening with this terrible man. The only things waiting for me at home were the smell of chlorine and the sound of drunk people arguing in the street.

We got another glass of wine and went farther into the recesses of the roof's patio. My date set our glasses down on an elegant table, and I noticed a giant water bug resting arrogantly beside them. Excuse me, in Florida they're Palmetto bugs. Either way, the bug won, and we moved even closer to the ledge, looking out over the empty beach.

"I used to be fun," I whined suddenly, a little drunk and

caught up in my own thing. I leaned against the glass parti-
tion, staring at what was now just solid blackness.

"The person I've met tonight seems pretty fun," he said,
encouragingly. I couldn't really explain, because what I actually meant was that I used to have fun. Adventures used to
happen to me without all this damned work. Back before I'd
withdrawn from dating and before I'd rediscovered it. Friendships were deep, parties went until dawn, each night held
promise. So much of that had faded away with getting older,
and I hadn't replaced it with anything that felt real. Here I
was, living out the fantasy of a hot hookup on my iconic
single-lady vacation, and . . . it was boring. It shouldn't have
been, which meant that I must be boring. There was something wrong with me that no amount of traveling or dating or
self-reflection was fixing.

Instead of explaining that, I asked if he wanted to make
out, and he instantly agreed. It was fine. After a perfectly
timed amount of kissing, he suggested we go to his hotel room.

For someone whose only hobby seemed to be sex, my date
did not impress me. I did come, after pointedly asking, "Do
you not eat pussy?" Otherwise, it was about the equivalent of
taking a HIIT class. Everything gets done, it's certainly rigor-
ous, but you don't really settle in and connect with your body.
I'd also never been rushed out of a room so fast. Moments
after we were finished, he was getting dressed, saying dolefully,
"And now I have to be up at six A.M. tomorrow," as though I
should apologize for keeping him up with sex.

My date insisted on escorting me downstairs, which read as
50 percent chivalry, 50 percent a suspicion that I would wan-

der around the hotel, get into some shit, and ruin his life. At the lobby door, he bade me farewell.

"Think of me when you blah-blah-blah," he said, and for the life of me I never could recall what was supposed to remind me of him in the future.

I smiled and waved, thinking, *Motherfucker, I will not dwell on you at all.*

That wasn't true. I did think about him as I continued on my journey, and what it was about our encounter that was so dissatisfying. I'd recently had plenty of sex with people I didn't love, and had mostly enjoyed it quite a lot. Eventually, I realized that I had never had sex with someone who kept so much of their self shuttered. For better or worse, sex brings down defenses, even when deeper emotions aren't involved. Peering into the window opened by physical intimacy is a big part of the divertissement for an unrepentant voyeur. It's a form of communication. He'd managed to share nothing honest, so I'd shared nothing. It was the most touristy encounter I'd ever had.

Discombobulated, I decided to walk home, thirty or forty short blocks along the boardwalk. A palm-lined walkway accidentally directed me toward the beach, then disappeared into the sand. The shore was desolate and hostile. Instead of turning back, I stared into the emptiness, the glare of the bars' bright lights at my back. Then I squatted and peed. After that, I called my mom, the only person I know who will always pick up.

I told her about the man I'd just been with and that it had left me feeling off-kilter.

"I went to Miami once," she replied. "It sounds like you

had a Miami experience. Shallow sex with a guy at a nice hotel. Did he buy your drinks?"

"No," I said glumly, and she gasped, outraged. We laughed.

Then I started to cry. She listened patiently as I cried about feeling so disconnected, so without roots anywhere, about how it sometimes seems like you just give and give and get nothing back in life and everyone just wants to take what they can get from you and move on. Then I blabbed about how lucky I am and how I shouldn't be complaining, before outlining more of my misfortunes.

None of it was really about my lousy hookup or my lousy hotel room or my fabulous life. It was about the vastness of some void inside that my soul couldn't seem to cross.

My mother is good at putting me at ease in moments when my flare for drama makes simple challenges seem insurmountable. She told me it was just the city (it's always just the city), and that journeys have their ups and downs. I calmed as she talked. I was about to answer more sensibly when a small black blob on the ground started to move in my direction. It was hard to tell if it was a bug or a crab, so I ran the hell out of there, telling my mom I'd call her later.

The walk home did me good. So did some microwaved fries leftover from lunch. After those, it was much easier to remind myself of all my many blessings. I fell into a fitful sleep listening to a couple talk outside my window, discussing their tattoos.

The trip continued. Plans made in a firmer frame of mind dragged me along inexorably. Eventually, I made it to Seattle, then took the train to Portland and then to San Francisco. There, I already had a date waiting.

We had matched months ago on Tinder, when I'd first started swiping on people. He'd "super liked" me, meaning he used Tinder's option to let people know you *really* want to match with them. Flattered, I'd swiped right and discovered he was actually based on the West Coast. He had persistently courted me via app ever since, checking in when he visited New York, though the timing never worked out, and repeatedly asking if we could meet when I arrived in his hometown. Ordinarily, someone who has never met me in real life being so invested would be an immediate no, but it was just so convenient. He'd sent some public verification info. Despite the red flags, he didn't really seem dangerous, only a run-of-the-mill level of intensity for someone running a tech startup.

When I arrived, I checked in to see if he still wanted to meet. Of course he did. He'd just gotten back from an event he described as "Burning Man on the water," a true nightmare sentence. I agreed to show up at a bar at the top of a hotel that he picked, curious how no one had died on the flotilla.

The lobby was nondescript and huge. It was like a hospital cafeteria or a small airport. Lots of busy people, very little personality. I was unconvinced about the quality of this mystery spot. Then, when I got off the elevator, the view was absolutely dumbfounding. Floor-to-ridiculously-high-ceiling windows showed an almost 360-degree panorama of the city. It was a godlike view, a taste of the sublime, or the all-seeing eye of Sauron. I decided that I was thankful to my date, whoever he turned out to be. I tried to take a photo, but a photo couldn't capture how it felt to stand at the top of the sky.

He turned out to be a small guy dressed in a crumpled suit,

with king-sized self-possession and a fascination with me. His eyes burned with it. We got our wine and sat on a banquet with an unobstructed look at THE VIEW and started chatting. Again, my date was in an open marriage. They both traveled a lot and found it had brought them peace in their relationship to have that freedom. He was a good conversationalist; his life had been different from mine, and I was enjoying talking to him. I felt no attraction.

Suddenly, my date offered to read my palm. It was an interest of his, something he once did avidly and still dabbled in. It was probably a ploy to touch me. Like most narcissistic navel-gazers, I was susceptible to being told about myself, so it worked. He cupped my hands in his, bending and twisting them gently, running a fingertip down my lifeline. He counted the number of notches on the edge of my hand.

"These represent the number of people you'll love in a lifetime," he said, tapping them. I wanted to ask if he could tell if I'd already loved them all, but I was afraid to.

He then traced a small curlicue coming down between my pinky and ring finger, saying this indicated I'd be famous for something intellectual—it was an indicator of success. Then he pointed to where my life and health lines crossed.

"Are you okay with bad news?" he asked after a slight pause.

"I think so," I said.

"Okay. This means that you may have an early death or some sort of health crisis in the future."

I looked at the betraying X, then glanced at his hands.

"Yours are the same," I accused, and he shrugged.

"So what? So I die young. That's my life."

My date seemed sincere when he said he didn't care about dying young. I, on the other hand, had discovered I actually didn't do well with bad news. The landscape outside suddenly felt like it was tipping toward me. Everything was so open, so gigantic, and there was so much left to do—and this man had told me I'd die before I could enjoy all this success he'd also predicted. It was a bold move. He soon got bolder. He leaned too close as I edged away. He asked me if I'd like to go to join him and his friends in their hot tub and I refused.

"I'm just so attracted to you. I don't know why," he said, his voice implying some divine connection.

"Because I'm attractive," I said, finishing my wine and thinking about death. It wasn't hard to understand where he was coming from. I, too, have been extremely horny for someone and thought it was profound.

"You're making me feel a little uneasy. It's not possible for me to feel an attraction to someone who isn't sensitive to that," I explained to him as he edged closer, wondering to myself why I wasn't getting up. He settled down a bit, admitting that was fair.

"Can we hold hands?" he asked, after a moment.

"Absolutely not!" I protested, though he'd just been cupping mine in his. It made me think of Vanessa, and how differently I'd responded to her asking the same question. There was just something so fervent about this guy, it seemed feasible that if I agreed to hold hands, he'd never let go. I'd drag him back, like a barnacle, to my guest bedroom at a family friend's home. It would be really hard to explain to my hosts.

Indeed, he did cling, walking me to my BART train, which thankfully arrived very quickly. There was some part of me that was perhaps undecided, and he sensed that. Who doesn't want to be worshipped? To have someone declare a cosmic understanding of you, saying they really see you, and have a passionate need to be at your side? Plus, he'd said I'd be dead soon anyway. Might as well go for it. I wondered if this would be the only way I'd ever get that kind of focused attention again: from someone completely delusional.

Even after we left in opposite directions, he messaged me, saying how much he wished I was with him. I informed him we would only ever be friends, and he enthusiastically agreed; I never messaged him again.

Being told you will die young, even by someone who is just trying to get you into bed, can stir up old issues. Death had been a big part of my life. It seemed like every three to four years, someone I cared about or was connected to had died, beginning in my preteens. My uncle, another uncle, a friend, a friend, a friend, a friend. I'd seen my mother rushed to the hospital again and again. I'd seen parts of my city crumble and thousands die in a day. During my most formative years, death had become a presence, hovering all around, moving close and then away. Death was inevitable, I knew, but it did seem to be lingering when there must have been better things to do than lurk in the moments when I most wanted to experience life.

I especially felt death whenever I tried to rest. I'd lie down for a nap, close my eyes on the couch, or pull the covers up at bedtime. Just as I'd begin to drift away, my pulse would speed up like I'd been running sprints. My eyes would snap open. I was convinced my heart would stop in my sleep, at least for those brief moments when consciousness dips back and forth between waking and dreaming.

Before I started dating again, the patterns of my life had been stiff as rigor mortis. Wake, work, nap, work, read, TV, sleep. I did other things, of course, performing, partying, walking the streets listening to music. I had friends, I had my cats, I had my pastimes. It was easy to imagine the years stretching ahead in exactly the same hourly increments of time-filling behaviors, until the end. Once I started to shake things up, I realized that what had really been waking me up at night wasn't death at all. It was the fear of never truly living.

The traveling had been an extension of that; the quest for adventure can be equal parts a search for something new and an attempt to outpace the speed with which life goes by. I remember reading once that time passes much faster when every day is the same. It is the days that are unlike any others that slow down our perception of our existence on this earth.

Dating had made a lot of days more memorable for me. Dating changed how I saw the future—and what was possible right now, if I would just reach for it. There were still revelations out there. Maybe even good ones. My creepy date's warning, however, spurred me to seize the day even harder. I arrived in Los Angeles possessed by a manic need to *live, live, live*. I bought my ticket with the credit from my eclipse trip, the one I'd canceled a year ago only to meet Adrian on a Bumble date—someone who made me feel so vibrant and present and full of possibilities instead of dead ends.

While traveling, structures had dissolved. Arriving at my destination, I had a focus again. All I wanted was to recapture that feeling at all costs.

CHAPTER 13

See You Again Soon

I arrived at Dylan's house nearish the beach to sleep on his lumpy couch. It was the middle of a heat wave, and his brother was staying with him, too. The three of us worked at our computers in the morning, gathered in the living room between the oscillating fans. I was blogging, and they were doing whatever inscrutable stuff people who work in tech do.

I was there less than a day before I emailed Adrian. It seemed safer than a text. I'd at least know it had probably been delivered. Hitting Send brought back that time I spent the previous winter, waiting for his replies, the excruciating way the time started to lengthen between each one as he lost interest. If I'd remembered that painful wait *before* sending the email, I might not have.

Dylan and his wife took me to the beach, and I found her much friendlier than in the past. My travel-worn self wasn't very threatening. She gave me a recommendation for a place to get laser hair removal, and we bonded.

The Pacific Ocean was colder than I'd anticipated. I was warned that a friend of a friend had recently stepped on a manta ray in the foam. Dylan had told me in the past that the enormity of the ocean made him feel slightly panicked. The horizon line made my heart expand, looking at how big the world was. There was another land across the sea, and another. Nothing ended, it just turned in on itself again.

My expansive view of the possibilities in life narrowed considerably when I thought of Adrian. When would he email me back? My return to an unworthy obsession earned Dylan's contempt.

"You can find someone better and more reliable," he told me, after I admitted to reaching out. He was wrong. Not only had I not met anyone else I'd felt more than a passing interest in, none of them had been particularly reliable. It made more sense to gamble on the person I really wanted, even if it was a losing bet.

About a day after I emailed him, Adrian replied. Sure, he'd meet up.

On the day of our plans, he canceled, saying he was sick. There, that's your answer, I told myself, feeling very sad. I'd moved to a sublet and spent most of my afternoons in a coffee shop. Obviously. Los Angeles has a reputation for being spread out and isolating, but I couldn't go anywhere without bumping into someone I knew. Other New Yorkers, old friends. I was always seeing them at restaurants and bars. There was so much residential space, with just these short little strips of activity that everyone congregated at.

Though he didn't live nearby, when the door would open at the coffee shop, I'd think, "What if Adrian walked in? Wouldn't that be funny?'"

Meanwhile, I went on more dates—with yet another poly-amorous fella, who took me to a secret bar where we bumped into his ex-girlfriend. With an older dude who worked at Universal Studios as a *Walking Dead* zombie. With a woman painter who took me to a very expensive vegan restaurant. With a man who brought a Hitachi wand in a giant bag to the wine bar.

Then, very surprisingly, Adrian emailed me again. He was feeling better. How about Friday?

My makeup was perfection. I wore a faded black dress covered in tiny flowers and let my freshly washed hair hang loose. As I walked to the nearby pub that he'd chosen, I put in earbuds and hit Play on my phone. The Haim song "Want You Back" came on. It made me grin. Hope unfurled in my heart, no matter how sternly I tried to tell the little sprout that this was only a meetup. It didn't mean anything.

At the door, a grizzled old bouncer checked my ID. He told me some joke I don't even remember, and I laughed, turning the corner to see Adrian standing up to greet me.

"Look at that smile," he said. He was exactly the same, and also completely different than I remembered. He was a little grayer around his temples, I thought. He seemed smaller than before, slightly shorter or skinnier. Those eyes were just as compelling to me, light green pools above the smooth planes of his cheeks.

We sat in the dark bar, drinking and making conversation. As usual, it was very easy to talk to him. Feeling like I can talk to someone all night has always entranced me. We talked and laughed about everything except what was clearly on both our minds. I didn't mention that he'd ghosted me, and he never mentioned it either. A soccer game was playing on a screen over the bar, drawing our attention for a moment.

"Soccer players are always so good-looking," I said, off-handedly.

"Oh?" he said, looking at me suggestively.

"What?"

"I was a soccer player. I thought you were paying me a compliment," he fished.

"Well, you're very handsome," I said, biting the hook. It was the first clear moment of flirtation.

The bar filled up. We saw a couple who seemed to be on an awkward date. It led to a discussion about dating apps, and he mentioned he was on a few. He was single, I thought.

We finished our third round. The question hovered if we should go to another bar. We ended up walking to the grocery store, buying beer and canned wine, then walking to my sublet, setting up chairs outside the door.

I knew that we were both deliberately getting drunk enough to make some bad choices. The moon was out, lighting the small courtyard fountain bubbling at its center. The shadows of fat palm leaves made the corners cinematic. A French bulldog that belonged to my neighbor appeared from under a bush with an orange plastic bone in its mouth.

"Look at this good boy!" Adrian exclaimed, leaning down to wrestle the animal over the bone. As they played, the talkative energy that had been carrying the evening left me. I grew more still and absorbed, watching him croon to the dog, muscles visibly shifting under his black T-shirt. Gradually, he grew quieter, too, giving the puppy one last pat. The bulldog took its toy and scampered off, leaving us in tense silence. With no more words in the way, we kissed.

We moved from the courtyard to my little room, quickly undressing, and doing what we did best together. With more recent affairs for comparison, the actual mechanics of the sex we had weren't quite as unbelievable as I had immortalized them in memory. We had a magnetic attraction and familiarity; it was also a bit awkward and hesitant. He was rougher than I remembered, in a way that was more about his needs than my inclination. The brief sense of disappointment was whisked away quickly, as the mystical effects of fulfilled cravings took hold.

Here was the thing I had wanted for months, long past the point it had seemed possible to have it. Gratification was delicious. Plus, now I was here in Los Angeles, only a short car ride away from him instead of an entire country. We could be together. Wasn't the whole problem just the distance and the lack of honest communication about how we felt? Now that he knew I wanted him and would forgive him for disappearing on me, he'd naturally want to date for real this time.

Yet, when Adrian wrapped his arms around me afterward to continue our endless conversation, I wished I could hit Pause to savor the moment much longer. I knew, even in my victory, that this was a momentary high. The voice singing with delight inside me was underscored by a deeper chord of woe. From my recent exploits, I'd learned a bit about personal evolution. I was much more malleable than I'd thought, and far less stuck than I'd thought. I'd managed to make many changes in how I related to other people, to my own body, even to where I'd lived my entire life. I'd also run up against many things that couldn't be forced to change overnight within myself. There were definitely things I couldn't change about Adrian, because you really cannot change another person. There was no reason for him to suddenly become the guy I needed him to be, to show up for me, reach out to me, to give more of himself than just sex.

I wanted Adrian to want me as much as I wanted him. I wanted him to say he wanted to see me again. As he left, he didn't look over his shoulder at me. He didn't text again either, so I messaged him a few days later and said I'd like to hang again. As friends only this time.

This was a horrid lie and he responded that not having sex "would probably be for the best."

We met again and were having sex within about ten minutes. Afterward, I hugged him from behind as he sat on the edge of my bed. I kissed him up and down his spine, fervently conveying my deepest wishes physically because I couldn't express them with words.

Let me sit in your shadow just to know you're near . . . take whatever I have inside, as long as a part of me is with you . . . deranged poetry filled me, because pragmatic language couldn't cover it.

What would I have said? Could I have said? A long time later, I would admit to a friend, "Sometimes I wonder what would have happened if I'd just told him I loved him."

A veteran of heartbreak as well, that friend would shake their head and simply say, "He already knew."

That's why I couldn't say it. Adrian did know I loved him, and putting it into words would have only forced him to tell me definitively that he didn't love me back. I couldn't face that.

As Adrian got dressed he suggested we meet up the following week, like Wednesday. I walked him to the door and we kissed one last time through the courtyard gate. Finally, he had been the one to suggest we hang out, and I was thrilled. All week I walked on air.

Hours before our scheduled meetup time, he texted to say he was sick and couldn't make it.

Bummer! I wrote. *Let me know when you're feeling better, if you still want to hang out.*

And then the cruelest response of all. None.

Over the next few weeks, a lot happened. I moved again to a longer term sublet in Silver Lake. I started a new job, one that flew me to Austin for a weekend. From there, I went back to New York, then back to Los Angeles again. It was funny to now skip from destination to destination with purpose after so recently crossing these same lines with none. Actual purpose in travel makes wandering look ridiculous, no matter how many wild adventures you have along the way. And then I lived one of the most triumphant moments of my life—I sold a book! (This book.) Something so glorious, I was sure it would be ripped away from me at any second. Suddenly, despite my disappointment in love, my life felt meaningful and directed again. All it took was external validation on a much higher scale than anything that had ever happened before.

As I ran around, worrying, celebrating, and exhausting myself, I tried to catch up with family and friends. People were having babies, and crises, and moving, and breaking up, and getting new jobs. The lives of everyone I loved had continued their ups and downs as I chased a new life across the country.

There was plenty for me to share as well that was probably

more important than getting ghosted again; too bad I couldn't stop thinking about what happened with Adrian. The most recent stuff. After nodding attentively at their stories, I told many friends either a long or an abbreviated recount of what had happened, depending on their openness to this kind of man-analysis. I wanted to know why he had disappeared on me yet again, especially when we were finally in the same city, finally so close to living out the relationship make-believe for real.

A married friend said, "When stuff like this used to happen, I'd tell myself, 'There's someone else.' It was just easier that way. There's someone else, that's it."

A single friend going through something similar with a guy who was always sliding into her DMs said, "They're just not thinking about it. Women think about it. All. The. Time. But men just don't! They're not thinking about us at all."

Billie and I sat in her car by the East River in a brief moment before she had to run home to her kids, talking about depression, and how sometimes people we knew would just go into hibernation. For a brief moment, I had compassion for whatever mental health issue was keeping Adrian from texting me. That had to be it, right?

A co-worker in Austin asked me how old he was. I told her thirty-six, and she said, "I really think men that age get scared. They're just freaking about their life and where they're at."

My mother helpfully suggested it was because I'd gained some weight back in the last year, unable to control herself. That seemed plausible for an awful minute, until I remembered he'd fucked me twice, two weeks apart. He knew what he was getting the second time, at least.

My therapist in New York mostly listened, as I told her via FaceTime that I suspected he had just found someone younger and hotter who he was actually willing to change for. Somebody he'd text back.

"Well, the patriarchal standard of beauty is something many men chase," she said, confirming my worst thoughts in so many words. "But I think it's a common misconception that someone changes for another person or becomes better because their partner deserves it—actually, their crap just fits in with that other person's crap!"

Dylan said, "Maybe he just thought you were good for sex, but too boring to date."

We paused and then laughed. Sadly, I suspected this was the correct take. I appreciated that the idea I was too boring was funny to Dylan.

"Look, he's keeping you hanging, and he'll pop back in when he wants to have sex again," Dylan continued, and I recognized the annoyed tone I used with my girlfriends when they wasted their time on total losers. "Because that's what you taught him he could do. Just let it go! Let him keep living in his sister's garage in the Valley or whatever and find someone else."

And to almost all of these suggestions I responded, "I know."

I knew also that I was being very repetitive and dull, as women trying to unravel the "mystery" of a shitty guy usually are. It was time to let it go. It had *been* time to let it go.

When I sold my book, I bought myself a tiny bottle of prosecco, drank it, and sobbed on the couch. Nothing else mattered. And I had to be thankful that I'd met Adrian, because

in pursuing love and thinking and writing about love and loneliness, I'd come up with something to say that someone was
now going to pay me to share.

But . . . he was a writer. Who was trying to sell a book. I
stopped asking why Adrian didn't want me and asked a few
people, "Should I tell him?"

I mean. C'mon. If there was ever a way to get back at
someone for being kind of a dick to me, this was it. I had
something he wanted, even if it wasn't me. It was me adjacent,
a level of success he aspired to, and the success of a woman
often seems particularly stinging to men in their field. It was a
petty idea and it had appeal. Petty ideas often do.

I saw a man I used to work for at a bar. He was a little
stoned and I was a little drunk, so I asked his opinion.

"Well, here's the thing," he said, gesticulating broadly to
emphasize his point. "Dude is keeping you on a tether, right?
And, sure, you can tell him about your book and be like,
'That's right, you baloney-sandwich bitch!' But then he probably will really never want to see you again."

Ultimately, that isn't what stopped me from texting him the
news. I considered it a few nights in a row, telling myself that
if I wanted to in the morning, I could. Each morning, I woke
up at peace with Adrian and the universe. Who knew what
was going on with him? There was no need to kick the hor-
net's nest of feelings again or sully my accomplishment with a
half-baked attempt at revenge.

That was what I thought I believed, anyway. Two months
after arriving in L.A., having finally settled back in after that
second round of traveling, I grabbed my computer and walked
down through the hills of Silver Lake to the neighborhood

coffee shop, planning to catch up on work. The sidewalk was so steep, I had to take baby steps, careful of my balance. Hummingbirds zipped around the trees, and I grinned at them, feeling like I was observing something secret. That's how someone felt about pigeons once, I thought, and that made me like them even more.

I was wearing a soft cotton dress and a pullover. It was a little too warm, but the sun seeping through my layers felt nice. Every single day felt like the most beautiful day of the year in Los Angeles. I hummed and composed in my head the words I'd type out soon.

I turned the corner into the coffee shop entrance and there he was.

I recognized Adrian's back, his shirt, his bag, the second they came into view, my mind hungrily jumping on the subject of its most intense scrutiny in the last month. He was waiting in line to order. I walked up directly behind him and tapped him on the shoulder.

It's very rare to witness the look in a man's eyes as he realizes he's about to have to deal with a woman he thought he'd never ever have to deal with. Shock, disbelief, dawning terror, and then an attempt to mask it all with a warped smile.

"I knew this would happen," I said. I laughed, a giant Ursula the Sea Witch laugh.

He recovered slightly, asking how I was, and leaned in for a hug. I wasn't composed enough to reject it. I held my body away from him and patted him, in an aggressively platonic gesture. His familiar smell that had lingered for days in my sheets wound around me for a brief moment, and my amusement fell away.

"What's going on?" he asked once more in a high-pitched voice. "How are you?"

At that, I smiled again, dropping all my good intentions and high-minded ideas about how Gloating Is Bad.

"Great. I just sold a book."

"What?" he said, like he didn't understand.

"I just sold a book," I repeated clearly, and watched him absorb what I was saying.

That's right, you baloney-sandwich bitch.

He seemed confused, though I'd told him before that I was trying to sell one. He asked the publisher and I told him and he looked even more confused. He asked me if I meant a subsidiary of that publisher. No, I said. Then he asked what I was doing at the coffee shop and I said I'd planned to work. So had he. On the edge of hysteria, I sarcastically suggested we sit and work together. He took me at my word and agreed.

I ordered an Americano. The barista, hugely misreading the situation, asked him if we were paying together and he held his breath. For a second, I considered making Adrian pay for me. In an unearned act of mercy, I stepped in and paid for myself. He watched as I signed for it. My voice was calm and I felt remarkably clear-headed, but it took everything to keep my hands steady, to keep the cup from clattering in its plate.

When we walked to the courtyard, I did have a moment of panic.

"We don't actually have to sit together—" I began.

"No, we should talk," he said. We found a bench secluded from the rest of the diligent writers clacking away on their keyboards and sipped. My heart was pumping so hard. I could feel the heat gathering under my clothes, sweat pooling at my temples. We talked about the book some more; he still seemed disbelieving.

It's hard to piece together how we segued, but eventually, I said it.

"You could have messaged me anything," I told him. "That you didn't want to date, that you didn't feel you could see me, that you just wanted to be friends. You just left me hanging."

"I was going to reach out," he protested.

"No, you weren't," I said.

"I was!"

We were quiet for a minute.

"I didn't intend to sleep with you that second time," he said, eventually. "I just have no self-control. And the truth is, I'm kind of a coward."

Sometimes I think people confess to shitty things about themselves and think that's the pinnacle of good behavior. That's the cue for the people they did the thing to to rush in and support them through the pain of being bad.

"Yeah, you are a coward," I said, looking him right in the face. It was a face I loved to look at, and I wish I could say that had no effect on me at that moment, but it did. "And I'm brave. And I'm honest. And I would have dealt respectfully with you, but you treated me like trash when you completely didn't have to."

My shoulders were tight, my eyelids aching. It should have felt like a relief to finally say all that. Instead, it felt very similar to when I said I'd be alone forever at that dinner party. It was the esophagus-clenching tension of knowing you have articulated something that has disrupted the norms of what you're *supposed* to say. This wasn't a speech I could smooth over or take back. I concentrated on not crying and waited for a response.

After a pause, he said, "I know," though I don't remember if he ever said he was sorry. That would have been the moment. I do not think he said the words. Instead, Adrian told me he'd been seeing someone, and it had very recently and very abruptly gotten serious. Indeed, it was so serious they'd just booked tickets for a trip to Mexico. And she wasn't the sort to ask him to be monogamous, but he wanted to try.

"The situation was always so strange with you and me," he added. "Maybe if it had been different, things would have worked out differently."

"Well, you can say that about anything."

"Yeah."

I could totally picture her. The Girl. I saw her as a twenty-seven-year-old, with colorful hair and tattoos and into punk music. Thinner than me and probably shorter than him, with very perky breasts and no bra and lots of style. Someone I imagined was simply better than me, instead of better for him. Only later did I wonder if Adrian told me some of the real details of their relationship as his own petty revenge for me having some success as a writer: the part about how he wanted so much to be faithful to her, the part about how he actually booked a plane ticket when she asked him to. I almost hoped that was the case, rather than him just hurting me with carelessness.

I shrugged. What could I say?

"Well, if you've found someone you can love, I'm happy for you," I said. I'm sure that sounded like a lie, but it really did seem better somehow for him to love someone else than to just not love me.

"Love?" he said. "I don't know about love."

That old line.

He got quiet again and my thoughts did cartwheels, not sure where to land.

"I was thinking about her and the trip just then," he said, suddenly. "I didn't want you to project onto my pensiveness."

I had no idea what that was supposed to mean, except that even when I was sitting directly in front of him, he wasn't thinking about me. I gulped down the rest of my coffee.

"Well, this has been about as much of a jolt as I need today," I said. "I'm gonna go home and work. I live up in the hills there now," I pointed, not wanting him to think I was covering miles to get away. He asked me what street with an intensity that suggested his girlfriend probably lived nearby, too. Great, I thought. I'll probably see them walking a puppy soon. I put down my cup and saucer.

"I'll let you bus that for me," I said, leaving it and probably a butt-sweat stain behind on the bench. I walked away without looking back. I got about a block and a half before my phone buzzed. Now he was texting me!

His message said it had been great to see me and to let him know if I'd like to have a coffee sometime. And congrats! I responded that it had been good closure, and then noncommittally about the coffee; it struck me as insanely tone-deaf to ask that I do the work of reaching out to him yet again. He most likely just wanted another shot at being a "good guy," but how many chances do you get?

Then I deleted his number. I deleted the photos of him petting my cat on my couch and kissing my cheek in a restaurant and, yes, of his dick. It was a largely symbolic gesture. Sometimes we do need symbolism.

That night, a huge storm rolled across the city. Thunder crashed, and lightning lit up the dripping lime trees outside my window. I pictured him somewhere, holding her as he'd held me not too long ago. My stomach cramped, the thought making me physically ill.

So I tried to picture myself as I'd like to be, one day. I kept returning to that moment when I strode down the street listening to that corny Haim song, looking and feeling my best. Determined, powerful, not knowing what would come and with the courage to try anyway. What a darling, bold idiot she was, and so different from the frightened woman texting her first date in years from a nail salon bathroom.

It still hurt, even knowing that everyone had been completely and totally right. It hurt so much. Having been in love before, I knew I would recover. Someday, I'd feel nothing at all about Adrian, not even mad. But I would feel again. I would be brave again, I promised myself, alone and shaking under the covers.

PART THREE

CHAPTER 14

. . . .

Single! And Fabulous!

It would be great to be able to say that was the end of my obsession. Embarrassingly, it was only the *beginning* of the *recovery* from my obsession. Our last meeting had some narrative clarity to it, despite what Dylan and I had discussed about the way life just continues without wrapping up loose ends. If this were a romantic comedy, there'd probably be a scene of me walking away from that coffee shop, settling in at a new one with a confident, wise smile on my face, and then glancing up and making eye contact with some cutie at the counter, implying this heroine would soon be in the *right* relationship after all. Because she finally earned it by having respect for herself, or something.

As I am as far from being a heroine as possible without becoming a villain, I actually spent the next few weeks mostly in bed watching TV. Hours of body heat turned my mattress into a nuclear reactor, and my most active choice was when to flip my pillow to find some trace of coolness beneath. I kept rolling back into the groove I'd been wearing in the center of the bed binge-watching *Sex and the City*. The laptop was overheated as well, whirring gently to keep itself from exploding in my face. Is this how I want to go? I mused, before reaching out to start the next episode.

After that chance meetup with Adrian, I'd balanced on the knife's edge between two choices. I could pick myself up, dust myself off, and strike out in yet another new direction. Or I could retreat and fall into despair. It was a very similar situation, in a way, to that first man I'd gone on a date with so long ago I couldn't even remember his name, the guy who had pushed me to make my resolution to go on date after date after date until I figured dating out. It was very similar to the first time Adrian had ghosted me, and I'd decided to keep right on trucking, dating, living, laughing, and leaving New York.

The recurring theme of disappointment followed by renewal wasn't lost on me. Most people repeat patterns in their life, and personal growth after a difficult moment isn't a bad pattern to repeat. This time, giving up beckoned with more power. It was perhaps the awful confirmation that the best self I'd been working so hard on had been rejected for someone else that made the thought of getting up and trying again absolutely ludicrous. Especially since I'd gone through this, like, three times with the same man. What was the fucking point?

After finding out about Adrian's girlfriend, I was quickly returning to my celibate past self's status quo of TV and sedation, now with a new hint of anger and unease I hadn't carried before. I'd started all this personal development in January of 2017; in a few months, there'd be another new year, 2019, and that would make almost two years of dating. By now, I knew what was on the other side of trying: more of the same.

I was disappointed in the story I'd told myself about what I deserved for being good, working hard, and trying to become worthy of love. I was heated about not getting it. That anger swirled around me like Pig-Pen's dust cloud.

To deal with it, I bought some weed gummies, shut my bedroom door, wrapped myself up in a duvet, and binge-watched *Chilling Adventures of Sabrina*. Fuck doing anything remotely constructive. After that, I started rewatching *Gilmore Girls*, discovering it was much more homophobic than I remembered. Now I was on *SATC*. I had a lot of hours to kill before the end of my life.

A few episodes in, I realized I was now closer to the age of Carrie Bradshaw in the series's later seasons than in its first. I'd originally watched the show when I was in high school, and now here I was, one of many single women who had slid gracelessly past the first bloom of youth into their midthirties without settling down, just like the show's heroines. It wasn't lost on me that so much of what was once considered revelatory or shocking about how the foursome handled dating was now pretty mundane. People were horrible to each other then, and they were horrible to each other now, twenty years later. The biggest change I observed between Carrie's time and my own was that ass eating is now fairly mainstream. Actually, most of the dynamics, disappointments, stigmas, and friction between single and partnered people on *Sex and the City* were super familiar.

Especially the stigmas. Throughout the show, every character is subjected to humiliations related to being single. They are excluded from work dinners centered around couples, they are mistrusted by other women with partners, they have to pay for every bachelorette and baby shower in the tristate area with no reciprocation, and then they sit through the dull torture of watching diapers get unwrapped for hours. The episode where Carrie Bradshaw gets dragged on the cover of *New York* magazine by an unflattering picture and the words "Single and Fabulous?" made me laugh. If my soul at the moment had been put in front of a camera, it would look as washed out as Carrie under the strobe light.

And only Samantha ever escapes using relationships as validation for her existence, and that doesn't even make it into the plotline until the first movie! I was so steamed.

One afternoon, the computer screen started to look hazy and distant. Or perhaps too close? I ran my hand along the gray fleece blanket, pushing the fibers this way and that. Or maybe it was the fleece petting *my* hand. That's when I remembered that I'd eaten those weed gummies.

When I could focus on the clock, I saw it was much later in the day than I had thought. I was in no condition to leave the house, but the place I was subletting had a long wood patio, built out over the roof of the apartment below. My roommates were two men in their late twenties who kept the space in about the condition of an off-campus frat house, except they were both very quiet, even courteously wearing headphones as they played *Red Dead Redemption* on the couch. They were happy to say hello whenever I floated by like a wraith. Otherwise, they were not interested in my antics.

Yes, I was back to living with people again. Looking for a new room on housing lists, I'd noticed how many people specified that they wanted someone in their twenties, or early thirties, tops. I'd wondered how long I would be able to live with other people before I became the living embodiment of the Steve Buscemi "How do you do, fellow kids?" meme. Someone my age was supposed to be rich or living in a one-bedroom apartment with their partner.

I padded out onto the gritty carpet and one of my roommates was sitting there, making his horse gallop down a digital lane on the widescreen TV. He nodded at me as I struggled to open the sliding door before realizing I was pushing the wrong direction.

The feeling of being high on THC had never been something I'd enjoyed, a fact I forgot every six months. It was so easy to access the drug in California, and there were so many ways to ingest it, so many variations on the same product and lots of appealing packaging. Surely, among all these choices was one that didn't make me feel like I was having an allergic reaction to my own tongue. Not this time. I stepped out into fresh air, finally, and wondered again if this was what everyone feels like when they're high, and if so, why did they like it?

Though the apartment was totally mediocre, the vista from the balcony was not. Set up slightly in the hills, the complexes and bungalows of the east side swirled on twisted streets below like streams in the valley. Far in the distance, the Hollywood sign was visible, and in the foreground, tall sycamores provided perches for giant birds. In the two months I had lived in this apartment, I'd spent enough time out there for some of the birds to be recognizable, like a large crow on its favorite branch, and a magenta-streaked Anna's hummingbird doing aerial maneuvers overhead, from one telephone wire to the next. The panorama was beautiful for the layers it offered, creating a universe with so many universes inside it. You could look out or in and be encompassed. It was close to sunset. The light was mellow, and gathering clouds along the mountain ridges were turning from gray to pale gold. Looking at nature was less disorienting than looking at a computer screen. I dragged a sagging lounge chair to face the beaming display and tried to settle my mind.

Why is the mind unsettled by rejection? It's destabilizing to think something is possible and then discover it's not. Not only was it not possible for me to be with Adrian in any significant sense, it really never had been, which made me question my own perception of reality, my reasons for being in a completely new city, and my ability to make judgment calls about relationships in future. Even without any hallucinogenic drugs involved, I felt fucking bad.

In a piece for *Gay* magazine, writer Alison Kinney interviewed the neuroscientist David Hsu. Hsu and his team were developing ways to measure rejection, building on previous findings that taking a couple of Tylenol helped some people with feelings of rejection, the same way it would alleviate physical pain. They discovered that after a rejection, the body releases opioids that bond with the brain's pain receptors to help regulate the negative emotions, much as it would if you stubbed your toe.

At least, that's what should happen in a healthy brain. The brains of people with depression release fewer opioids, and many of them retreat after a rejection to a much worse place than what would be considered healthy. Hsu's aim was to figure out how people can recover from rejection when they're having an "unhealthy" response. He told Kinney: "If someone becomes depressed, because they just broke up with their significant other, and they go to see a psychiatrist, they're still in that environment of *being* single or broken-up. It's not like a punctuated, single event: 'I just broke up with boyfriend or girlfriend, now I'm depressed, now there's this thing called depression I have to deal with now.' They're *still* interacting with that event, beyond their diagnosis."

Rejection, like loneliness, like love, isn't just an idea. It's a chemical process inside of us. We respond to and recover from the pain of rejection in much the same way we respond to and recover from physical pain. Since the wound of rejection isn't visible, monitoring the healing process of rejection is an invisible project. No one on the outside can necessarily tell you're still mentally interacting with the event, being negatively stimulated by it over and over.

There are answers people have come up with for how long this process should officially take. Love has a half-life, like radioactivity; that's a common equation of colloquial advice, actually. People say it takes half the time of the relationship to get over it. Some think you're not fully healed until you've lived as long without your lover as you did with them. Or it's one week for every month you were together, or the percentage increases depending on how stunned you were by the rejection. Were they cheating? That's a time increase. Your first love? Forget it, you'll be carrying them to the grave.

With Adrian, none of these rules truly applied. We hadn't been together. If I measured our "relationship" by days spent side by side, I should have been over the whole thing in a week. I needed to rewrite the rule to say, "Half the amount of time you felt hope."

He hadn't cheated on me, had he? There was no guarantee

of fidelity in our interactions, quite the opposite. If anything, he'd probably been cheating on the woman he was about to visit Mexico with when he spent those nights with me. I still felt like I'd been betrayed. The usual definitions of cheating and dating didn't apply to us at all, though I was suffering like they had. Whether or not I had legitimate grievances, I wanted the pain to stop. I wanted to stop interacting with the event or series of events that had brought me to this place.

I was still working through my haze. In between TV episodes, I pitched stories and ended up writing a piece about grief. I was thinking about death when I started. Then a therapist named Emily Adams expanded my scope. Adams worked as a marriage and family therapist at the Center for Mindful Psychotherapy in San Francisco. In an email, Adams told me that not everyone experiencing grief has lost someone to death. People grieve over the ends of relationships. They even grieve over the end of an idea, a dream they had for themselves or their lives.

She said that people tend to think of healing as a linear process. Most of us know the five stages of grief that are supposed to lead ultimately to acceptance. Apparently, recovery from loss is not like that at all.

"In my experience, people who are grieving bounce around from one stage to the next and not always in any particular order," she wrote. "It is common that the grief process begins with denial and anger, but these experiences will come up much later in the grief process as well. Sometimes depression and acceptance show up first and anger is much later to rise."

Adams's explanation made me picture a spiral, dipping in and out of all these feelings, the rings getting wider so you can spend longer in acceptance, then, as the spiral turns, you feel angry about someone you haven't thought of in ages. It wasn't a perfect explanation for why it was taking so much out of me to get over Adrian, but it did make me understand I was mourning the loss of possibility I had felt in our time together much more than him as a person. I was mourning being a person in love, a state I hadn't known in so long and was very aware was not guaranteed to come again. One moment I walked in acceptance, the next, I stepped into difficult feelings to walk for a stretch.

And I did then connect my feelings to grieving much bigger losses; I thought of my high school friend Raymond, who drowned in our late twenties, and how sometimes I'd see a picture memorializing him posted by mutual friends and weep like he died yesterday. And I remembered that loss took place around the start of my six years alone, marking the beginning of a retreat from the risk of loving someone you can lose.

In the midst of my angst, I told my mother about this connection, and how it just didn't seem worth it to love anything you can't keep.

"Don't be ridiculous," she exclaimed. "Do you refuse to love a flower? Or a sunset? Things aren't important because they never end, it's because they're fragile."

A few years later, when coronavirus arrived and things shut down, grief hung in the air even as government officials pushed people to move past it and get back to work. As I write this, over six hundred thousand people in the United States have died of COVID-19. Along with these deaths leaving gaps in families, there were smaller losses to grieve in every individual: the end of a career, the separation from loved ones in quarantine, the loss of expectations around so many things people had planned and dreamed of for who knows how long before they were extinguished by a pandemic.

One of the most painful parts of all that loss was the rush to move on, when that's not the way the heart heals at all. We can't be forced to recover from pain and loss—it's supposed to be a slow trudge, with lots of backward steps.

Researchers have been trying to figure out a way to skip all the pain. Hsu isn't the only one working on the ways emotions are traced in the body's pain receptors.

Stephanie Cacioppo is a scientist, and widow of the late scientist John Cacioppo. The two studied loneliness and its effects together. Then John died, leaving Stephanie to continue the work without her husband. She has been developing what could essentially be described as a daily pill for loneliness and is often discussed that way in articles about its development, whether Cacioppo would describe the pill that way or not.

Cacioppo works with a neurosteroid called pregnenolone, which has been shown to help with stress-related disorders and hypervigilance as a response to social threats, including chronic loneliness.

"If we could successfully reduce the alarm system in the minds of lonely individuals, then we could have them reconnect, rather than withdraw from others," Cacioppo told *The Guardian* in 2019. When I first read about these pills, they sounded very similar to an antidepressant or antianxiety medication, even if the chemistry they're working with is different. A pill can help people break out of their spirals; taking antidepressants helped me recover from grief after Raymond's death, like a rope thrown to me in the water.

Reading about a medical "cure" for loneliness disturbed me anyway. That rope wasn't a cure, if there *is* such a thing as a cure to fluctuating emotional states. I still had to pull myself hand over hand out of the stormy waves of depression. It had to be anchored to something, to friends and family, and there had to be a place for me to climb out and dry off that was safe and stable: I had an income, a home, a therapist. Cacioppo probably isn't suggesting that her experimental medication would be the only recommended treatment for someone experiencing chronic loneliness. Frighteningly, the way the medical industry works now, it's all too likely that lots of people who really need social services might end up getting a prescription instead.

When writing about Hsu's research, Kinney talks about how recovering from rejection is seen as a character-building mission in American culture. Mental and physical health is treated like an individual responsibility in a similar way, yet mental health isn't just something wrong with the chemical balance in your brain; it is largely influenced by what's around you. Again, during COVID-19, a great deal of emphasis was put on personal responsibility, on social distancing and having things delivered and avoiding contact between households—disregarding that these weren't options for many people.

The rate of hospitalization and death from coronavirus was highly disproportionate by race, with Black and Latino communities hit much harder than white ones. The Cleveland Clinic attributed much of this to economic factors, like working in front-facing "essential" jobs; living in more populated areas and multigenerational households, which disallowed isolation if someone got sick; and the lower likelihood of having

medical insurance that would offer early treatment and testing. It was part of a long-established pattern of systemic rac-
ism in the medical industry playing out at a much more rapid
pace, and not something any individual could manage alone.

The devastation of coronavirus was in some ways just a
heightened version of what is happening to BIPOC communities all the time. Kinney wrote her piece before COVID-19,
but much of what she says applies generally to surviving the
structures of Western societies that demand so much and return so little:

> Self-help guides, therapy, schooling, and all our cultural
> rules and norms determine whether our reactions to re-
> jection are appropriate or excessive, reasonable or de-
> ranged. According to these standards, our ability to
> cope with rejection depends on maturity, resilience, and
> the hard work of self-improvement: we get over it, we
> shake it off, we cope, we move on, and, nevertheless,
> we persist. But what we call resilience comes at a huge
> material, financial, and psychological cost for those
> who, through no fault of their own, can rarely or never
> prevail against a system stacked against them.

A pill might help someone suffering from feelings of
chronic loneliness who has a great deal of support. The systems created by white supremacy, ableism, transphobia, xeno-
phobia, and more are what Kinney is referring to; a lonely
person at the intersection of these types of discrimination is
facing a very different battle to heal from rejection and isola-

tion. Even the most chemically stable person would be exhausted and traumatized by them.

In *Sapiens: A Brief History of Humankind,* Yuval Noah Harari discusses happiness in the context of human evolution, examining whether humanity has become happier or more dejected overall since the dawn of man. Since modern society is fascinated with how to feel and maintain happiness, there are many studies approaching the question: from sociological perspectives, from historical ones, and from basic chemical ones. The biochemist's thoughts on happiness, from Harari's account, is that a healthy brain tries to moderate our feelings. Even if you have a momentary burst of joy, you will eventually even out. The mind doesn't like high highs any more than it likes low lows.

"To be happy is no more and no less than experiencing pleasant bodily sensations," Harari writes. "Since our biochemistry limits the volume and duration of these sensations, the only way to make people experience a high level of happiness over an extended period of time is to manipulate their biochemical system."

Harari suggests that the key to happiness is controlling how people feel through biochemical engineering, not through widespread improvements to their quality of life via social progress. From my reading, he's being a little facetious; shortly after, he backs off the idea of distributing happiness pills, and writes that a more complicated and more accurate notion of happiness is a sense of meaning in life, the feeling that what you do is worthwhile, and a connection to those around you.

My understanding of what Harari is saying is that the recipe for happiness is feeling like you're a meaningful part of the world and that the social barriers impeding you have been removed. Finding meaning in life is a very ill-defined directive, left to the individual; happiness is always more available to people who fit easily into the dominant, oppressive culture as it is. Kinney's article makes a distinction between recovering from personal versus systemic rejection. By the latter standard, I had no serious problems at all. I'll admit, though, that if I'd had a pill to take to never feel wretched about my personal rejections again, I might have swallowed it.

Time marched on. I came to the end of my HBO rewatch. I started to do things like enter coffee shops again. The intensity of my feelings faded, even if I occasionally sat straight up in bed muttering some variation of "How dare he!"

By this point, it was a few weeks until Christmas. I planned to return to New York for the holidays on the early side, to catch all the friends soon leaving for their own homes of origin. I'd been in L.A. for less than six months, so they probably didn't miss me too much, but I missed them. I was packing my battered suitcase when the phone choo-chooed softly. It was a text from Xavier, one of my friends from the dinner party that inspired my original essay, the one that had set me off on a dating spree and caused me to fall in love then get heart-stomped. I hadn't heard from him in a minute.

I'm writing 'cause I'm getting married, and I'd love it if you can join us to celebrate, he wrote, naming a date when, serendipitously, I would be in town. He sent a picture of himself grinning in the park with his bride-to-be, plus an image of the homemade block-print invitation to their reception.

She's gorgeous! I enthused. *And stylish. Can't wait to meet her.*

She's really great and I'm so very happy, he replied. Direct, impactful words. The last we had talked, Xavier had been dating a woman in an open marriage who had a young child, and he hadn't seemed content. We'd known each other a long time. Sometimes when you know a friend for a long time you don't check in with them as frequently as you should; it's easy to take the relationship for granted, and I'd let things slide because it felt like anytime we wanted we could pick up right where we left off.

In a way, that was correct. I arrived on the day of Xavier's wedding at the same house where that dinner had taken place more than two years ago, the same place where Rachel and Jon had been married. There were a lot of familiar faces. Again, it was mostly people whom I hadn't spoken to in a long time. Jon and Rachel were there, wearing their wedding rings. I met Xavier's new wife, Bella, whom he'd married at the courthouse that morning. She was a bit reserved and looked at her husband with a reverence that felt almost too intimate to witness.

The house was bubbling over with people and food. The tables were piled high with fresh baked bread, sliced cheese and fruit, homemade tamales, rice and beans, three kinds of soup (which proved difficult to distribute), roasted vegetables, kale salads, and desserts. A small table soon overflowed with bottles of wine as more well-wishers arrived, the brownstone's stairs creaking incessantly under the tread of visitors' feet.

I tried to do my part by grabbing a glass of champagne, and ran into one of Xavier's old roommates, Dan, a guy who always brought up his girlfriend in conversations with me by the second or third sentence.

"Hey, Dan!" I said. "Nice to see you. What's new?"

"Well, my girlfriend and I are just making plans for the holidays," he said.

"Okay," I replied, sipping my drink. We traded a few more pleasantries, and then I wandered down the hall to join Jon and Rachel.

"Dan always does this thing where he immediately mentions his girlfriend to me, like he's trying to let me down gently," I said. It seemed like the time to air this very specific complaint.

"Oh my goodness, yes," exclaimed Jon. "He does this. I've noticed him doing this to other women, too."

Rachel confirmed she'd also heard him say similar things. I wondered aloud, "Does he really think he needs to warn everyone off?"

Jon shook his head. "I think he is reminding himself."

This conversation produced some gloomy thoughts about commitment at a party celebrating it. I thought about Adrian, who should have reminded himself he had a girlfriend before sleeping with me again. To address those feelings, I went looking for more cheese. As I turned away from the buffet table, a woman with glasses and a head of short curls smiled and waved hello, then embraced me.

"Hiiiii," I said, not really knowing who she was. A man behind her was carrying an older toddler, and they were clearly together. That's when I realized it was Xavier's former lover, attending his wedding. Not surprising, considering their ability to navigate complicated situations. It was a reminder of how much of this story I didn't know.

I found Xavier standing alone for a moment by the staircase. He was smiling gently to himself, a beatific expression that made me impulsively reach out and hug him. We drew apart, holding each other's forearms.

"It's so good to see you!" I said.

"I know! I'm so glad you could be here, but it's so hard to talk to people as the host. Quick. What is going on with you?"

I gave a very short summary of life in Los Angeles. He told me a bit about how long he and his wife had been seeing each other, and their plans for where they would soon be living. Eventually, I leaned in to ask if I could inquire about something more personal.

"Of course," he said.

"What happened with you and your last girlfriend? I just saw her and was curious how that all ended."

Xavier told me that he had been seriously dating the married woman for three years when she and her husband had decided to move upstate. Something already challenging was compounded by a lengthy commute.

"It just got to the point where I was feeling so fed up and so bad," he said. "One day I just decided, 'Today I'm going to be really nice to myself.' I went out and bought a new pair of running shoes, because I love running. And I took myself out for a nice meal. And I sat in the park. And then I got a text from a friend."

The text said that the friend had another friend, a girl named Bella. Bella had seen a picture of Xavier on Tinder that she recognized from a photo series made by their mutual pal.

"I had deleted Tinder off my phone. I never looked at it," he said. But Bella had thought he was cute and asked their photographer friend to reach out and see if he'd be interested in getting a cup of coffee.

"Sure, why not," he told his friend. He met Bella that very same day. Their date lasted four hours.

It was exactly the kind of story I'd always hated being told as a single person—just alter your headspace and love will slide right in. The only real difference was that this wasn't some anecdote I was hearing from my mom about her doctor's niece's stepsister's catsitter. This was a story from my friend. I could see for myself how happy he was.

The thing to focus on was probably that Xavier had met his true love. Instead, I kept thinking about him deciding to be nice to himself instead of waiting for somebody else to be nice to him. It was similar to my impulses toward expensive self-care, except Xavier hadn't seen that care as part of a self-improvement campaign. He'd just wanted to feel good again, with no other purpose. His voice when he described making that decision had been so full of relief. I could almost taste the wonder of setting aside a failed love affair and finally moving the fuck on. Almost.

It was a formless dream. I wasn't sure anymore how to do it: to feel good with no agenda, to do something with no thought of it being recognized by anyone except you. Not asking for anyone else to choose you and say you were worthy, nothing to satisfy except your own expectations of what makes a worthwhile life. It was suddenly a much more arresting subject than what a relationship with another person would look like. Even if I didn't know how, I was inspired to try to wake up sometime very soon and say, "Today, I'm going to be really nice to myself."

CHAPTER 15

New Ceremonies

I flew back to Los Angeles on New Year's Day because it was cheap. I arrived late at night, enervated and unable to sleep. Visiting home had made me wonder why I'd bothered to leave. I missed my family, and there was no good reason to be somewhere else except for the hankering to feel different. Being in a new city wasn't that different, mostly because I hadn't been trying that hard to branch out.

With Xavier's life lesson in mind, I tried to approach this new year with the intention of being really nice to myself, if I could figure out what that entailed. I took things slow. I walked. I walked so much I developed plantar fasciitis in my heel and started wearing inserts, crossing a line in my mind from suffering regular aches and pains to being old.

"Things aren't gonna bounce back the way they used to, bitch!" I told my reflection, noticing grays at my temples that I'd never seen before. Being nice to myself wasn't getting off to a good start.

I was working hours that were disjointed and solitary. There was no office to go in to. There wasn't enough for me to do with my days besides wandering—to the coffee shop, the grocery store, a bar, a Pilates class if I was feeling decadent. I didn't know how to drive, and there wasn't anywhere to drive to, really.

Often, I would walk all the way to Griffith Park and then up to the Observatory, observing other people trudging up the main winding path from the base of Los Feliz Boulevard. They were families or groups of friends, with a smattering of lone runners showing off absolutely unbelievable bodies.

I rarely walked at night. I had a rule now about being out by myself past 10:00 P.M. in L.A. In New York, I had walked alone in all sorts of places during most times of night and felt perfectly safe. New York becomes more itself in the dark. Buildings in Midtown are lit to mimic Gotham City sets, neon illuminates the façades of busy stores with blinding fluorescents inside, and streetlamps hang in reliable rows, like pearls along the hem of a neighborhood. Everything about that was familiar to me. Familiarity feels a lot like safety, and I didn't know L.A. the same way. Los Angeles fell through the looking glass at night and became an entirely new place. On some roads I could walk through solid blackness for most of the block as giant palm fronds blocked the faint illumination from scattershot yard lighting. There would be periodic strips of activity filled with Lyfts and Ubers dropping people off and escorting more away. These isolated blocks were like villages in a medieval forest. You wanted to get to one before sunset. Everyone seemed to be closed into their houses or their cars, zipping from one to the other without any thought of anybody outside.

One night, I was out breaking my own rules. I'd been on a date. Yes, I was still dating, not having much else to do to fill my evenings, though I wasn't enjoying it much. Dating had become kind of a social crutch. I was lonely, lonely in a way that didn't really have to do with romantic love anymore. I missed the sense of place that came from walking streets I'd walked a million times through all the stages of my life. I missed being able to always find something to do and someone to do it with. Meetups in L.A. felt so scheduled, forty-five-minute dinners written into the calendar weeks in advance. I was lonely from lack of acquaintanceship, the sensation of walking into a place and having everyone know your name. The *Cheers* effect, a very specific kind of connection that can only be developed over time and a little bit by accident. Show up to a place too many times and it will happen. I hadn't been here long enough to show up anywhere too many times.

All this loneliness was somewhat amplified by the fact that I was spending so much time thinking, reading, and writing about what it meant to feel alone, usually actually sitting all alone at my desk. Often, by the end of the day, I wouldn't have spoken aloud to anyone. Even the emptiness of the streets was hard to take as I wandered them, L.A.'s sole pedestrian.

Not knowing what to do, I turned to my old standby. Any time I felt like sitting among a group of people in a public place on a beautiful night having a conversation, I could usually find someone else to do that with on an app. There are always more lonely people trying to find someone to grab their hand and pull them to the other side of the relationship divide. I mostly just wanted someone to talk to.

That night, this date had wanted to give me a ride home and I hadn't wanted to get into their car. Insisting I lived close by, I'd said goodnight, swerving away from a kiss to run off in an impractical direction. The path I took curved through a residential area—a much prettier, less direct route. Up ahead, another street connected with mine, sloping down off an even emptier hill. Walking down it at about the same pace as mine was a coyote. We caught sight of each other at the same moment and both stopped. The coyote was probably around twenty feet away from me, and it looked very much like a dog, except it wasn't. Not all wild animals convey humanlike intelligence. When they do, it's unsettling. The coyote and I were clearly having the same thought, which was, Should I risk it?

Again, at the same moment, we both decided, "Nah," and each turned back the way we had come. I had gone a few feet when I changed my mind, thinking that if the coyote was going back where it came from, there was no reason to go out of my way even farther. I turned back and saw it had come to the same conclusion. It paused again, however, and I kept going, taking a fork in the road while attempting to pass by it as unconcernedly as possible. It wasn't until I was out of sight that I started to run. That was inadvertently wise. A wildlife expert told me later that you're never supposed to run in front of a predator, because it will feel the drive to give chase, even if all it really wanted to do was eat some trash out of a garbage can. As potential prey, the urge to run is almost as irresistible.

When I got far enough away that it felt safe to stop, I had run farther than I ever did under any circumstances not involving a wild carnivore. I gasped, a stitch straining in my side, shuddering from a burst of adrenaline. I started to laugh as I hadn't laughed in a long time—at the sheer preposterousness of everything there was to consider and look out for and protect yourself from. The laughter lifted a numbness I hadn't been aware of.

That curtain didn't stay up for long. But it was looser, fluttering to allow me to feel all sorts of things I hadn't been feeling. Not all of them were good. That's why we sometimes get numb, even to joy. I began to wonder if something was seriously wrong with me when a brand-new symptom of potential incipient lunacy arrived soon after my coyote encounter. It happened a few times, one afternoon walking through another empty street, once in a yoga class, once sitting in my own bedroom, and once, horribly, on a date at a pizzeria.

It always started the same way. Suddenly, I'd feel like I was losing touch with what was right in front of me, like my body was a puppet I was operating from a great distance. Where from, I couldn't say. Another planet? Another point in time? Who was I? Did this date roofie my pizza?

After a few moments (or eons) of intense breathing and focusing on a specific point ahead, I would come back to myself and inhabit my body again. What was scariest about this sensation of being unanchored was the temptation to let go completely. Some part of me was curious about what would happen if I didn't attempt to return to my historical standard of sanity. I would wake up naked in the hills, or mentally travel to a distant galaxy. I might never come back, and that would be okay.

This disembodiment finally visited me when I was with someone I could explain it to. Dylan and I had bought tickets to a comedy show and even managed to get there in time to grab seats. It was sold out, in an auditorium downtown. Dylan bought the first round, and as I sipped my glass of house red, my head started to balloon off my shoulders.

No, no, no, I thought. I tried very hard to calm down, to reconnect, reminding myself that I was in a safe place, that nothing would happen, not really.

You might die from fear, I told myself, *but then it will be over.*

It occurred to me that someone I knew was there to call an ambulance if the situation deteriorated, and I turned—very slowly, it felt—toward Dylan.

"I've been having this feeling lately, like I'm losing my grip on reality," I said. To Dylan's credit, he almost convinced me that he wasn't alarmed by this news.

"Is it happening right now?" he asked.

"Yes," I said, realizing that just being able to tell someone else was helping. I tried to describe the puppeteering feeling, and my worry that this was the beginning of some sort of serious mental breakdown.

"I promise I'll get you to a hospital if you take off your clothes and start running up and down the aisle," he said, after I mentioned the potential naked-in-the-hills outcome. Soon I started to feel better, or at least well enough to sit through the rest of the show with my clothes on. I couldn't depend on having someone there to talk me back to lucidity every time this happened, though. I needed to figure out what was going on.

My sliding-scale therapist in New York had seen me when I last visited. I didn't know how to find the right person in L.A. I ended up choosing one who was close enough to my house to walk to, one who did EMDR, or Eye Movement Desensitization and Reprocessing. A friend of mine who had gotten assaulted on the street had started doing it after he couldn't escape paranoid thoughts about being attacked in his apartment. The promise of EMDR is that it can rewrite the story of things that happened to you and make you see them in a different light. I'd been caught in a loop so long and that sounded like something I needed. Also, I sold a story based around EMDR so I could write the whole session off.

What was kind of too bad was that the therapist actually seemed really good, and I knew I wouldn't be able to afford her on a weekly basis—or do the write off trick a second time. I told her about this feeling I had of being stuck in the past, in my patterns, in my feelings; conversely, it seemed like I was losing my grip. The strain of these two things was pulling me apart. Wanting to let go, scared to let go. She let me monologue, which is why therapy is good.

"What I'm really asking," I concluded, finally, "is, am I going crazy? Like, is that disconnected feeling the beginning of, like, complete mental collapse?"

"Oh," she said. "No."

What a relief.

"It sounds like what you're describing is disassociation," she continued. "It's a response to trauma or stress or feeling unsafe."

That seemed a bit much; I wasn't traumatized, I was just someone who moved to Los Angeles from New York. I thought anxiously of that sense of disconnect I'd had on the road the previous summer, the feelings that had followed me throughout my life of being separate and apart all the time. Where did my mind take me when it was scared of where it was?

Where does anyone retreat to when they feel excluded, left

out, out of step, and isolated for reasons they can't quite articulate? For me, it was like being very far away from everything that mattered and feeling fuzzy about why those things *did* matter and why I should get back to them. All of this exploration of loneliness hadn't alleviated it. If anything, it had become more acute, because I could see now how far the distances were between us all. This disassociation, though, was about the distance from me to myself, and that had become a much longer trip to take than I had ever known it could be.

Whatever, I thought, brushing that off. All that mattered was that this wasn't the beginning of the end of my mind. One step at a time. The therapist let me hold her weird EMDR kit handles that buzzed in my palms as she talked me through a series of meditations. She asked me to picture someone who seemed wise, someone who seemed loving, someone strong, and to imagine them gathered all around me.

This was harder than it sounded. Reading the struggle on my face, she told me I could choose fictional figures, and for some reason this made me think immediately of Tony the Tiger. I couldn't make Tony the Tiger my caretaker, so I picked out some friends: Dylan. Billie. My grandmother.

"Now imagine yourself someplace safe and beautiful," she said, and I imagined the balcony at my apartment that looked out over the glimmering city at sunset. She instructed me to imagine each one of those people I'd thought of joining me there, bringing all of the wisdom, kindness, and support I associated with them. The balcony filled up as I focused on the exercise, trying as hard as I could to squeeze everything out of this therapy session as possible.

Whoever else rejected me or dismissed me or mocked me,

there were other people out there who knew who I was, who cared what happened to me, who understood my flaws and decided I was still worth knowing. I let myself remember that, let myself live in that acceptance for the half hour I was led through her exercises. Briefly, I was really nice to myself.

Most love stories tell you that love is contained in one perfect other who recognizes your perfection. As my therapist murmured to me, I saw more and more people I cared about and who cared about me without demanding anything close to perfection. My hands clung harder to the handles. The crowd in my mind grew, filling me with gentle gratitude. The buzzing in my palms came to a stop and I blinked my eyes open.

It's possible that all I really needed was the reassurance that I wasn't losing my mind, but over the next week, I felt better. Loving only one person had taken so much out of me and offered so little in return. I didn't want to pour that much energy into or dedicate that much mental space to finding another Adrian, or another anybody. Nor did I want to withdraw again, into my bedroom or into the distance of disassociation. The past year had been about the danger of extremes. I wanted to walk a middle path, one that wasn't hiding from the ups and downs of loneliness, one that wasn't making escaping loneliness via a romantic relationship the primary motivation of my life. Go slow, be nice to yourself, I repeated, trying to allow myself some actual space and time to heal rather than finding ways to avoid or distract.

If I'd had a newsletter about my emotional progress, I would have written to those followers and said, "Hey, everybody who is keeping track, I really tried this time and I did fall

in love and it cost me so much effort and heartache and ultimately wasn't very beneficial. I know some people will tell me
to keep on trying and trying and trying, even if it eats up my
whole life. Well, I don't want to keep trying, because I think
that my life is more valuable than the pursuit of someone else
to validate it."

At least, I wanted to believe that was true, even when it was
hard to. I wanted to remember that there were more people to
reach out to, more things to do than walk to nowhere from
nowhere until my feet fell off. What I needed to do was to keep
filling my balcony, even if it took a long time. Even if it was a
project that would never end.

I'd rushed from doing nothing to change my life to doing
way too much. Those things were mostly what everyone else
thought I should do to find love and escape loneliness. The
people who suggested them were as influenced as I was by the
narrative that couplehood is the ultimate reward in a person's
life. We were stuck in a loop together. Judith Williamson writes
in the introduction to her book *Consuming Passions: The Dynamics of Popular Culture* about how, too often, the creativity of the
human mind gets forced down the same old routes by the stories around us. "We are consuming passions all the time," she
writes. "Passions born out of imbalance, insecurity, the longing for something more, find forms in the objects and relations
available; so that energies fired by what might be, become the
fuel for maintaining what already is. . . . What I am concerned
with is the way passions are themselves consumed, contained
and channeled into the very social structures they might otherwise threaten."

I'd read that a very long time ago, when I'd been research-
ing romance novels for something I was writing. Romance
novels had been one way of channeling my sexual energy in
those long years without sex, and I'd felt pretty ambivalent
about that. I understood Williamson's point to be that often
the things we want or care about are much more curated and
controlled than we admit, even if only by the lack of alternatives. Did I want to be in love with another person, or was that
the clearest example of satisfaction, safety, and validation I
was familiar with? What if all the single people out there were
able to imagine something completely new for their lives besides not being single? What if everyone were able to explore
new ways of connecting? What current systems would fall
apart if we stopped channeling our energy into them?

The stuff I started to try to care about instead probably
wouldn't have passed whatever Williamson's criteria were for
innovative thinking; I was pretty regular. I only wanted to find
things to care about that felt new for me.

The common advice lonely people are given isn't completely wrong, even if it is trite and only addresses a fraction
of the problem: do stuff you enjoy doing and you might meet
people who like doing it, too. I started by volunteering, first at
a food bank in Silver Lake, filling grocery bags for families
lined up around the block, then at the Audubon Society, showing up to help water shrubs that provided perches for feath-
ered families. I worked alongside twenty high school students
who were there to fulfill community service requirements.
Two girls and I were assigned to arduously cart buckets up a
hill to drown a few nondescript scrub brushes over and over.

They were from different schools. I drifted, hypnotized by the water pooling and soaking into the parched ground as they made small talk about what had brought them there.

"How about you?"

The inquiry was directed at me.

"Oh," I said, "I just like birds."

This was clearly a bizarre reason to be at the Audubon Society at 9:00 A.M. on a Saturday, in their opinion. As an adult, being judged by teens didn't phase me *too* much. They had no idea what socializing after mandatory schooling would be like. I did remember their reaction and smile to myself with every new hobby or activity or attempt to build out my life over the next few weeks. It is hard to try something new, especially by yourself. I managed to drag a few people I knew in L.A. to events or activities, but a lot of stuff I tried on my own. I was putting myself out there. The more you put yourself out there, the weirder you seem.

I went to a breathwork class, which is where a group of adults literally lie on the ground and hyperventilate until they scream and cry. Afterward, we sat in a circle to reflect on the shared delirium, and I mentioned I was new to the city and if anyone had any other workshops or events, I'd love to go! No one replied, not even the Kundalini yogi in the circle. I was so ripe for joining a cult, and no one wanted me. I went to the Rainbow LGBTQ+ night at a roller-skating rink and watched crowds of young queer people in their best fashion zoom backward as I clung to the velvet walls. A person with a purple undercut floated up to me, watching my struggles.

"Like this," they said in a German accent, exaggerating

putting their feet one in front of the other with the toes turned out. "Like a penguin."

"Okay! Thank you!" I said after ten seconds of trying, returning to the wall like a bisexual limpet. They sped off with a shrug.

I resolved to come back for an actual lesson. Progress was painstakingly slow, much slower than I wanted, despite my new "go slow" mantra. Trying to get around the rink without stopping, trying to build up community, trying to find things that fill up our lives that aren't our phones or comparing what we don't have to what other people do. These things require patience and occasional boredom and false starts. Their rewards are far slower to arrive and much richer when they do. The first time I did a circuit by myself, feeling confident and free, it was with a warm glow of accomplishment that depended only on my own ability. I did not have to wait to hear from anyone else to know I felt good about myself. A small thing that made me feel more powerful than I had in a long time.

Then I had some luck, getting invited to a writers' group for women that was mostly sitting around a living room, eating snacks, and gossiping. Sitting on a pink plush couch, I felt included in something, even if the gossip was mostly about people I didn't know. Just hanging out was enough. Damn, I had missed just hanging out—no goal, no time frame, no need to hurry or get the check or get to work. The way conversations built and collapsed and picked up, then churned along on the steam of shared laughter. The quiet moment when the laughter ends and then someone introduces a new topic instead of calling it a night, because the talk is so delicious.

A comedy person in L.A. who I knew from New York texted to ask if I wanted to join an improv practice group. Of course; anything, I'd do anything, and I loved improv, my usual cult. When I arrived, I was informed that they were practicing for auditions at an improv theater. What the hell, I thought, let's do it. I auditioned and got put on a house team. The number of people I knew and could text or call or get a drink with was growing. That centered me even more. So did being onstage, feeling that electric exchange between an audience and a performer that I hadn't realized I missed so much.

And then I got a text from Billie. She was flying into Los Angeles for just a few days. A school that an old colleague worked at was looking for a teacher, and she'd been recommended. They were buying her ticket and asking her to lead a lesson to see if she'd be the right fit.

Can I stay with you?! she asked.

Of course! I answered, ecstatic.

I went shopping for groceries, planning what I'd make for her breakfast and dinner, laundering my sheets so she could sleep in my bed, even mopping the floor. That was a very big deal. She arrived in a rented car and leapt out into my arms. It felt so nice to hug her, to be hugged. It occurred to me that I never hugged anyone like this in L.A., like it was okay to just sit in each other's arms without wondering if it had gone on too long.

I left her alone in my bedroom to work on her lesson plan. She came out after a bit with a laptop and folder, keyed-up energy shimmering around her like a halo.

"I need to go to the library," Billie announced.

"Oh, okay, I can come, I have to renew those books anyway," I answered, looking at a giant pile of hardcovers I had been dreading carrying on foot.

"I'll take them!" she said, following my eyeline. Half-heartedly, I objected, but soon Billie was out the door. I started making dinner, salmon and green beans, laying out the former over a bed of thinly sliced lemons in a pan, then sprinkled with dill. The peace of preparing a meal I would share for the first time in ages stole over me. I turned on some music and danced around the kitchen a little before settling to pick the beans.

When Billie got back, the food was ready.

"Your books were overdue. I paid the fine!" she said, dumping the pile on the floor. "But I renewed them all."

I offered to pay her back, and she waved it away.

"Well, how much was it?" I asked.

"I think less than forty dollars, I have to look at my change. They only took cash, so I had to go to an ATM."

"Why on earth did you do that?" I exclaimed.

"Yeah, even the librarian was like, 'You're sure going to a lot of trouble,' but I told him you were worth it."

Billie and I ate and talked, and she explained her plans for the classroom tomorrow. I asked her if she really wanted to move out here, and she said, "It's hard to imagine leaving Brooklyn, but we've been talking and talking about it. If I had a job here, it would be a clear sign to do it. And I've also kinda realized that a lot of the people who are important to me aren't there anymore."

Her extended family all lived in California. Her parents were finding it much more difficult to live on the sixth floor in their rent-controlled walk-up. If Billie could get a job in L.A., she could bring them, reuniting the older members of her family with their kin and rescuing her mom and dad from an unmanageable living situation. There was a lot of potential in the air.

Before bed, I convinced Billie to let me give her a facial, using all my little product samples and a face mask to pamper her. She had a naturally lovely complexion, which she did very little to take care of and probably didn't need to.

"This is ret-in-ol," I enunciated carefully, holding up the bottle, and she nodded gravely. I tucked her into bed and went to sleep on the pull-out couch.

Billie and I have the same internal clock for waking up. She tiptoed out early the next morning to find me already scrolling on my phone to see what the enraging news of the day was and slid in next to me. When we were kids, we would have sleepovers several times a week. She threw a heavy leg across my hips in a gesture I had forgotten from then and asked, "What's for breakfast?"

Billie got the job, just like I knew she would, though she didn't find out for certain for a few more weeks. After her successful lesson plan for a few dozen rapt fourth-graders, she picked me up and we drove to the beach.

It was too cold to swim, but Billie kicked her shoes off and walked into the water, still dressed in a gray business-casual dress. She held her arms up over her head and tilted her face into the sun. I wished I had insisted she wear sunscreen. Then she looked down at her feet, spotted something, and leaned closer.

"Look at this," she said. From the water she pulled a perfectly formed sand dollar a bit smaller than her palm.

"It's a sign," I told her, wanting her to find the signs she needed to justify uprooting her life to be closer to mine.

"I think so."

Before long, my best friend would be living in the same city as me, after a brief break on different coasts. Billie had a family, and they'd come with her. A husband, two children, and her folks would all soon be living together in a house in Pasadena. I couldn't fit into that house, and I didn't believe I should try. That was her life.

It still made all the difference that she would be there, another point from which I could wind more and more attachments, weaving together a future. Very slowly.

. . . .

CHAPTER 16

O Hunting Heart,
Shall You Find It

I planned to spend a lot of money to celebrate my thirty-fifth birthday in February. Several friends were visiting at once, most for work reasons, a few for vacations. Thrilled, I rented an apartment in Venice Beach big enough for ten people. It was stupid expensive, like, actually a very stupid use of money once again, but I really wanted to do it. I wanted to make a big deal about myself, because no one else was remotely obligated to do so.

At Billie's wedding, five or six years earlier, I was elated to see my beautiful friend being celebrated. It was so special to watch other people acknowledging this important change in her life. The reception was in the backyard of her ground floor apartment in Brooklyn. I watched her greet guests and felt a fervent, weepy love for the girl I'd grown up with who had turned into this kind, accomplished, beloved woman. I had ingested an entire bottle of wine. We were both hideously sunburned from the small ceremony earlier that morning on Coney Island Beach.

We met soon after the event to rehash it all, and she told me how the next morning she'd cried as she went through all the cards and gifts they'd received, filled with messages about how fantastic she was, from all the people she cared about. From joy, of course. I was once more moved, happy to think of my friend being showered in all the love she deserved.

Then, for a horrible moment, I thought about how I would likely never have a day like that.

When I first read about sologamy, or self-marriage, I tried to imagine my grandparents solemnly attending a ceremony in which I married myself and collected gifts afterward. Stories about self-marriage generally focus on women, often highlighting that they're ladies who've recently been dumped. In some cases, the cancellation costs of an actual planned wedding were so high they decided to just have a big party anyway. In 2017, on assignment for *Vogue*, Patricia Garcia followed several women who had gone viral after sharing photos and videos of their sologamy ceremonies on Facebook; the responses they received ran the gamut from cheerful support to hate mail.

Life coach Sasha Cagen, one of the women profiled, who has written extensively about her solo commitment to herself, commented on the fact that there are far fewer self-commitment ceremonies enacted by men. "Clearly women feel much more pressure to be married [in order] to feel validated as women and adults," she said. "The mythology of completion on your wedding day with the dress, the ring, the man—these are all the stories that are sold to girls from day one in a way we don't sell them to boys. So there is a deep anxiety and longing in women for a ritual of acknowledgment. I believe men, too, love to be seen and acknowledged, but marriage just doesn't have the same weight for them."

Cagen's ceremony was witnessed by only two people and had few similarities to a big, traditional wedding ceremony. Even if she'd eschewed the traditional trappings, her point about desiring acknowledgment via formal ceremonies is accurate. I wanted very much to be acknowledged, and I was disgusted by my inability to stop wanting that acknowledgment, especially in the ways it was woven into monogamous couplehood. My birthday party was an attempt to shrug off this weight, if that was possible.

My friend Marian was flying in, setting up meetings with the West Coast branch of her acting agency. By a week before the event, she and several other visitors were texting me constantly about logistics and requests for a couch to crash on before our big beach night. I was enjoying it enormously, feeling very busy and important.

I walked into a coffee shop a ways from my house, planning to do some work. I liked to mix it up, and this particular place had a really good fried chicken sandwich I wanted to eat. My phone buzzed. I checked more of Marian's messages, waiting in line to order.

I glanced up. Sitting at the marble coffee shop bar, typing away, was a very familiar figure. A slender man in a black T-shirt. Momentarily, I questioned my senses. I'd often thought I was seeing Adrian around town. There are a lot of curly-haired dudes of average height wearing black T-shirts in L.A. The frequency of the second looks I had to take at random men had made me consider that he was much more basic than I'd believed. Copies of him were everywhere.

They were just copies. My body knew. This was the real man.

I turned and walked into the bathroom.

Adrian is in this coffee shop, I texted Marian from the toilet, releasing my shock through my bowels. *Why the fuck can he not get out of my life.*

LOLOL, she texted back, a compassionate friend.

There were two choices. I could get off the toilet and leave, sparing myself the awkwardness of speaking to him again. Or I could go and tap him on the shoulder one more time, because I never learn. I chose the latter strategy, as I'm not the sort of coward who runs away from creating a problem.

His pupils dilated like a startled cockatoo's when he recognized me, and then we both started to laugh. All the dramatic meetings and partings couldn't stand up to the absurdity of another coffee shop run-in.

"Just wanted to say hello," I told him, then stepped back in line to order. Instead of turning to his computer he got up and followed me as I retrieved my coffee, stirred in cream and sugar, then found a seat. We didn't talk about much, only the general how-are-yous. He shared his observation that this place was always like the gym on Mondays—everyone was here! He leaned against my table, waiting for something. I didn't know what.

"Well, I'm gonna try to do some work," I said.

He stood up.

"Oh, yeah, me too," he said, then hesitated. "Would it be okay if I asked you out for a coffee sometime?"

"Um, yes," I answered, thinking about how hilarious Marian would find that.

"Great!" he said and offered me his hand for a high five. Bemused, I slapped it, and he went back to work at the counter.

There he sat, just five feet away. I could have walked up to him again, touched him, demanded his attention once more. I patted myself on the back for resisting the urge to make a scene. Somehow, I managed to focus for a few hours. My stomach settled.

Finally, I packed up my stuff to go, looking his way. Adrian had his headphones on and appeared engrossed. I passed him to go to the bathroom one more time, and when I came out he was turning the corner to use it himself. I wondered if he'd followed me, but we both laughed again, like it was all a hilarious farce.

"So, coffee?" he asked, weighting the word with significance.

I'd barely trained myself to stop chasing Adrian. Resisting even this minimal gesture coming from him was beyond me. I had learned one thing: if I said yes and left this coffee shop, I would probably never hear from him again. I would still wait, hopeful and yearning.

"What are you doing right now?" I asked.

The sun was setting, and the air had turned cool. As we walked to a bar, he told me about his trip to Mexico in January to connect with his father's country, and was surprised to find his dad had flown to meet him there for some bonding time. Adrian explained the tenuous peace he'd made with his father's hit-or-miss parenting, saying it had been remarkable to receive an apology he'd long since stopped waiting for. I understood giving up on waiting for apologies.

He told me he had quit his bartending job before his trip and wasn't quite ready to find another one. He'd been considering grad school, naming MFA programs in other cities. Though I could have easily gone without ever receiving any of this information, it was disquieting to imagine Adrian in yet another city far away from me. I'd never known exactly where he was, but sometimes, thinking he was somewhere in Los Angeles had given it a certain significance. When the sun would set, he could be looking at it. Every time I turned a corner he could be standing there. And I'd been right, hadn't I? Today, I'd been right.

He didn't mention his girlfriend.

That's how every line of conversation went. It flowed as pleasurably as usual, from one topic to the next, as we found a good happy-hour special at a French-style bistro and sat at a table by the window. In every exchange was this void in the shape of a woman I didn't know. When he said he'd been camping on the beach recently, I knew he meant with her; when he described eating at an amazing restaurant in Mexico, I knew she'd been sitting across from him. He didn't say her name, whatever it was.

There was no avoidance of the topic of romantic entanglements on my end. I was fine with telling him about relatively recent dating misadventures, even glad that I could. It was mostly surface-level stuff about the differences in dating between New York and Los Angeles, basically a stand-up routine on what flakes and phonies people are in both cities.

"But in L.A., people cancel plans like *this*. . . ."

He murmured agreeingly in all the right places, commiserating with me over the difficulties of dating as though he hadn't been one of my biggest problems personified: chasing people who don't want me. This was my unspoken part of the conversation, another hole. The *other* thing that couldn't be mentioned. Eventually, the two bubbles of silence rubbed up against each other and popped.

"I guess I'm just trying to do my work and not think about romance too much," I said, because it sounded like the kind of thing people with self-esteem say. He sighed and shook his head.

"Yeah, man, romantic love is just—" he began.

"I have to go pee," I yelped, leaping out of my seat and speed-walking to my favorite emotional refuge. I didn't want to hear whatever Adrian was about to say, another comment about love being fake, especially when he was probably going to go home to someone who thought the love they shared was very, very real.

If anyone knew love was fake, it was me, after all the reading I'd been doing for this book. Love was just a mess of reactions in the body, heightening your focus on another person to a level of intensity that will cause you to mate with them, then raise a child until it's big enough to peel a banana on its own. The more the object of your affection is separated from you, the more you want them. Half the reason I wanted Adrian for so long was that he had never been truly available, which only activates desire more. Really. It's science. He was a delicious apple, just out of reach. Here he was, back again, tempting me with an undeliverable promise.

It didn't matter what I knew. In the bathroom mirror, I looked beautiful. I looked happy. For the last few hours, I'd been given the focused attention of a man I still, on some level, completely adored. Knowing he was a dishonest and manipulative guy hadn't altered whatever that chemical reaction was, or the twisting path he'd taken across my love map of cultural volition. Any recovery I'd made in the last four months had been completely swept away by the look in his eyes and our third half-priced drink.

In Peter Godfrey-Smith's book *Other Minds: The Octopus, the Sea, and the Deep Origins of Consciousness*, he describes the development of the uncannily complicated octopus brain. Compared to humans, octopuses are not very social at all, and it is sociability that is most often a marker of complex minds in animals. Just the same, they do have a very sophisticated intelligence.

Godfrey-Smith says that the octopus is smart in the sense of being "curious and flexible; they are adventurous, opportunistic," and that this intelligence developed from the complexity with which they travel across the ocean floor "roving and hunting" in search of food. Neurons built up in the octopus's body over years and years of evolution, and then one day "an octopus wakes up with a brain that can do more."

Humans developed higher intelligence for similar reasons to the octopus, with all our habits of complicated omnivorous foraging. That led to speech and, for *Homo sapiens*, gossip, or so claims Yuval Harari in *Sapiens*. The evolutionary step of being able to talk shit allowed *Homo sapiens* to run rings around our other human competitors, eventually leading to their extinction and our disastrous takeover. That's just one theory, of course, but the hunt being the spark that lights the mind to things like wonder, a concept of self, and complicated forms of expression makes sense to me.

Godfrey-Smith doesn't claim that an octopus thinks and feels in the same way a human does. For one thing, despite their measurably prodigious brain power, most species of octopus generally live for only three to five years. But they possess mischief, curiosity, recognition, the ability to learn, and a need for playful stimulation. There is a wide separation between the development of consciousness in octopuses and in humans; however, we share a common ancestor, and both species found a path toward awareness through the search for something life-sustaining.

The longing for connection encourages people to do and develop more within themselves. At the moment, much of humanity is still caught up in a cycle of searching for the same old conventional union, even if they don't think they'll find it. Looking at myself in the bathroom glass as Adrian sat waiting across the restaurant, I felt like an octopus. I was someone who had to search further, feeling in the murky depths for a different path, for another morsel, kicking up sand with my flailing appendages, the influence of my environment flickering across my body. I imagined the hunt waking me up one day to a deeper understanding, something more than I'd started out seeking. Being alone makes many people see and question things as they are in a way that people satiated by couplehood simply cannot. They're too settled, too sure. They haven't had to look for what else is out there.

Pontificating to myself in the bathroom, I thought, It didn't matter that the basic building blocks of the thing we called love are just extraneous sensations. Like the octopus, we've all evolved in the course of feeling around for survival and propagation. I could try to diminish love by calling it chemical or fake, but that was like calling the moon a giant rock. Love has evolved past its practical necessity, far past the basic affection we recognize and personify in animals. The mystery of love isn't where it came from, it's where it is going. There is no other living creature on this earth with the capacity to love with the complexity we do. There is no limit to what we're capable of in love, or what love can look like, or how love can be expressed.

These thoughts were cruder in that moment, as I looked at my shining, buzzed reflection. It mattered, it didn't matter; my love was fake, and also the realest thing about me. Soon I'd be cut off from the locus of its energy yet again. When I walked back out there, it would be about time to get the check, and then that would be it until the next time we ran into each other somewhere, if ever. Nothing else would happen with this person. He could be attracted to me still; he could be basking in my obvious attraction to him. He could just need a little thrill. I didn't want to let him go again, even as I recognized he wasn't really there with me in the first place. The glow inside was still valid to me, even if I couldn't glow for him again.

When I returned, we got the check and then walked out onto the street.

"There's this great bookstore around here," he said.

"Oh yeah!" I exclaimed, recognizing a reprieve. "I love that place. Should we go?"

He shrugged, "Yeah, why not."

I moved in that direction and he grabbed my coat.

"That's the wrong way."

"I don't think so," I said, having no idea. I started to walk the wrong way again, and he took hold of my hand, pulling me along.

His hand. His hand.

We dipped into the bookstore, chatting in a subdued manner in the sudden bright light. I picked up a book on marine life, commenting, "This looks cool."

"Really? Oh, right. You were reading that octopus book."

"Yes, I was," I said, surprised he remembered what I'd been reading over a year ago, when he'd come to pick me up from Dylan's house—that weekend when I had first visited him in L.A.

Eventually, we ran out of spines to finger and went back outside. It seemed like we were close, very close, to making the usual mistake. Suddenly, he leaned in and gave me a quick squeeze, patting me jovially.

"Well, I gotta go. See you soon!" he said. He walked briskly away, waving backward in a slightly drunken manner.

He reminded himself, I thought. *Good for him.*

Then I was alone on the sidewalk. There are many shades of loneliness and not enough words to describe them. This was the loneliness of knowing there are no more dreams to dream about someone. A very flat sort of feeling. Loving someone had given shape to a lot of my days, added poignancy to a lot of my nights; it had motivated me, made me feel anger, sorrow, passion. It was even part of the final decision to move my life from one place to another, both internally and externally.

Love is a story, one I'd heard many, many times before. While in love, I could very easily picture what a future would look like, if Adrian (or anyone) would only love me back. Even knowing he never would, I'd been waiting for some denouement to make sense of it all. This was the moment of truly accepting it would never happen, no matter how many unplanned encounters we might have, in coffee shop after coffee shop. In fact, I would see him again over the coming months, and each time he'd be a little more faded, a little less animated by my love, until he was just a regular guy. I'd understand then how much importance I'd constructed within another person, instead of building a world of love inside myself. I'd placed it in somebody to follow, instead of planting it inside to grow.

. . .

The evening of my thirty-fifth birthday arrived. My friends and I ended up at a crowded bar that I almost immediately wanted to leave. After an hour or so, I took a break on its slightly less busy patio, then sat on a short storage box by the garbage. I needed a break from celebrating myself. Since nine out of my eleven party guests were queer, we'd searched for a gay bar in the neighborhood to dance at. Disappointingly, aside from some gay pornography wallpapering the two bathroom stalls, the venue seemed aggressively straight. It was clearly a birthday bar, and many parties were happening that same night.

I took a deep breath and lifted my face toward the sky, my head feeling too heavy on my spine. Throwing my own party had been a bad idea. Sitting around the rented house in Venice was awkward until my friends poured a case of wine on the situation. It wasn't yet midnight, and everyone was sloshed. I had remained mostly sober, not wanting to forget my special occasion. I was too tense to really enjoy myself, dissatisfied over expectations I hadn't admitted to having. I'd wanted the night to be effortless and fun and to feel loved. Instead, I was feeling the weight of my friends' attention and none of the joy of it. Is this fun? Are you having fun? I wanted to see *them* have fun, to feel like someone so delightful they make other people happy just by being around. Instead, I felt like a burden no one quite knew how to handle—my usual personality motif. Sensing my discomfort, my friends tried even harder to inject the night with merriment, which made me feel even guiltier for having a bad time.

This is why you can't have nice things, I thought. They'd all been gamely trying to start a dance party for at least an hour, to no avail, and now I was literally hiding.

Just then, a drunk woman wearing a birthday tiara fell into the trash can next to me. Four other women rushed forward to fish her out, crowding around my knees.

"Where's your purse?" one asked her fallen pal. The drunken birthday girl shook her head, so her friend persisted, "Is it inside?"

She nodded. I reached down into the can and grabbed the strap of the woman's clearly visible missing purse and said, "Here it is."

They stared at it like I'd pulled a rabbit out of a hat, then all began thanking me profusely at once.

"It's her birthday!" one announced, as though that were a clear explanation for the mix-up.

"Mine too," I said, a little shyly.

"*Really?*" my birthday doppelgänger demanded.

"Yes," I answered, with a serious nod.

"Magic," one of them whispered, then asked. "How old are you?"

"Thirty-five," I replied. They reacted with such collective shock that I was fairly certain they misheard me and thought I said forty-five. I looked slightly younger than my age due to an intense commitment to constant sunscreen use, but not much. I think they were just trying to give me a birthday gift.

"I'm thirty-two!" yelled the birthday girl, grabbing my hand.

"Well, happy birthday!"

"Happy birthday!"

Soon we were all murmuring happy birthday to one another and holding hands.

"Come inside and sit with us," said the birthday girl. I told them I'd be right in, then continued to hide on the patio for much longer than was appropriate for a party host.

I didn't really believe in birthday magic. When my mom was thirty-five, I'd just been born. I'd been born via emergency C-section, and she'd had no anesthesia in effect when they cut into her. She'd been hospitalized for a month afterward. When the nurses brought me to see her, she said she cried because my armpits were too big. She would always laugh when she told me that story and imitate her own weepy voice, making herself sound like a child instead of a woman who'd just been vivisected while fully conscious.

I remember the first time I thought, It's too late for that for me. I was watching a film of Ginger Rogers and Fred Astaire dancing and realized that to be able to dance like that I would have had to start years and years ago. That's how aging feels sometimes, as though it's too late to start doing things. Thirty-five was still young, but being the same age as my mom was with no children of my own, it felt too late to start a family. It was too late to be married in my twenties, too late to have ended up with my college romance, too late to grow up with my high school honey. And the years would only speed up, leaving more and more things I didn't have time for behind.

On my ninth birthday, I had a temper tantrum in the middle of the party. My mom had a bunch of people over, her friends and mine, and I hid away from them in the bedroom, crying. I don't know what set me off—I just kept on crying, because I knew I was ruining the party by crying in the first place. It was this godawful pattern I couldn't break out of. Finally, I cried until I was exhausted and thus calm enough to rejoin the festivities. Here I was, once again having a tantrum, ruining my party by feeling too old to enjoy life, even though it was right there in front of me.

I was tired of my tantrum. I was tired of probing for meaning in everything that had happened over the last three years, over the entire course of my life. I was tired of looking for love and answers. I was tired of my primal urges and of societal expectations and of romcoms dictating what I should be spending this one precious life wanting.

There is so much urgency about finding something external that even when you have that thing, there's the next thing, and the next. There's a greater state of completion that's always then accompanied by a constant, gnawing sense of dissatisfaction with what you already have.

I closed my eyes and pictured the inner pond I'd always thought of as a metaphor for depression or loss or loneliness, cold and deep with a thin frozen surface barely keeping me safe from the murk underneath. I stood on the creaking shield of glossy ice, surrounded by another ring of frost, the borders beyond that lost in fog. The ice began to melt. It thinned until cracks fractured the surface; water poured through, sucking the fragments below, churning them, filling my shoes, sucking me downward, where my body dissolved and the cold didn't matter. The water flooded the banks, melting the snow, lapping beyond its known borders until they eroded. Then the pond wasn't a pond; it was a glass-smooth lake stretching as far as the horizon. It was a river passing outside the train window. It was waves breaking around the feet of a gull. The water filled a well where I could always drink. The water fell as rain, restoring the dry earth and then returning to the sky then falling, eternally. The water was a lagoon, a bay, and then a pond once more, filled with slippery koi, carefully planted with lilies, skipped across by dragonflies.

Beside the water was a patch of grass where I could sit, myself again. For a moment I rested there, feeling the warmth and life within. Then I opened my eyes, stood up, and went inside.

My friends were waiting. I joined them and we kept dancing, pretending to enjoy it until a subtle shift happened and we weren't pretending anymore at all.

A Lost-Loved Human Face

About one year later, in March of 2020, my mom got sick. I was in Los Angeles, talking to her over the phone until she was too out of breath to answer. Her doctors were certain she had COVID, but at the time tests were very scarce. They warned her to stay home unless she absolutely couldn't breathe. I spent the days in my apartment, where I now lived alone, walking from the bathroom to the kitchen to my desk, reading the reports of how New York City had become emptied as the wealthy fled, how ambulance sirens wailed all day and night, how there were refrigerated trucks driven up to hospitals for morgue overflow. I wanted so badly to be home, and traveling home seemed incredibly irresponsible.

Worry and indecision was the story for so many people, so I will skip ahead and say my mother recovered. She got better, though the virus kicked up new symptoms of her degenerative illness. Worry didn't dissipate. How could it?

Then, in September, my grandmother died. Not from COVID-19. She had a stroke, and I said goodbye to her unconscious form over FaceTime. I wished so much then that I had gone home, that I could have waved to her from the street one more time before she left.

In the first month of the pandemic, I realized I was living as I had lived for many years in my past: sedentary, self-soothing with food and television and romance novels. Slightly agoraphobic yet forcing myself to at least go for a walk so I'd be able to sleep that night. Wearing a groove into the center of my mattress again. It was ludicrous how familiar pandemic life felt.

When I stayed in bed because I was certain I'd never find anyone to share my life with and not because I was trying to prevent the spread of a deadly virus, it felt like running the clock out. Time slid across me like a rock in the creek bed. I did nothing because it felt like there was nothing to be done. I'd let the spring pass, miss the flowers on the trees, and think, *next year*. The next year would go by, and the other people would wake up again to possibility as I remained frozen through another season.

I did change my life. Through determined effort and small steps and different choices, I became someone who could do things again. Then a pandemic put me right back in the same place. In bed. Alone. Staring into an opaque future without much faith that I would ever find anything worth looking for again. Loneliness can feel like a kind of emotional enclosure from which you can't escape. It does not have the same literal boundaries of a shelter-in-place order.

There was no universal experience at the beginning of the pandemic, even if it did seem like everyone was feeling lonely in some way those first few months. They were lonely for different reasons, even if those reasons were all triggered by a singular virus. They were lonely because they were isolated due to their age or physical necessity, as people believed at first that it was only the elderly or immunocompromised who really had anything to avoid. They were lonely because they couldn't travel, or because they were trying to adhere to social distancing rules and "flatten the curve," a phrase that soon came to seem meaningless as U.S. policies pushed us toward a herd-immunity model of "recovery" that equated to mass death. They were lonely because their work was labeled "essential" and put them in danger, creating a separation between their value and everyone else's. They were lonely because they lost their jobs or lost opportunities or lost dreams that had been so close to being realized.

During that first month, I wanted so much to be with my family. Yet, I kept thinking, "Your family can't keep you safe."

There might be times in your life when quite the opposite has felt true, when a parent or brother or the responsibility of having a child has saved you. COVID-19 didn't care about any of that. The highest transmission rates were in family units, where people lived and breathed together, passing the virus among generations and seeing multiple deaths under one roof. Family was a liability that made being alone the surest way to survive. The coronavirus revealed how flimsy that "us against them" mentality ends up being. Your family cannot ever really be safe when other people aren't.

It's not surprising to me how swiftly the federal and many state governments shifted the pandemic narrative from "we'll get through this together" to "surviving is your personal responsibility." If avoiding a highly contagious and deadly virus is left to the individual, that means the government doesn't have to pay out unemployment, or cover healthcare, or address the housing crisis, or invest in social services at all, really. They could, but they won't, because that would mean that whenever the pandemic ended, they might not find it so easy to take those things back.

The pandemic was obviously a moment of crisis, but it's much more honest to say that there has been a crisis for a long time and the people shielded from it by their race and class were feeling the effects of that crisis in ways they hadn't conceived of before.

A lot of the people who knew I was writing about loneliness would tell me that it was a timely subject. Over text, of course. It didn't feel that way to me. The loneliness I'd felt before the pandemic was quaint; it had involved meeting new people in crowded bars, hugging, holding hands, dancing. Before, I was lonely in a way that contained far more delights. I appreciate that loneliness differently now.

It is true that the things I already thought were separating people have been amplified by the pandemic. Even the divide between single people and married people with kids was revved up, with periodic Twitter discourse breaking out over who had it harder: the parents who could no longer take any breaks from parenting or the single person who hadn't touched another human in almost a year. Most of the people with the time to argue about this on Twitter will be fine, though the passion around these subjects bordered on desperation.

My friend Tessa, the one who never wanted kids, had actually worked in childcare before she gained success in an entertainment career.

"It really seems like parents are just becoming aware of all the work of raising their kids that they don't have to deal with, because someone else is always doing it," she told me, on a masked meetup at the park.

Another single friend with asthma, who didn't leave her apartment for six months, told me over Zoom, "Couples never check in on me. They don't get what this is like, being completely alone all the time."

But it wasn't just the parents who ordinarily paid for childcare who were suffering. For every person typing furiously online there are thousands more without help, who were still expected to show up at jobs outside their homes every day even as schools closed. In New York, it was revealed that some of the resistance to closing schools in early March was because over 114,000 homeless children depended on them for basic necessities like food or even laundry. Over one hundred thousand homeless children in one of the richest cities in America, and the story became a blip as more and more cracks in our systems were split wider by the mounting pressure.

There wasn't really a "silver lining" in 2020, in my opinion, so please don't take this as one: catastrophes are an opportunity for redesigning things. It might be years before we know if this opportunity is being utilized to make people's lives better or worse. For myself, whenever I can return to what "normal" was, I hope I'll have grown beyond it. At the moment, I am thinking about the ways I've failed other people. I am thinking about how I never want to do that again, and I wonder if that is possible.

When I first started writing this book, I envisioned writing something about how I conquered loneliness or, at minimum, found management strategies for it. I wanted answers to the question of what we can do to make life fuller, more joyful when we're alone. I wanted it to be helpful for the individual.

I also wanted to have an answer to the question I know people will ask: Do I still think I'll be alone forever?

To the latter, I'll say that since the timeline of this story ended, I have felt again, felt deeply, affectionately, and with a heart full of hope; I've been hurt again, disappointed, and kicked in all the tender spots I'll probably never learn to armor. I have continued to date (as public health allows) and will keep doing so for as long as it's more fun than not. There is no answer to the question of whether I think I'll be alone forever, because I can't see the future, but its importance recedes as time passes. There are many more interesting questions. One day, I might find the right person with whom to share whatever answers I've found.

About the former, I now believe there are definitely things you can do to alleviate a sense of isolation—small movements that will help you to make friends, find new hobbies, feel better for a brief interval. Even learning how to talk to another person takes practice. Through these interventions, your life could completely transform, and that's an awesome accomplishment. Taking on these practices myself, I learned there were certain things about me that needed to change: my passivity, my fear of loss, my inability to be truly vulnerable with another person. Through dating, I rediscovered how to take chances, learned to become less reactive to rejection, to mature in the ways I'd avoided for six years. Through falling in love, I came to understand that I can't accept the very least from someone, even if I want to take anything I can get. I learned everyone is on their own journey that has nothing to do with yours. And that even when feelings aren't reciprocated, they're meaningful. I honor my own ability to have them.

These were all things I personally needed to do. The only problem there is that thinking about loneliness solely through the lens of what an individual can do is in itself isolating. Now I think that when talking about loneliness, it should never focus on what each person can do to make themselves more compatible with things as they are, more attractive, more self-actualized, more whatever you're told you need to be to *deserve* connection. We should talk about loneliness in order to identify the ways in which we are disconnected by structural systems external to us. Let's think about how we regard others outside of our homes, and how much we really need them. Let's think about collectivity.

The economic and social conditions that separate people now aren't the natural order, and the idea that a romantic relationship will do all the work to alleviate loneliness isn't that old. The news that loneliness is on the rise and that its consequences are disastrous to public health means we're at a point when a lot can change, if we have the imagination for it.

In regards to having imagination, there is an example that comes to my mind a lot; I'm sorry to say it's kind of an awful one, which might be why it lingers. I'm not sure what someone who doesn't live their life plugged in to the Internet knows about incel culture. To simplify the modern meaning of the word, incels are generally cis men, usually young, who believe they have been forced to be involuntarily celibate because of rejection from women. As a group, they might be one of the most well-known faces of loneliness outside of the trope of the single career girl.

More specifically, incels believe that they're *owed* sex. And not from women who might reasonably be considered on par with them for looks and charm—they want young, attractive, virginal women, despite the fact they speak of those women in the most denigrating and hateful ways possible and see themselves as physically repellent as well. Many incels believe the only reason they can't get laid is their looks. And yet. Their anger toward women is wrapped up in feeling like they're not getting what they deserve.

Who among us hasn't felt like they aren't getting what they deserve? It's a relatable feeling. Had I been angry over the years when I didn't find the relationship I'd been implicitly promised by rom-coms and love songs? Yes. There was also a part of me that believed if I were just more attractive, I'd get the devotion so many other women seem to get from their partners—partners who appeared to be in a long line to love those women.

The original incel was actually a woman named Alana, who lived in Toronto. She started a website called Alana's Involuntary Celibacy Project in 1997 about her difficulties with dating, and it became a kind of forum where mostly other women shared the difficulties of feeling disconnected from sexual adulthood. After that period, she moved on and did start dating, according to an interview she did with the BBC more than two decades later. She left her project behind, not realizing how her description, "involuntary celibacy," was co-opted by communities on Reddit and notorious forums like

4chan and 8chan, mutating and merging with misogynist Men's Rights ideologies. She only found out years later when a series of men describing themselves as incels started murdering people.

In 2014, a man named Elliot Rodger killed six people and injured over a dozen more in Isla Vista, California, then died by suicide, leaving behind a video manifesto about all the ways women had rejected him and driven him to mass murder. His name would be cited by Alek Minassian, who in 2018 would run a van onto the sidewalk in Toronto, deliberately targeting pedestrians and killing ten.

"I didn't notice what was going on because I wasn't paying attention. My dating life was going okay. I didn't want to think about my history as a late bloomer," Alana told the BBC. Why did anyone expect Alana to be paying attention at all? She'd started a project about self-reflection, discussion, and support for lonely people. Then she'd moved on. What a difference in approach Alana had compared to the men who corrupted her ideas.

Reactions to the violence of white men always seem to be far more compassionate than they are for anyone else. Shortly after Minassian's mass-murder spree, *The New York Times* published an opinion piece by staff writer Ross Douthat. He seemed to take the complaints of male incels quite seriously.

In the article, Douthat claims that modern society focuses so intensely on sexual conquest, it's bound to warp any man's perspective on how much sex they should be having. Douthat suggests that the breakdown of family values, chastity, and moderation have oversexed the population, and that is what led to violence, not male entitlement. He then examines the fringe idea that the solution would be the "redistribution of sex."

"By this I mean that as offensive or utopian the redistribution of sex might sound, the idea is entirely responsive to the logic of late-modern sexual life, and its pursuit would be entirely characteristic of a recurring pattern in liberal societies," he opines. "First, because like other forms of neoliberal deregulation, the sexual revolution created new winners and losers, new hierarchies to replace the old ones, privileging the beautiful and rich and socially adept in new ways and relegating others to new forms of loneliness and frustration."

Beautiful, rich, and charming people didn't have a leg up before? I think he really means that women were once forced to marry whomever they could find because they didn't have the alternative of supporting themselves. As that changed, fewer heterosexual men were guaranteed a woman in the house. What pretzels Douthat is willing to bend himself into to justify all sorts of heinous things, like state-mandated sex. He goes on to say that sex robots will eventually be able to relieve some of these pressures, confirming his perception that women are objects meant to satiate men's demands.

There isn't really anything new to what Douthat suggests, since what he essentially wants is to turn back to an even worse time. It is rare, however, to see people talking so soberly about how society could be dramatically restructured to help with loneliness, because the people who need it can't help themselves. Douthat isn't telling incels to try to make themselves more attractive, try to get some new hobbies, go to therapy, or work harder to connect. He thinks the government could intervene here! Personal loneliness can become a political issue for anyone under the right circumstances.

It's possible that the lonely single gal has been in the collective imagination for too long to inspire innovation, or it's because guys like Douthat think there's a clear solution for single women—just get married to whoever will take us.

In justice to the incels who don't kill people, single, sexless men were right that as a moderately attractive woman I'd been able to instigate sexual contact as soon as I really tried, a belief they hold about all women. I think anyone who identifies as an incel is very wrong, though, that what they want is just sex with the most submissive young virgin they can find. An incel is only another person whose perspective has been so influenced by what they're told is normal that they've cut off all avenues of escape from the idea.

What other avenues could we take? Can we do better than suggesting what's been done before?

In *All the Single Ladies,* Rebecca Traister offers a few practical solutions for how single people can safely remain single, and for making marriage more egalitarian for those who choose it. She wants strong equal-pay protections, a higher minimum wage, a national healthcare system, mandates that insurance companies cover IVF and reproductive care, subsidized housing for single people (it is currently not illegal at the federal level to discriminate against potential renters because of marital status), reform of local laws that make it difficult for people to live communally who aren't related, universal childcare, and government-mandated and -subsidized paid leave for both parents after the birth of a child.

This list of transformative, radically progressive suggestions is thrown into her book's Appendix. In her last para-
graph, she writes:

"We are increasingly a land of free people, who at various
times in our lives enjoy companionship and care, and, at other
times, do not. We must not continue to function as if every
worker has a wife caring for his home and his children for free,
or as if every wife has a worker on whose paychecks she must
depend."

Author Bella DePaulo, who wrote *Singled Out: How Singles
Are Stereotyped, Stigmatized, and Ignored and Still Live Happily Ever
After*, also has some uncompromising suggestions in her book
for how society could transform. DePaulo's ideas for ending
obligatory couplehood would be an extreme overhaul of current systems. She suggests breaking down the power of marriage immediately by taking the government out of it. It would
be an institution left entirely to churches or secular businesses
to handle, essentially demolishing all government protections
created through the marriage ceremony, truly separating
church and state.

Obviously, that would be a dangerous proposition for a
great many people, especially those in the United States who
depend on a marriage certificate for a visa. That danger illus-
trates just how much power the marriage ceremony has—one
of the "simplest" ways to reside in the United States safely and
legally as an immigrant is to bind yourself to someone. I knew
a number of couples who had done exactly that, some of
whom were in love, and some of whom married so one partner could stay in the country.

DePaulo's focus isn't on the complications or perils of this idea. She's more interested in seeing the benefits of legal marriage funneled toward progressive policies. She also wants universal healthcare and a huge expansion of the Family and Medical Leave Act to accommodate caretakers who help *anyone* ill or disabled, within or without their immediate family unit. She wants to abolish joint tax filing and to make it illegal to question someone's reason for taking time off at work. Interestingly, married people with children feel they're stigmatized for taking time off related to family, and single people think their reasons for needing time off are taken less seriously than their counterparts with family obligations. A change in policy might be to everyone's benefit.

Marriage won't truly end, according to DePaulo, until the sense of validation that comes with it fades. If her legislative suggestions came to pass, people would see less material or social safety in the act of coupling. Couples would be less inclined to attach so much of their identity to the process of dating and cohabiting, and perhaps even the sense of ownership around biological children would dissipate, allowing people to recognize a wider need for all kids to share and receive care in society, whoever their technical parents are.

With this freedom, being in love could become a much more joyful venture, something to participate in simply for the satisfaction of connection, the power of intimacy, and the fun of sex, rather than as the supreme confirmation of human value.

In most of the studies on the subject, the word "loneliness" is used even when what is being described are the effects of poverty and discrimination: isolation, unstable housing, de facto age segregation, a need for healthcare, or even a basic lack of leisure time. Constant stress and dejection. I really believe there is so much focus on singleness because grappling with these other issues would require a change of everything around us. I also believe change is possible.

There are some transformational changes already happening, often very slowly, because it's quite hard to organize single people around a common cause. People are single for all sorts of reasons, from every demographic, with a limitless number of perspectives on their lives. And DePaulo's claim that making singleness synonymous with loneliness causes discrimination is likely correct. But thinking about how to make unmarried people's lives better is a helpful way to conceive new legislation, because there are still so many ways that pairing off is financially and politically rewarded, leaving everyone else behind.

There are people who have been on the front lines of making these shifts happen on local and national levels, especially in historically marginalized communities. LGBTQ+ people have long been establishing networks of support to survive the often violent rejection by the dominant culture and even their own biological families. A "chosen family" is one made up of people who may or may not be lovers, who may live together or not, but who consider themselves a cohesive unit. A chosen family acknowledges that frequently, the most important people in your life, the ones who really show up to take care of you, aren't related to you at all.

Gay marriage has only been legal on a federal level in the United States since 2015. Younger gay couples might choose to marry, but in 2010, 64 percent of LGBTQ+ baby boomers said they had a chosen family, according to a survey from the MetLife Mature Market Institute. Chosen families remain a stabilizing and supportive part of queer culture, and they've exerted a powerful influence on how families in general are categorized in the United States. Chosen families have been officially recognized in New York, L.A., and Chicago; members can now use paid time off if those families need care. In 2015, President Barack Obama signed an executive order guaranteeing federal contractors paid sick leave to care for any family members of "blood or affinity whose close association with the employee is the equivalent of a family relationship." Similar local laws have arrived in Austin, Texas; Rhode Island; New Jersey; Arizona; and Cook County, Illinois, the county that contains Chicago.

Despite these expansions, for a lot of couples, getting married is the most streamlined way to have their union recognized by the state, and the most familiar framework for protecting financial assets and property, making it easier for courts to know what to do should that marriage end in divorce. That leaves people without a marriage certificate in a difficult position—including people who aren't romantically involved but who have built a life together.

The nonprofit Unmarried Equality, which advocates for the rights of unmarried people, suggests on their website that people throw parties to celebrate their friendships—for your BFF, or for an entire friend group. But, Unmarried Equality warns, these events do not "involve laws or government agencies in any way."

What if friendship commitments were recognized by the state, or the benefits of legally recognized chosen families were extended? How might that change the statistics about, for example, who can expect elder care? In 2017, Hawaii enacted

Kupuna Care, a stipend offered to anyone providing care to an older adult, regardless of family ties. I know of a commune on Staten Island formed in the seventies where members are aging out, unable to maintain their structure without younger members entering to help maintain and run the household. What if New York State provided younger families with a stipend to come in and provide care? It would mean stabilized housing and a continuation of a communal living situation that had benefited dozens of people over the years.

When I lived in a communal home in my midtwenties, I had seriously discussed with some of my roommates what it would be like to raise children together. It was largely a hypothetical, but one that sounded much more possible to me than raising a child with one other person who was, additionally, my committed romantic partner. Most modern jurisprudence on child guardianship is dictated by the "rule of two," meaning only two people are allowed to be legal parents of a child—generally the person who gives birth and the person they are married to or whose name is on the birth certificate, or the two legal parents in an adoption. With the complicated nature of conception, birth, and family relationships, it has begun to be recognized that in some cases more than two people should legally retain the right of parental guardianship. Most notably, in 2013, California passed SB-274, a bill allowing that in very rare instances, three or more adults could be legal parents to a child. Any state could change their rules around parental rights and not delineate so firmly who matters in a child's life.

Beyond the scope of family life, we could make a bigger leap to the other ways people connect with and support each other in the places they live. How can we create the financial security needed to put down roots? If you want to alleviate loneliness, join a union. Worker protections mean higher wages and more stability, leading to stronger communities. Better yet, support worker-owned co-ops, so employment in a town or city isn't contingent on corporations and monopolies based far from home. The work week could be shorter, the minimum wage far higher. Changing how work figures in our lives could accommodate lifestyles that center family and socialization over survival.

Or we can talk about how urban planning can alleviate loneliness. Instead of cordoning off the elderly in distant communities, they could be integrated into family neighborhoods. We could invest in crumbling infrastructure, especially public transit services, making it easier for people to socialize, get to work, attend events outside of their work life. Accessible transportation services for the disabled could remove them from the default state of exclusion that's so institutionalized by abled society. We could have town squares that give people a place to gather instead of rows of unwalkable streets far from city centers. We could have tenant unions fighting for affordable rents or promoting co-operatives, instead of a housing crisis and empty buildings.

Universal healthcare, which both Traister and DePaulo mention, would alleviate loneliness. Traister mentions family-planning services like IVF, but that's just one aspect of how guaranteed healthcare would support lonely people living untraditional lifestyles. The studies by Eric Klinenberg on elder-care and Julianne Holt-Lunstad on the loneliness epidemic all emphasize that people experiencing social isolation are often those who are homebound because of health issues, especially as they age. In the United States, many people are pushed into vast amounts of debt by an accident or illness. The stress of damaged physical health and financial ruin isolates people. Reliable mental health services, especially therapy, could reduce a sense of isolation. Loneliness is called an epidemic, and yet we avoid connecting the dots when it comes to the cost and scope of healthcare.

We could abolish punitive systems that create "loneliness" as the least of their ills, from the racist prison-industrial complex to the violently xenophobic U.S. Immigration and Customs Enforcement. Both break up families, with the burden falling disproportionately on Black, Latino, and Indigenous people. During the pandemic, news outlets reported that hand sanitizer produced in New York State was being made by inmates at their Great Meadow Correctional Facility, even as coronavirus ravaged prisons where few had access to hand sanitizer themselves. The situation was the perfect encapsulation of how people are dehumanized and disenfranchised by the prison-industrial complex, then expected to remain out of sight and suffer. Even if it were true that prisons function as a way to reform character or extract "debts to society" (they don't), there could be no excuse for the stigma and separation that can dog a formerly incarcerated person the rest of their life.

In the summer of 2020, when protests over the murder of George Floyd by officer Derek Chauvin began, it wasn't only about racist police violence. It was about how the pandemic was already killing Black people at a far higher rate than white people in the United States. It was about racial justice in healthcare, housing, and the workplace, and the need for meaningful reparations. Many of the issues white people are just becoming aware of under the extremity of a pandemic have been suffered by Black and Indigenous people since the United States was colonized. COVID-19 put a lid on a pot that was already simmering. All the justified rage and pain boiled over.

Protesting was one of the few group activities of 2020, and it felt meaningful to participate. Prison abolition and defunding the police had been relatively fringe proposals, as activist for prison abolition Mariame Kaba says in an essay from her 2021 book, *We Do This 'Til We Free Us.* The essay was originally published in 2014, and addresses the protests in Ferguson in response to the murder of Michael Brown by officer Darren Wilson, and the ensuing proposals for police reform.

"Advocates call for reforms suggesting that the current practices and systems are 'broken' and/or unjust. There is a (racist) backlash by people who support the police. A very few people whisper that the essential nature of policing is oppressive and is not susceptible to any reforms, thus only abolition is realistic. These people are considered heretics by most. I've spent years participating in one way or another in this cycle."

According to Kaba, only six years ago, abolishing the police was a proposal from "heretics." It became a common phrase on protest signs across the country in the summer of 2020. It's a testament to the speed with which ideas can become mainstream when evidence of their validity mounts— and to the widespread recognition that community health is more underfunded every year as the police become more militarized. Even people sensitive to the words "defund the police" were likely to understand "fund education, fund healthcare, fund community centers," and that money is better spent on these things than policing.

"Everything worthwhile is done with other people," Kaba says in her book, as she's interviewed by sociologist Eve L. Ewing. That's the framework within which she approaches activism and organizing, and I find myself thinking it often since I read the words.

To implement even a few of the changes above would require a huge shift in political power. We'd need representatives who push to tax the ultrawealthy, and put those taxes back into the communities that prop them up. Change like this requires a huge shift in thinking, in how we see one another and what we think we owe one another.

Each of these issues is limitless, and the movements based around them are interconnected. Mentioning them seems far outside the scope of my personal story, but as the pandemic unfolded, it became more and more ridiculous *not* to mention them. I've realized that ignoring the much bigger reasons why people are isolated denies that they are often *purposefully* isolated. Together, we could change so much, but not if we think we're alone in loneliness, spending all our time scrambling to find a way out by ourselves.

We are all grappling with ways to break out of the narrow story we're told about what's possible, either by choice or necessity. One person can't alleviate every issue that intersects with the "loneliness epidemic," but these are the suggestions I've come up with for a very small start: if you're lonely, pick one thing you can do to make the world a more just place and find the other people trying to do the same. Pick one thing you can do that separates you from other people's humanity and refuse to do that thing. And pick one thing you think is wrong with you that justifies your loneliness and ask, "Who gains power from me believing this about myself?"

The deepest love has to include the work of solidarity: sometimes messy, boring, painful, sometimes violent and frightening. It's a love that goes beyond the sensations of body and mind, beyond the euphoria of romance, past the door-step of my home. The capacity to love and to let it encompass more instead of less is the only thing that has ever made me feel less lonely.

ACKNOWLEDGMENTS

....

First, I must thank the people who have been most key in shaping my psyche, for better or worse, in particular my mother, my grandparents, my dad, and my friends, especially the ones who appear in this story.

This book would absolutely not exist without Susan Golomb. I don't think anyone else has ever before taken the kind of chance she did on me, and it's really a big deal and a gift I'll value always. Thank you also to Mariah Stovall for her notes and time invested in corralling my thoughts when they were becoming a proposal.

Thank you to my editor, Whitney Frick, who supported and guided me throughout this process, and gave my writing direction whenever it went astray. I have been so lucky to be in your care.

There are a bunch of people who helped me who might not even remember doing so, but I do: Malin von Euler-Hogan, Beth Newell, Kelsey Murphy, and Rosalie Knecht answered all my emails when it would have been very easy to ignore them. Thank you! You never know when answering an email might change someone's life.

Thank you to the team at The Dial Press and Random House, including Rose Fox, Avideh Bashirrad, Debbie Aroff, Jessalyn Foggy, Karen Fink, Luke Epplin, Mimi Lipson, Donna Cheng, and Grace Han. Thank you so much to Sarah Braybrooke at Scribe and her team. Thank you to the staff at *Jezebel*, who let me write essays people would actually see.

And finally, thank you to the people whom I've fallen in love with, especially when it was against my better judgment. You know who you are.

BIBLIOGRAPHY

·················

Administration for Community Living, U.S. Department of Health and Human Services. "Costs of Care." Long Term Care, last modified February 18, 2020, acl.gov/ltc/costs-and -who-pays.

Beck, Julie. "The Concept Creep of 'Emotional Labor.'" *The Atlantic*, November 28, 2018. www.theatlantic.com/family/ archive/2018/11/arlie-hochschild-housework-isnt -emotional-labor/576637/.

Berman, Robby. "COVID-19 Has Produced 'Alarming' Increase in Loneliness." Medical News Today, November 25, 2020. www.medicalnewstoday.com/articles/alarming-covid -19-study-shows-80-of-respondents-report-significant -symptoms-of-depression.

Bertoni, Steven. "WeWork's $20 Billion Office Party: The Crazy Bet That Could Change How the World Does Business." *Forbes*, October 23, 2017. forbes.com/sites/ stevenbertoni/2017/10/02/the-way-we-work/?sh= 321e6d131b18.

Blau, Melinda, and Karen L. Fingerman. *Consequential Strangers:*

Turning Everyday Encounters into Life-Changing Moments. New York: W. W. Norton & Company, 2010.

Blei, Daniela. "The False Promises of Wellness Culture." JSTOR, January 4, 2017. daily.jstor.org/the-false-promises -of-wellness-culture/.

Bricker, Darrell, and John Ibbitson. *Empty Planet: The Shock of Global Population Decline.* New York: Penguin Random House, 2020.

Brodesser-Akner, Taffy. "Losing It in the Anti-Dieting Age." *The New York Times Magazine,* August 2, 2017. www.nytimes .com/2017/08/02/magazine/weight-watchers-oprah-losing -it-in-the-anti-dieting-age.html.

Chozik, Amy. "Adam Neumann and the Art of Failing Up." *The New York Times,* May 18, 2020. www.nytimes.com/2019/11/ 02/business/adam-neumann-wework-exit-package.html.

Coontz, Stephanie. *Marriage, a History: How Love Conquered Marriage.* New York: Penguin Books, 2006.

Cox, E., G. Henderson, and R. Baker. "Silver Cities: Realising the Potential of Our Growing Older Population." IPPR North 2014. ippr.org/publications/silver-cities-realising-the -potential-of-our-growing-older-population.

Crispin, Jessa. "How Not to Be Elizabeth Gilbert." *Boston Review,* July 20, 2015. bostonreview.net/books-ideas/jessa -crisipin-female-travel-writing.

DePaulo, Bella. "Everything You Think You Know About Single People Is Wrong." *The Washington Post,* February 8, 2016. www.washingtonpost.com/news/in-theory/wp/2016/02/ 08/everything-you-think-you-know-about-single-people-is -wrong/.

DePaulo, Bella. *Singled Out: How Singles Are Stereotyped, Stigma-*

tized, and Ignored and Still Live Happily Ever After. New York: St. Martin's Press, 2006.

Douthat, Ross. "The Redistribution of Sex." *The New York Times,* May 2, 2018. www.nytimes.com/2018/05/02/ opinion/incels-sex-robots-redistribution.html.

Ehrenreich, Barbara. *Bright-Sided: How the Relentless Promotion of Positive Thinking Has Undermined America.* New York: Metropolitan Books, 2009.

Entis, Laura. "Scientists Are Working on a Pill for Loneliness." *The Guardian,* January 26, 2019. theguardian.com/us-news/ 2019/jan/26/pill-for-loneliness-psychology-science -medicine.

Farkas, Carol-Ann. "Bodies at Rest, Bodies in Motion: Physical Competence, Women's Fitness, and Feminism." *Genders 1998–2013.* University of Colorado, Boulder, April 1, 2007. www.colorado.edu/gendersarchive1998-2013/2007/04/01/ bodies-rest-bodies-motion-physical-competence-womens -fitness-and-feminism.

Fetters, Ashley. "The Five Years That Changed Dating." *The Atlantic,* December 21, 2018. www.theatlantic.com/family/ archive/2018/12/tinder-changed-dating/578698/.

Fisher, H. E. "Lust, Attraction, and Attachment in Mammalian Reproduction." *Human Nature* 9, no. 1 (March 1998): 23–52. doi.org/10.1007/s12110-998-1010-5.

Garcia, Patricia. "Why Women Are Choosing to Marry Themselves." *Vogue,* October 6, 2017. www.vogue.com/article/ women-marrying-themselves-sologamy.

Godfrey-Smith, Peter. *Other Minds: The Octopus, the Sea, and the Deep Origins of Consciousness.* New York: Farrar, Straus and Giroux, 2017.

Harari, Yuval Noah. *Sapiens: A Brief History of Humankind*. New York: Harper, 2015.

Harris, Aisha. "A History of Self-Care." *Slate*, April 5, 2017. slate.com/articles/arts/culturebox/2017/04/the_history_of_self_care.html.

Hochschild, Arlie Russell. *The Managed Heart: Commercialization of Human Feeling*. Oakland: University of California Press, 1983.

Holt-Lunstad, J., T. F. Robles, and D. A. Sbarra. "Advancing Social Connection as a Public Health Priority in the United States," *American Psychologist* 72, no. 6 (2017): 517–30.

Indiana University. "Study Finds Participants Feel Moral Outrage Toward Those Who Decide to Not Have Children." *ScienceDaily*, March 1, 2017. www.sciencedaily.com/releases/2017/03/170301084924.htm.

Jennings, Rebecca. "Facebook Has Always Been About Relationships. Now It's in the Dating Game." *Vox*, September 5, 2019. vox.com/the-goods/2019/9/5/20851020/facebook-dating-app-feature-how-to-use-news.

"The Jo Cox Loneliness Commission." n.d. The Jo Cox Foundation. www.jocoxfoundation.org/loneliness_commission.

Kinney, Alison. "The Rejection Lab." *Gay*, September 4, 2019. gay.medium.com/the-rejection-lab-89c69d2babe0.

Klinenberg, Eric. *Going Solo: The Extraordinary Rise and Surprising Appeal of Living Alone*. New York: Penguin Books, 2013.

Klinenberg, Eric. "Is Loneliness a Health Epidemic?" *The New York Times*, February 9, 2018. nytimes.com/2018/02/09/opinion/sunday/loneliness-health.html.

Lorde, Audre. *A Burst of Light*. Ithaca, N.Y.: Firebrand Books, 1988.

Marks, Nadine F., and James David Lambert. "Marital Status

Continuity and Change Among Young and Midlife Adults: Longitudinal Effects on Psychological Well-Being." *Journal of Family Issues* 19, no. 6 (1998). doi.org/10.1177/019251 398019006001.

Martin, Joyce A., Brady E. Hamilton, and Michelle J. K. Osterman. "Births in the United States, 2019." Centers for Disease Control and Prevention, National Center for Health Statistics. October 2020. www.cdc.gov/nchs/products/databriefs/db387.htm.

Metlife Mature Market Institute. "Still Out, Still Aging: The MetLife Study of Lesbian, Gay, Bisexual, and Transgender Baby Boomers." American Society on Aging, March 2010. www.asaging.org/sites/default/files/files/mmi-still-out-still-aging.pdf.

Molteni, Megan. "The World Might Actually Run Out of People." *Wired*, February 4, 2019. wired.com/story/the-world-might-actually-run-out-of-people.

Musick, Kelly, and Larry Bumpass. "Reexamining the Case for Marriage: Union Formation and Changes in Well-Being." *Journal of Marriage and Family* 74, no. 1 (2012): 1–18. onlinelibrary.wiley.com/doi/abs/10.1111/j.1741-3737.2011.00873.x.

Perel, Esther. *Mating in Captivity: Reconciling the Erotic and the Domestic*. New York: HarperCollins, 2006.

Putnam, Robert D. *Bowling Alone: The Collapse and Revival of American Community*. New York: Simon & Schuster, 2000.

Roseneil, Sasha. "It's Time to End the Tyranny of Coupledom." *The Guardian*, November 14, 2020. theguardian.com/commentisfree/2020/nov/14/coupledom-couple-norm-social-change.

Roseneil, Sasha, Isabel Crowhurst, Tone Hellesund, Ana Cristina Santos, and Mariya Stoilova. *The Tenacity of the Couple-Norm: Intimate Citizenship Regimes in a Changing Europe.* London: UCL Press, 2020.

Sachs, Andrea. "The Importance of Consequential Strangers." *Time,* September 22, 2009. content.time.com/time/health/article/0,8599,1925288,00.html.

Taormino, Tristan. *Opening Up: A Guide to Creating and Sustaining Open Relationships.* San Francisco: Cleis Press, 2008.

Taylor, Jim. "The Woman Who Founded the 'Incel' Movement." BBC News, August 30, 2018. www.bbc.com/news/world-us-canada-45284455.

Tiffany, Kaitlyn. "The Tinder Algorithm, Explained." *Vox,* March 18, 2019. www.vox.com/2019/2/7/18210998/tinder-algorithm-swiping-tips-dating-app-science.

Traister, Rebecca. *All the Single Ladies: Unmarried Women and the Rise of an Independent Nation.* New York: Simon & Schuster, 2016.

Treleaven, Sarah. "The Enduring Appeal of Escapism: A History of Wellness Retreats." *Elemental,* April 16, 2019. elemental.medium.com/the-obsession-with-wellness-retreats-goes-back-centuries-5c491cf2baa3.

Unmarried Equality. n.d. "Commitment Ceremonies F.A.Q." Unmarried Equality. www.unmarried.org/commitment-ceremonies/faq.

Walsh, Colleen. "Young Adults Hardest Hit by Loneliness During Pandemic." *The Harvard Gazette,* February 17, 2021. news.harvard.edu/gazette/story/2021/02/young-adults-teens-loneliness-mental-health-coronavirus-covid-pandemic.

Weigel, Moira. *Labor of Love: The Invention of Dating.* New York: Farrar, Straus and Giroux, 2016.

Whiteman, Honor. "Loneliness a Bigger Killer than Obesity, Say Researchers." Medical News Today, August 6, 2017. medicalnewstoday.com/articles/318723.

Whole30. n.d. "Whole30." Step 1. whole30.com/do-the -whole30/.

Williamson, Judith. *Consuming Passions: The Dynamics of Popular Culture.* New York: Marion Boyars, 1986.

Yglesias, Matthew. "The Controversy over WeWork's $47 Billion Valuation and Impending IPO, Explained." *Vox,* May 24, 2019. www.vox.com/2019/5/24/18630126/ wework-valuation-ipo-business-model-we-company.

PHOTO: JOANNA C. TILLMAN

AIMÉE LUTKIN is a writer and performer from New York City, where she was born and raised. Her writing has been featured on *Jezebel, Marie Claire, Glamour* online, and *Elle*, among other places.

aimeelutkin.com
Twitter: @alutkin
Instagram: @aalutkin

ABOUT THE TYPE

This book was set in Baskerville, a typeface designed by John Baskerville (1706–75), an amateur printer and type-founder, and cut for him by John Handy in 1750. The type became popular again when the Lanston Monotype Corporation of London revived the classic roman face in 1923. The Mergenthaler Linotype Company in England and the United States cut a version of Baskerville in 1931, making it one of the most widely used typefaces today.